תומר דבורה

Rabbi Moshe Cordovero

The Palm Tree of Devorah

תומר דבורה

Rabbi Moshe Cordovero

The Palm Tree of Devorah

Translated and Annotated by
Rabbi Moshe Miller

TARGUM/FELDHEIM

First published 1993

Copyright © 1993 by Moshe Miller
ISBN 1-56871-027-5

Phototypeset at Targum Press

Printing plates by Frank, Jerusalem

Published by:
Targum Press Inc.
22700 W. Eleven Mile Rd.
Southfield, Mich. 48034

in conjunction with Mishnas Rishonim

Distributed by:
Feldheim Publishers
200 Airport Executive Park
Spring Valley, N.Y. 10977

Distributed in Israel by:
Targum Press Ltd.
POB 43170
Jerusalem 91430

Printed in Israel

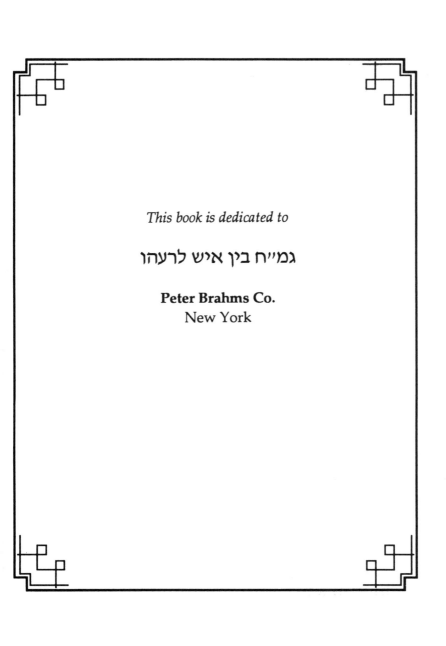

This book is dedicated to

גמ״ח בין איש לרעהו

Peter Brahms Co.
New York

INTRODUCTION

1. The Author

Among the great luminaries of Kabbalah, Rabbi Moshe Cordovero holds a particularly important place as one of the most prolific and systematic exponents of the teachings of the *Zohar* as well as the writings of almost all the early Kabbalists.

Moshe Cordovero — or Ramak (an acronym taken from the first letters of his name), as he is commonly known — was born around 1522 to a distinguished family of Spanish descent, apparently originally from the town of Cordova. Although it is not certain that Ramak himself was born in Safed, he spent most of his life in that holy city, the home of Kabbalah.

In the revealed aspects of Torah — the Talmud and associated works — Ramak was a student of the renowned Rabbi Yosef Caro (circa 1488-1575), author of

Shulchan Aruch. The latter highly praised the acumen and vast knowledge of his young student. His greatness in Talmudic law is further confirmed by the fact that at the tender age of eighteen, Ramak was ordained by Rabbi Ya'akov BeRav. Of the four men accorded *semichah* by Rabbi Ya'akov — the others were Rabbi Yosef Caro, Rabbi Moshe of Trani, and Rabbi Moshe Galanti — Ramak was by far the youngest. According to the testimony of Rabbi Menachem Azariah DeFano, Ramak served Safed as a Talmud teacher and legal authority.

At age twenty, Ramak became a student of his brother-in-law, Rabbi Shlomo HaLevi Alkabetz (author of the *"Lecha Dodi"* hymn), in the hidden aspect of Torah — the Kabbalah. Despite Ramak's formidable achievements in Talmud, he states that until he began learning Kabbalah, he was as if asleep and pursuing idle thoughts (*Pardes Rimonim,* intro.).

Ramak became one of the leading Kabbalists in Safed. He acted as spokesman for the group of Kabbalists headed by Rabbi Alkabetz, and he wrote several treatises explaining the fallacies of philosophy. In addition, he exhorted Torah students everywhere to study Kabbalah.

Ramak led an ascetic life, part of it in self-imposed exile. These exiles are detailed in his *Sefer Geirushin* (Venice, 1543). Through such self-purification and penances, Ramak became worthy of the revelation of Eliyahu (*Shem HaGedolim*).

Among Ramak's most famous students were Rabbi Eliyahu DeVidas, author of *Reishit Chochmah*; Rabbi Chaim Vital, later a student of the renowned Rabbi

Yitzchak Luria (the Arizal); Rabbi Avraham Galanti, author of *Yerech Yakar* on the *Zohar*; Rabbi Eliezer Azcari, author of *Sefer HaChareidim*; and Rabbi Menachem Azariah DeFano (Maharam MiPano), author of many works, including *Asarah Ma'amarot*, *Kanfei Yonah*, and *Responsa of Maharam MiPano*. As Europe's leading Kabbalist, Rabbi Menachem Azariah was instrumental in promoting the study of Kabbalah all over the continent, and he taught Ramak's *Pardes Rimonim* regularly. Similarly, Rabbi Yeshayahu Hurwitz, author of *Shelah* (*Shnei Luchot HaBrit*), considered himself a student of Ramak and quoted extensively from his works. And in the last year of Ramak's life, the Arizal came to Safed. He, too, studied under Ramak, to whom he refers as "our teacher."

At the young age of forty-eight, Rabbi Moshe Cordovero passed away in Safed on 23 Tammuz, 1570. In his eulogy, the Arizal declared Rabbi Moshe so pure and saintly that his death could be attributed only to the sin of Adam. According to the Arizal's testimony, the bier bearing Ramak to his burial in Safed was preceded by a pillar of fire.

2. Ramak's Works

Ramak wrote prolifically. Among his works are:

Pardes Rimonim: The most renowned of Ramak's writings, the *Pardes* systemizes and expounds the entire spectrum of Kabbalistic thought until his time, resolving many apparent contradictions and hundreds of long-unanswered questions.

Or Yakar: A monumental, line-by-line commentary on the *Zohar*, this work explains numerous passages from *Tikkunei Zohar*, *Zohar Chadash*, *Sefer HaBahir*, *Sefer Yetzirah*, and other Kabbalistic classics.

Or Ne'erav: An introduction to Kabbalah.

Sefer Geirushin: A journal of events, insights, and revelations that occurred during the author's self-imposed exile.

Shiur Komah: A treatise dealing with the structure of the worlds and the *sefirot*.

Eilimah Rabbati: A systematic and highly explanatory approach to the *Or Ein Sof* and the *sefirot* as well as other central Kabbalistic themes. The book begins with a polemic against those "who distance themselves from learning Kabbalah."

Tomer Devorah: One of the seventy *temarim* (date palms), or subsections, of *Eilimah Rabbati*. The curious titles of these two works derive from two verses: "Then they came to Eilim, and there [were] twelve springs of water and seventy date palms..." (*Shemot* 15:27), and "And [Devorah] sat under the palm tree of Devorah..." (*Shofetim* 4:5). Although the author does not explain the significance of these titles, they clearly suggest an oasis. Perhaps Ramak intended these Kabbalistic works to quench the thirst and satisfy the appetites of those searching for "the sweet and goodly light" of Torah. Alternatively, the date palm signifies wholeness in man's service of G-d, as in "The righteous will flourish like the date palm..." (*Tehillim* 92:13) (see *Pardes*, sha'ar "Archei HaKinuyim," ערך תמר).

Tomer Devorah is essentially an ethical treatise devoted to a Kabbalistic understanding of the commandment to imitate G-d. Based on the verses "...you shall go in His ways" (*Devarim* 28:9) and "to go in all His ways" (ibid. 11:22), the Sifri ("*Eikev*") explains, "just as the Holy One, Blessed Be He, is called 'Compassionate,' you should be compassionate; just as the Holy One, Blessed Be He, is called 'Gracious,' you should be gracious; just as the Holy One, Blessed Be He, is called 'Righteous,' you should be righteous; just as the Holy One, Blessed Be He, is called 'Pious,' you should be pious." Expounding the verse "Follow the L-rd, your G-d..." (*Devarim* 13:5), the Gemara derives the practical implications of this concept: "Emulate the attributes of the Holy One, Blessed Be He. Just as the Holy One, Blessed Be He, clothes the naked...so should you; just as the Holy One, Blessed Be He, visits the sick...so should you; just as the Holy One, Blessed Be He, consoles the bereaved, so should you..." (*Sotah* 14a).

In *Tomer Devorah*, the Thirteen Supernal Attributes of Mercy mentioned in *Michah* 7:18-20 are analyzed in detail, apparently for the first time. Ramak's treatment is uniquely clear, Kabbalistic, and practical. Rightfully acclaimed throughout the Jewish world, *Tomer Devorah* has become a classic of Jewish thought. Said the saintly Shelah: "If you have been worthy of the light of the secrets of Torah, you know that the Ten Days of Repentance correspond to the ten *sefirot* Above. During these ten days, study *Tomer Devorah* in order to rectify the corresponding *sefirah* each day" (*Shelah*, "*Kuntres Eser Hillulim*"). Similarly, Rabbi Yisrael Salanter, the founder of the *Mussar* movement, told his students to learn *Tomer Devorah* from the beginning of Elul until after Yom Kippur, and many other *gedolei Yisrael* have made it customary to study the work at this time.

3. The Basic Principles of Ramak's Kabbalah

The *Sefirot*:

The nature of the Emanator, the King of kings, the Holy One, Blessed Be He, is to pour forth abundant goodness and benefit to all His creatures. He imparts His attributes to them — such as kindness by way of the *sefirah* of *chesed*, and so on — revealing His greatness in order to become known to them. In His kindness, He desires to reveal His exaltedness — which is called *keter* — to lowly creatures. But since they cannot grasp it, He has emanated the *sefirot* of *chochmah, binah*, and so on, for by way of these *sefirot*, He is comprehensible (*Pardes, sha'ar* 2, ch. 6).

The *sefirot* are the attributes of the Holy One, Blessed Be He (*Shiur Komah*, ch. 3, par. 4). A brief analysis of the word '*sefirah*' will clarify the function of the *sefirot*. The word may be derived from: 1) a word meaning "number" or "counting" (מספר), thus signifying a Divine limitation on Creation; 2) a word meaning "book" (ספר), signifying a well-ordered and defined blueprint of Creation; 3) a word meaning "inventory" (ספירת דברים), signifying the inventory of the deeds of the Holy One, Blessed Be He; 4) a word meaning "shining" (ספירות), like a luminous precious stone (cf. sapphire), signifying the purpose of the *sefirot* — to illuminate and radiate revelation; 5) a word meaning "border" or "boundary" (ספר), signifying division and limitation; 6) a word meaning "story" (סיפור), signifying the story of G-d's acts of Creation, man's deeds, and the unfolding of past, present, and future (*Eilimah Rabbati*, pt. 1, *tamar* 6, ch. 2).

 Tikkunei Zohar sums up all these definitions: "You are He Who has brought forth ten 'garments,' which we call ten *sefirot*, through which to direct both hidden worlds — which are never revealed — and revealed worlds; through them, You conceal Yourself from man.... Each *sefirah* has a specific name.... You, however, have no specific name, for You permeate all names, and You are the perfection of them all.... You are wise, but Your wisdom is unknowable; You understand, but Your understanding is unknowable; You have no specific place. [You have clothed Yourself in the *sefirot*] only to make known to mankind Your power and strength and to show [us] how the world is conducted through law and mercy — for there is righteousness and justice, which are dispensed according to the deeds of man..." (intro., פתח אליהו ד"ה).

 There are ten *sefirot*: *keter*, the crown; *chochmah*, wisdom; *binah*, understanding; *chesed*, kindness; *gevurah*, severity or judgment; *tiferet*, truth, beauty, or compassion; *netzach*, endurance, eternity, or victory; *hod*, glory or splendor; *yesod*, foundation; and *malchut*, royalty, kingship, or sovereignty. Each *sefirah* performs a distinctive function, often symbolized in Kabbalah by a corresponding human limb: "*Chesed* is the right arm, *gevurah* the left arm, *tiferet* the torso, and so forth" (ibid.). Each *sefirah* is defined by its function:

1) *Keter*, the crown, is the highest and most encompassing *sefirah*. It is so sublime that it is called "the most hidden of all hidden things" (*Zohar*, vol. I, p. 147a; *Pardes, sha'ar* 5, ch. 4) and is thus referred to as "*ayin* (nothingness) (*Zohar*, vol. III, p. 256b). It is completely incomprehensible to man (*Pardes, sha'ar* 23, ch. 1). *Keter* is also absolute compassion (*Zohar*, "*Idra Rabba*," vol. III, p. 129a; *Pardes, sha'ar* 8, ch. 3), where no harsh judgments exist. Accordingly, *keter* is the source of the Thirteen Supernal Attributes of Mercy, as explained in the first two chapters of this work.

2) *Chochmah*, wisdom, represents G-d's first creative activity (*Pardes, sha'ar* 5, ch. 4; *Targum Yerushalmi, Bereishit* 1:1). It is thus called "the beginning" (*Zohar*, vol. I, p. 3b) whence everything else derives. *Chochmah* is incomprehensible until it becomes enformed in *binah* (ibid., p. 15b). *Chochmah* is also called the source from which life flows forth (*Pardes, sha'ar* 3, ch. 5, and *sha'ar* 12, ch.1)

3) *Binah*, understanding, entails deriving one matter from another (*Chagigah* 14a; *Zohar Chadash*, p. 4a). *Chochmah* becomes known only through *binah* (*Tikkunei Zohar, tikkun* 22, p. 63b), which expands and elucidates it. It is often called '*teshuvah*' (repentance) (*Pardes, sha'ar* "*Archei HaKinuyim*," ערך תשובה). Although *binah* is the first source of severities and harshness, in·essence it is the source of kindness and compassion (*Pardes, sha'ar* 8, ch. 8).

4) *Chesed*, kindness, manifests and actualizes G-d's absolute, unlimited benevolence and kindness (*Zohar*, vol. II, p. 168b; *Pardes, sha'ar* 8, ch. 1). When a person cleaves to his Creator in total love from the depths of his heart and soul, the Holy One, Blessed Be He, showers him with love, kindness, and benevolence. This is the secret of the verse "As in water the face reflects the face, so does the heart of man to man" (*Mishlei* 27:19) (*Reishit Chochmah, sha'ar* "HaAhavah," ch. 1, p. 53c; *Likkutei Amarim*, ch. 46).

5) *Gevurah*, the power of restraint, is often referred to as *din*, law and judgment, for it demands that *chesed* be distributed justly, i.e., in proportion to the recipient's merit (*Zohar*, vol. II, pp. 175b, 51b; *Tikkunei Zohar*, intro., p. 17b). *Gevurah* represents harsh judgment or severity, and it seeks to limit the outflow of *chesed* (*Pardes, sha'ar* 8, ch. 2). *Chesed* and *gevurah* thus oppose each other, but they are balanced and synthesized through *tiferet*.

6) *Tiferet*, truth or beauty, harmonizes and synthesizes the boundless outpouring of *chesed* with the severe restrictions of *gevurah*. The resultant blend is endurable by the intended recipients and hinges on their ability and worthiness to receive its outflow. Thus, *tiferet* is referred to as 'truth,' for it depends on the merit of the recipient (*Zohar Chadash*, "Toldot," p. 26c, and "Yitro," p. 31b). Nevertheless, ideally, *tiferet* tends towards *chesed* (*Pardes, sha'ar* 8, ch.2, and *sha'ar* 9, ch. 3) and is therefore called *rachamim* — mercy or compassion (*Zohar Chadash*, "Yitro," p. 31b). In addition, *tiferet* is referred to as "beauty," for its harmonious blending of the *sefirot* is beautiful (*Tikkunei Zohar, tikkun* 70, p. 133b; *Pardes, sha'ar* 8, ch. 17).

7-8) *Netzach* (victory, endurance, or eternity) and *hod* (majesty or splendor) are usually paired. The *Zohar* refers to them as "two halves of one body, like twins" (vol. III, p. 236a). They are an extension of the *sefirot* from which they derive — *chesed* and *gevurah*, respectively. Thus, *netzach* conquers the barriers between the outflow of Divine benevolence and its intended recipients, while *hod* restrains this outflow lest it be dissipated among unworthy recipients. Divine majesty and splendor are thereby preserved.

9) *Yesod*, foundation, unites Emanator and recipient, or, in the language of Kabbalah, *yesod* unites *malchut* with the other *sefirot*. Just as *tiferet* mediates between *chesed* and *gevurah*, *yesod* mediates between *netzach* and *hod* (*Pardes, sha'ar* 8, ch. 24). Moreover, *yesod* blends, channels, and receives light from all the *sefirot* above it (*Tikkunei Zohar, tikkun* 21, p. 55b). Thus, their emanations can issue forth to creatures.

10) *Malchut* (kingship, royalty, or sovereignty) is the last of the ten *sefirot*. It is uniquely "passive," having nothing but that which other *sefirot* pour into it (*Eitz Chaim, sha'ar* 6, ch. 5, and *sha'ar* 8, ch. 5). Thus, the *Zohar* compares *malchut* to the moon, which has no light of its own (vol. I, pp. 249b, 251b, and vol. II, p. 245b; *Tikkunei Zohar, tikkun* 44, p. 82b). Nevertheless, *malchut* includes all the other *sefirot*, which pour their light into it. *Malchut* is therefore compared to the sea, into which all rivers flow. *Malchut* brings creation into being, for everything occurs among the lower beings by way of this *sefirah* (*Tikkunei Zohar, tikkun* 19, p. 40b; *Zohar Chadash*, p. 11a).

Indeed, *malchut* is referred to as "the architect with which the entire creation was made" (*Pardes, sha'ar* 11, ch. 2). *Malchut* also corresponds to the mouth (*Tikkunei Zohar,* intro., p. 17a) and thus represents the word of G-d (cf. *Avot* 5:1) and the revealed world (*Zohar,* vol. I, p. 1b, and vol. II, p. 127a).

The *sefirot* are arranged in three columns. The right column comprises the *sefirot* of *chesed: chochmah, chesed,* and *netzach.* The central column comprises the *sefirot* of *tiferet: keter, tiferet, yesod,* and *malchut.* And the left column comprises the *sefirot* of *gevurah: binah, gevurah,* and *hod* (*Pardes, sha'ar* 6, chs. 1, 7). Kabbalah parallels this configuration with the human body. Thus, *chesed* is the right arm, *gevurah* the left arm, and so on (*Tikkunei Zohar,* intro., אליהו ד"ה פתח), and the configuration is sometimes referred to as *Adam HaElyon,* "Supernal Man" (*Pardes, sha'ar* 4, chs. 5-6; *Shelah,* "Beit Yisrael," p. 5c).

The Soul:

The soul is an indivisible essence concealed with the *Ein Sof*—the Infinite One (*Pardes, sha'ar* 4, ch. 7). It emanates from Above via the ten *sefirot.* The ten powers of the soul derive from these *sefirot* (*Pardes, sha'ar* 24, ch. 11).

Similarly, the three levels of the soul — *nefesh, ruach,* and *neshamah* — each derive their character and path in Divine service from the *sefirah* via which they emanate: *neshamah* from *binah; ruach* from the six *sefirot* from *chesed* to *yesod* (which are often referred to collectively as *tiferet*); and *nefesh* from *malchut* (*Pardes, sha'ar* 31, ch. 1).

The soul is enclothed within the body via a fourth level: the *tzelem*, or "image." The *tzelem* of man is the human mold of his physical form, which links his body and soul. This mold derives from the configuration of *sefirot* via which man's soul descends. The soul reflects the *Atzmut*, or "Infinite Light," which illuminates the six *sefirot*. This reflection is the *demut* (likeness) of man (*Pardes, sha'ar* 31, ch. 4; *Shelah*, "*Beit Yisrael*," p. 6c; *Nefesh HaChaim, sha'ar* 1, ch. 1; Rashi, *Bereishit* 1:26). This way, man includes all of creation within him, from the loftiest spirituality to the most mundane physicality (*Pardes, sha'ar* 4, ch. 10).

When man does good, his soul disseminates G-d's abundant goodness and reveals His greatness. Through man's good deeds, certain *sefirot* prevail. For instance, if he occupies himself with Torah, he causes *tiferet* to prevail. Thus, Avraham represents kindness and love, which derive from the *sefirah* of *chesed*, for his deeds were concentrated in this direction (*Pardes, sha'ar* 31, ch. 1; *Eilimah Rabbati*, pp. 1, 43).

To be privileged to channel G-d's blessing and benefit into the world, man must emulate his Creator. It is insufficient that man is created in the Divine likeness — he must constantly, consciously, and willingly cleave to G-d by emulating Him in every way. This emulation is the subject of *Tomer Devorah*.

This translation abounds with footnotes for both layman and scholar. It also includes some of the explanations and textual references found in Hebrew editions of *Tomer Devorah*, such as those of Rabbi Ze'ev Wolf Ashkenazi (Jerusalem, 1928) and Rabbi Chaim Yitzchak Lipkin. In addition, I have tried to annotate sources in the Gemara, Midrash, Rambam, and *Shulchan Aruch* as well as parallels in the *Zohar*, *Tikkunei Zohar*, *Zohar Chadash*, *Reishit Chochmah*, *Shelah*, and, most of all, other major works by Ramak himself.

Rabbi Moshe Miller
23 Tammuz 5753
(the *yahrtzeit* of Rabbi Moshe
  Cordovero)
Jerusalem

Tomer Devorah

Chapter 1

[handwritten margin notes: gemilus chassadim = divinity / Have to do things, to act godly]

It is proper for man to emulate his Creator, for then he will attain the secret of the Supernal Form in both image (*tzelem*) and likeness (*demut*). For if a person's physical form reflects the Supernal Form, yet his actions do not, he falsifies his stature. People will say of him, "A handsome form whose deeds are ugly." For the essential aspect of the Supernal 'Form' and 'Likeness' is that they are the deeds of the Holy One, Blessed Be He. Therefore, what good is it for a person to reflect the Supernal Form in physical form only if his deeds do not imitate those of his Creator? Thus, it is proper that man's actions imitate the Thirteen Supernal Attributes of Mercy — the functions of the *sefirah* of *keter* — hinted at in these verses:

[handwritten margin notes: Chillul Hashem / when person doesn't act in accordance with divinity / i.e. acting according to divine will]

[handwritten note above "falsifies his stature": betraying own form]

> Who is G-d like You, who pardons iniquity
> and forgives the transgression of the remnant
> of His heritage? He does not maintain His

פֶּרֶק רִאשׁוֹן

הָאָדָם רָאוּי שֶׁיִּתְדַּמֶּה לְקוֹנוֹ וְאָז יִהְיֶה בְּסוֹד הַצּוּרָה הָעֶלְיוֹנָה, צֶלֶם וּדְמוּת. שֶׁאִלּוּ יְדֻמֶּה בְּגוּפוֹ וְלֹא בַּפְּעֻלּוֹת, הֲרֵי הוּא מַכְזִיב הַצּוּרָה וְיֹאמְרוּ עָלָיו צוּרָה נָאָה וּמַעֲשִׂים כְּעוּרִים. שֶׁהֲרֵי עִקַּר הַצֶּלֶם וְהַדְּמוּת הָעֶלְיוֹן הֵן פְּעֻלּוֹתָיו, וּמַה יּוֹעִיל לוֹ הֱיוֹתוֹ כַּצּוּרָה הָעֶלְיוֹנָה, דְּמוּת תַּבְנִית אֵבָרָיו, וּבַפְּעֻלּוֹת לֹא יִתְדַּמֶּה לְקוֹנוֹ. לְפִיכָךְ רָאוּי שֶׁיִּתְדַּמֶּה אֶל פְּעֻלּוֹת הַכֶּתֶר, שֶׁהֵן שְׁלוֹשׁ עֶשְׂרֵה מִדּוֹת שֶׁל רַחֲמִים עֶלְיוֹנוֹת וּרְמוּזוֹת בְּסוֹד הַפְּסוּקִים (מיכה ז׳, י׳׳ח–כ׳): "מִי אֵל כָּמוֹךָ נֹשֵׂא עָוֹן וְעֹבֵר עַל פֶּשַׁע לִשְׁאֵרִית נַחֲלָתוֹ לֹא הֶחֱזִיק לָעַד

anger forever, for He delights in kindness. He will again show us compassion, He will vanquish our iniquities, and You will cast all their sins into the depths of the sea. Show faithfulness to Ya'akov, kindness to Avraham, which You have sworn to our fathers from days of old.

(*Michah* 7:18-20)

Consequently, it is proper that these Thirteen Attributes, which we will now explain, should also be found in man.

1. *Who is G-d like You:*

This attribute refers to the Holy One, Blessed Be He, as a tolerant King Who bears insult in a manner beyond human understanding. Without doubt, nothing is hidden from His view. In addition, there is not a moment that man is not nourished and sustained by virtue of the Divine power bestowed upon him.

Thus, no man ever sins against G-d without G-d, at that very moment, bestowing abundant vitality upon him, giving him the power to move his limbs. Yet even though a person uses this very vitality to transgress, G-d does not withhold it from him. Rather, the Holy One, Blessed Be He, suffers this insult and continues to enable his limbs to move. Even at the very moment that a person uses that power for transgression, sin, and infuriating deeds, the Holy One, Blessed Be He, bears them patiently.

אַפּוֹ כִּי חָפֵץ חֶסֶד הוּא; יָשׁוּב יְרַחֲמֵנוּ יִכְבֹּשׁ עֲוֹנֹתֵינוּ וְתַשְׁלִיךְ בִּמְצֻלוֹת יָם כָּל חַטֹּאתָם תִּתֵּן אֱמֶת לְיַעֲקֹב חֶסֶד לְאַבְרָהָם אֲשֶׁר נִשְׁבַּעְתָּ לַאֲבֹתֵינוּ מִימֵי קֶדֶם".

אִם כֵּן, רָאוּי שֶׁתִּמָּצֶאנָה בּוֹ שְׁלוֹשׁ עֶשְׂרֵה מִדּוֹת אֵלּוּ. וְעַכְשָׁיו נְפָרֵשׁ אוֹתָן הַפְּעוּלוֹת, שְׁלוֹשׁ עֶשְׂרֵה, שֶׁרָאוּי שֶׁתִּהְיֶינָה בּוֹ.

הָא' — מִי אֵל כָּמוֹךְ

מוֹרֶה עַל הֱיוֹת הַקָּבָּ"ה מֶלֶךְ נֶעֱלָב, סוֹבֵל עֶלְבּוֹן, מַה שֶּׁלֹּא יְכִילֵהוּ רַעְיוֹן. הֲרֵי אֵין דָּבָר נִסְתָּר מֵהַשְׁגָּחָתוֹ בְּלִי סָפֵק, וְעוֹד, אֵין רֶגַע שֶׁלֹּא יִהְיֶה הָאָדָם נִזּוֹן וּמִתְקַיֵּם מִכֹּחַ עֶלְיוֹן הַשּׁוֹפֵעַ עָלָיו.

וַהֲרֵי תִמְצָא שֶׁמֵּעוֹלָם לֹא חָטָא אָדָם נֶגְדּוֹ שֶׁלֹּא יִהְיֶה הוּא בְּאוֹתוֹ הָרֶגַע מַמָּשׁ שׁוֹפֵעַ שֶׁפַע קִיּוּמוֹ וּתְנוּעַת אֵבָרָיו, וְעִם הֱיוֹת שֶׁהָאָדָם חוֹטֵא בַּכֹּחַ הַהוּא לֹא מְנָעוֹ מִמֶּנּוּ כְּלָל, אֶלָּא סוֹבֵל הַקָּבָּ"ה עֶלְבּוֹן כָּזֶה לִהְיוֹת מַשְׁפִּיעַ בּוֹ כֹּחַ תְּנוּעוֹת אֵבָרָיו, וְהוּא מוֹצִיא אוֹתוֹ כֹּחַ בְּאוֹתוֹ רֶגַע בְּחֵטְא וְעָוֹן וּמַכְעִיס וְהַקָּבָּ"ה סוֹבֵל.

One cannot say, G-d forbid, that G-d cannot withhold His benevolence from a person, for it is within His power to shrivel up a person's arms or legs instantly, just as He did with Yaravam. Yet even though it is within G-d's power to withdraw vitality, and He could argue, "Since you sin against Me, sin with that which belongs to you, not with that which belongs to Me," He does not withhold His goodness from man. He bears the insult and continues to bestow His power and benevolence on man. Such an insult and the forbearance thereof defy description.

For this reason, the ministering angels refer to the Holy One, Blessed Be He, as the long-suffering King. This is the meaning of "Who is G-d like You" — "You, G-d, are kind and benevolent, possessing the power to exact revenge and claim what is rightfully Yours, and yet You are patient and tolerant until man repents."

This, then, is a virtue man should emulate — namely, tolerance. Even when he is insulted to the degree mentioned above he should not withdraw his benevolence from those upon whom he bestows it.

2. *Who pardons iniquity*:

This attribute is greater than the previous one, for when a person transgresses, a destructive creature is created. As stated in the Mishnah, "He who commits a single transgression acquires against himself a single accuser" who stands before the Holy One, Blessed Be He, and states, "So-and-so made me."

Considering that no being in the world exists except

וְלֹא תֹאמַר שֶׁאֵינוֹ יָכוֹל לִמְנוֹעַ מִמֶּנּוּ הַטּוֹב הַהוּא, חַס וְחָלִילָה, שֶׁהֲרֵי בְּכֹחוֹ בְּרֶגַע כְּמֵימְרֵיהּ לְיַבֵּשׁ יָדָיו וְרַגְלָיו, כְּעֵין שֶׁעָשָׂה לְיָרָבְעָם (מלכים א' י"ג, ד'). וְעִם כָּל זֶה, שֶׁהַכֹּחַ בְּיָדוֹ לְהַחֲזִיר הַכֹּחַ הַנִּשְׁפָּע הַהוּא, וְהָיָה לוֹ לוֹמַר כֵּיוָן שֶׁאַתָּה חוֹטֵא נֶגְדִּי תֶּחֱטָא בְּשֶׁלְּךָ וְלֹא בְּשֶׁלִּי, לֹא מִפְּנֵי זֶה מָנַע טוֹב מִן הָאָדָם וְלֹא סָבַל עֶלְבּוֹן, וְהִשְׁפִּיעַ הַכֹּחַ וְהֵטִיב לָאָדָם טוּבוֹ. הֲרֵי זֶה עֶלְבּוֹן וְסַבְלָנוּת מַה שֶּׁלֹּא יְסֻפָּר.

וְעַל זֶה קוֹרְאִים מַלְאֲכֵי הַשָּׁרֵת לְהַקָּבָּ"ה מֶלֶךְ עָלוּב (פרקי היכלות פכ"ה). וְהַיְינוּ אוֹמְרוֹ "מִי אֵל כָּמוֹךָ", אַתָּה אֵל בַּעַל חֶסֶד הַמֵּטִיב, אֵל בַּעַל כֹּחַ לִנְקֹם וְלֶאֱסוֹף אֶת שֶׁלְּךָ, וְעִם כָּל זֶה אַתָּה סוֹבֵל וְנֶעֱלָב עַד יָשׁוּב בִּתְשׁוּבָה.

הֲרֵי זוֹ מִדָּה שֶׁצָּרִיךְ הָאָדָם לְהִתְנַהֵג בָּהּ, רְצוֹנִי: הַסַּבְלָנוּת, וְכֵן הֱיוֹתוֹ נֶעֱלָב אֲפִילוּ לַמַּדְרֵגָה זוֹ, וְעִם כָּל זֶה לֹא יֶאֱסוֹף טוּבָתוֹ מִן הַמְקַבֵּל.

הַב' — נוֹשֵׂא עָוֹן,

וַהֲרֵי זֶה גָּדוֹל מֵהַקּוֹדֵם, שֶׁהֲרֵי לֹא יַעֲשֶׂה הָאָדָם עָוֹן שֶׁלֹּא יִבְרָא מַשְׁחִית, כְּדִתְנַן (אבות פ"ד, י"ג): "הָעוֹבֵר עֲבֵירָה אַחַת קוֹנֶה לוֹ קַטֵּיגוֹר אֶחָד": וַהֲרֵי אוֹתוֹ קַטֵּיגוֹר עוֹמֵד לִפְנֵי הַקָּבָּ"ה וְאוֹמֵר פְּלוֹנִי עֲשָׂאַנִי.

by virtue of the fact that the Holy One, Blessed Be He, grants it life, how does this force of destruction stand before Him? The strict letter of the Law would justify that the Holy One, Blessed Be He, should claim, "I do not nourish destructive creatures! Go to him who made you, and derive your sustenance from him." Then the destructive creature would immediately descend and take the life of the sinner, or cut him off from his spiritual source, or punish him according to his just desserts, until the destructive being would cease to be.

Nevertheless, the Holy One, Blessed Be He, does not make this claim. Rather, He bears the sin and endures it, and just as He sustains the entire world, He sustains this destructive creature until one of three things happens:

1) The sinner repents, destroying or nullifying the destructive creature by his acts of penance.

2) The righteous Judge nullifies it through the suffering or death of the sinner.

3) The sinner descends to Gehinom to pay his debt.

This is also the explanation of Kayin's plea, "Is my sin too great to bear?" (*Bereishit* 4:13), which our sages interpreted as: "You bear and desire and nourish and sustain the entire world! Is my sin so severe that You cannot sustain it [i.e., the destructive creature] until I repent and rectify the sin?"

It is thus with tremendous tolerance that G-d nourishes and sustains the evil creature created by the sinner until he repents. From this, man should learn to what extent he, too, should be tolerant and bear the yoke of his fellow and his evil, even though his transgressions are of

וְאֵין בְּרִיָּה מִתְקַיֶּמֶת בָּעוֹלָם אֶלָּא בְּשִׁפְעוֹ שֶׁל הַקָּבָּ"ה, וַהֲרֵי הַמַּשְׁחִית הַזֶּה עוֹמֵד לְפָנָיו, וּבַמֶּה מִתְקַיֵּם, הַדִּין נוֹתֵן שֶׁיֹּאמַר הַקָּבָּ"ה, "אֵינִי זָן מַשְׁחִיתִים, יֵלֵךְ אֵצֶל מִי שֶׁעֲשָׂאוֹ וְיִתְפַּרְנֵס מִמֶּנּוּ", וְהָיָה הַמַּשְׁחִית יוֹרֵד מִיָּד וְנוֹטֵל נִשְׁמָתוֹ, אוֹ כּוֹרְתוֹ, אוֹ נֶעֱנָשׁ עָלָיו כְּפִי עוֹנְשׁוֹ עַד שֶׁיִּתְבַּטֵּל הַמַּשְׁחִית הַהוּא.

וְאֵין הַקָּבָּ"ה עוֹשֶׂה כֵן, אֶלָּא נוֹשֵׂא וְסוֹבֵל הֶעָוֹן, וּכְמוֹ שֶׁהוּא זָן הָעוֹלָם כֻּלּוֹ, זָן וּמְפַרְנֵס הַמַּשְׁחִית הַזֶּה, עַד שֶׁיִּהְיֶה אֶחָד מִשְּׁלֹשָׁה דְבָרִים, אוֹ יָשׁוּב הַחוֹטֵא בִּתְשׁוּבָה וִיכַלֵּהוּ וִיבַטְּלֵהוּ בְּסִגּוּפָיו, אוֹ יְבַטְּלֵהוּ שׁוֹפֵט צֶדֶק בְּיִסּוּרִים וּמִיתָה,

אוֹ יֵלֵךְ בַּגֵּיהִנָּם וְשָׁם יִפְרַע חוֹבוֹ.

וְהַיְינוּ שֶׁאָמַר קַיִן (בְּרֵאשִׁית ד', י"ג): "גָּדוֹל עֲוֹנִי מִנְּשׂוֹא", וּפֵרְשׁוּ רַבּוֹתֵינוּ זִכְרוֹנָם לִבְרָכָה (תַּנְחוּמָא בְּרֵאשִׁית סִי' ט'): "כָּל הָעוֹלָם כֻּלּוֹ אַתָּה סוֹבֵל", יִרְצֶה, זָן וּמְפַרְנֵס, "וַעֲוֹנִי כָּבֵד, שֶׁאֵין אַתָּה יָכוֹל לְסוֹבְלוֹ", פֵּירוּשׁ, לְפַרְנְסוֹ, עַד שֶׁאָשׁוּב וַאֲתֻקַּן.

אִם כֵּן הֲרֵי זוֹ מִדַּת סַבְלָנוּת גְּדוֹלָה, שֶׁיָּזוּן וִיפַרְנֵס בְּרִיָּה רָעָה שֶׁבָּרָא הַחוֹטֵא, עַד שֶׁיָּשׁוּב. יִלְמֹד הָאָדָם, כַּמָּה צָרִיךְ שֶׁיִּהְיֶה סַבְלָן, לִסְבֹּל

such magnitude that the evil remains. He should tolerate one who sinned against him until the sinner mends his ways or the sin disappears of its own accord.

Even relate to oneself & how we relate to our personal situation

3. And forgives...transgression:

This attribute is even greater than the preceding one, for when G-d forgives a sinner, He does not convey His pardon through an emissary. Rather, the Holy One Himself, Blessed Be He, grants the pardon, as it is written: "For with You is forgiveness..." (*Tehillim* 130:4). What is the nature of this forgiveness? He washes away the sin, as it is written: "When G-d has washed away the filth of the daughters of Tziyon..." (*Yeshayahu* 4:4). Similarly, it is written: "And I will sprinkle purifying waters upon you..." (*Yechezkel* 36:25). This, then, is the quality of forgiveness of transgression — G-d sends purifying waters and washes away the sin.

A person should behave in exactly the same way. He should certainly not say, "Why should I be the one to rectify so-and-so's sins or perversions?" For when man sins, the Holy One Himself, Blessed Be He, rectifies the perversion, not by way of an emissary, and He washes away the filth of a person's sins. From this, one can also understand that a person should be too ashamed to return to his sinful ways, for the King Himself cleanses the filth of his garments.

A person should pray for others to do teshuva

& H' in turn will cleanse that person.

עֹל חֲבֵירוֹ וְרָעוֹתָיו שֶׁהֵרַע, עַד שִׁעוּר כָּזֶה, שֶׁעֲדַיִן רָעָתוֹ קַיֶּמֶת שֶׁחָטָא נֶגְדּוֹ, וְהוּא יִסְבּוֹל עַד יְתַקֵּן עַד שֶׁיִּתְבַּטֵּל מֵאֵלָיו, וְכַיּוֹצֵא.

הַג׳ — וְעוֹבֵר עַל פֶּשַׁע

זוֹ מִדָּה גְדוֹלָה. שֶׁהֲרֵי אֵין הַמְּחִילָה עַל יְדֵי שָׁלִיחַ, אֶלָּא עַל יָדוֹ מַמָּשׁ שֶׁל הַקָּבָּ"ה, כְּדִכְתִיב (תהלים ק"ל, ד'): "כִּי עִמְּךָ הַסְּלִיחָה וְגו'", וּמַה הִיא הַסְּלִיחָה. שֶׁהוּא רוֹחֵץ הֶעָוֹן, כְּדִכְתִיב (ישעיהו ד', ד'): "אִם רָחַץ ה' אֵת צוֹאַת בְּנוֹת צִיּוֹן וְגו'", וְכֵן כְּתִיב (יחזקאל ל"ו, כ"ה) "וְזָרַקְתִּי עֲלֵיכֶם מַיִם טְהוֹרִים וְגו'". וְהַיְנוּ "עוֹבֵר עַל פֶּשַׁע", שׁוֹלֵחַ מֵימֵי רְחִיצָה וְעוֹבֵר וְרוֹחֵץ הַפֶּשַׁע.

וְהִנֵּה מַמָּשׁ כִּדְמוּת זֶה צָרִיךְ לִהְיוֹת הָאָדָם, שֶׁלֹּא יֹאמַר, וְכִי אֲנִי מְתַקֵּן מַה שֶׁפְּלוֹנִי חָטָא אוֹ הִשְׁחִית. לֹא יֹאמַר כָּךְ. שֶׁהֲרֵי הָאָדָם חוֹטֵא וְהַקָּבָּ"ה בְּעַצְמוֹ, שֶׁלֹּא עַל יְדֵי שָׁלִיחַ, מְתַקֵּן אֶת מְעַוֵּתָיו וְרוֹחֵץ צוֹאַת עֲווֹנוֹ. וּמִכָּאן יִתְבַּיֵּשׁ הָאָדָם לָשׁוּב לַחֲטוֹא, שֶׁהֲרֵי הַמֶּלֶךְ בְּעַצְמוֹ רוֹחֵץ לִכְלוּךְ בְּגָדָיו.

4. [*And forgives the transgression of*]
the remnant of His heritage:

The Holy One, Blessed Be He, conducts Himself towards Israel in this way: He says, "What shall I do for [the people of] Israel, who are My relatives? I have the obligations of My own flesh [*she'er bassar*] towards them!" For the people of Israel are the spouse of the Holy One, Blessed Be He, and He calls them, "My daughter," "My sister," and "My mother." As our sages explain the phrase "the children of Israel, a people close to Him" (*Tehillim* 148:14), "He has an actual blood relationship with them, and they are His children."

This, too, is the meaning of the words "the *she'erit* [remnant] of His heritage," implying *she'er bassar*, a blood relationship. In the final analysis, the children of Israel are G-d's inheritance. Says the Holy One, Blessed Be He: "If I punish them, the pain is Mine!" as it is written, "In all their trouble, He is afflicted..." (*Yeshayahu* 63:9). The verse is written לא צר (with an *aleph*), implying that the pain of Israel extends to the level of *keter* called *peleh*, and how much more so to the level of the 'dual visage,' *tiferet* and *malchut*, through which the world is mainly run. [But] the verse is read לו צר (with a *vav*), signifying that the pain is His. This is also the intention of the verse "...His soul became impatient with the misery of Israel" (*Shofetim* 10:16), for He cannot bear [the Jews'] suffering and disgrace, since they are the *she'erit* of His heritage.

A person should conduct himself the same way towards his friend, since all [the people of] Israel are

הד׳ — לִשְׁאֵרִית נַחֲלָתוֹ

הִנֵּה הַקָּבָּ״ה מִתְנַהֵג עִם יִשְׂרָאֵל בְּדֶרֶךְ זֶה, לוֹמַר, מָה אֶעֱשֶׂה לְיִשְׂרָאֵל וְהֵם קְרוֹבַי, שְׁאָר בָּשָׂר לִי עִמָּהֶם, שֶׁהֵם בַּת זוּג לְהַקָּבָּ״ה, וְקוֹרֵא לָהּ בִּתִּי, אֲחוֹתִי, אִמִּי, כִּדְפֵירְשׁוּ ז״ל (שִׁיר הַשִּׁירִים רַבָּה פ״ט), וּכְתִיב (תהלים קמ״ח, י״ד): ״יִשְׂרָאֵל עַם קְרוֹבוֹ״, מַמָּשׁ קוּרְבָה יֵשׁ לוֹ עִמָּהֶם וּבָנָיו הֵם.

וְהַיְינוּ ״לִשְׁאֵרִית נַחֲלָתוֹ״, לְשׁוֹן שְׁאָר בָּשָׂר, וְסוֹף סוֹף הֵם נַחֲלָתוֹ, וּמָה אוֹמֵר, אִם אֲעַנִּישֵׁם הֲרֵי הַכְּאֵב עָלַי, כִּדְכְתִיב (ישעיה ס״ג, ט׳): ״בְּכָל צָרָתָם לוֹ צָר״, כְּתִיב בְּאָלֶ״ף, לוֹמַר שֶׁצַּעֲרָם מַגִּיעַ לַפֶּלֶא הָעֶלְיוֹן וְכָל שֶׁכֵּן לְדוּפַרְצוּפִין, שֶׁבָּהֶן עִיקַר הַהַנְהָגָה, וְקָרִינַן בְּוָא״ו ״לוֹ צָר״, וּכְתִיב (שופטים י׳, ט״ז): ״וַתִּקְצַר נַפְשׁוֹ בַּעֲמַל יִשְׂרָאֵל״, לְפִי שֶׁאֵינוֹ סוֹבֵל צַעֲרָם וּקְלוֹנָם, מִפְּנֵי שֶׁהֵם שְׁאֵרִית נַחֲלָתוֹ.

כָּךְ הָאָדָם עִם חֲבֵירוֹ, כָּל יִשְׂרָאֵל הֵם שְׁאָר בָּשָׂר אֵלּוּ עִם אֵלּוּ,

blood relatives, being that all souls are united, and each person has a part of all others. This is why an individual who carries out the commandments can't compare to a multitude of people who do so, since they all complement one another. And thus, our sages explain regarding one who numbers among the first ten to arrive at the synagogue that even if one hundred come after him, he receives a reward equivalent to [the combined reward of] them all. *One hundred* is to be understood literally, since the souls of each of the first ten are included in each other, so there are ten times ten, equaling a hundred. Thus, the ten include a hundred souls. Therefore, even if a hundred people come after one of the first ten, his reward equals all of theirs. This is why "all [the people of] Israel are guarantors for one another," since each individual Jew has a portion of all the others. When one individual sins, he blemishes not only his own soul but the portion of him that every other Jew possesses. It follows that his fellow Jew is a guarantor for that portion.

Hence, all Jews are family, and one should therefore desire the best for his fellow, view his neighbor's good fortune benevolently, and cherish his friend's honor as his own — for they are one and the same! For this reason, too, we are commanded to "love your fellow Jew as yourself" (*VaYikra* 19:18) — and it is proper that a person desire the well-being of his fellow, and he should never speak ill of him or desire that evil befall him. Just as the Holy One, Blessed Be He, desires neither our disgrace nor our suffering, because we are His relatives, a person should not desire to see his fellow's disgrace, suffering,

מִפְּנֵי שֶׁהַנְּשָׁמוֹת כְּלוּלוֹת יַחַד, יֵשׁ בָּזֶה חֵלֶק זֶה, וּבָזֶה חֵלֶק זֶה,
וּלְכָךְ אֵינוֹ דוֹמֶה מְרֻבִּים הָעוֹשִׂים אֶת הַמִּצְוָה (ספרא לויקרא כ״ו,
ח׳), וְכָל זֶה מִפְּנֵי כְּלָלוּתָם. וּלְכָךְ פֵּירְשׁוּ רַבּוֹתֵינוּ זִכְרָם לִבְרָכָה
(ברכות מ״ז, ב׳) עַל הַגְּמָרָא מֵעֲשָׂרָה רִאשׁוֹנִים בְּבֵית הַכְּנֶסֶת, אֲפִילוּ
מֵאָה בָּאִים אַחֲרָיו, מְקַבֵּל שָׂכָר כְּנֶגֶד כּוּלָם, מֵאָה מַמָּשׁ כְּמַשְׁמָעוֹ,
מִפְּנֵי שֶׁהָעֲשָׂרָה הֵם כְּלוּלִים אֵלּוּ בְּאֵלּוּ, הֲרֵי הֵם עֶשֶׂר פְּעָמִים עֲשָׂרָה
— הֵם מֵאָה, וְכָל אֶחָד מֵהֶם כָּלוּל מִמֵּאָה, אִם כֵּן אֲפִילוּ יָבוֹאוּ
מֵאָה, הוּא יֵשׁ לוֹ שְׂכַר מֵאָה. וְכֵן מִטַּעַם זֶה יִשְׂרָאֵל עֲרֵבִים זֶה לָזֶה
(שבועות, ל״ט, א׳), מִפְּנֵי שֶׁמַּמָּשׁ יֵשׁ בְּכָל אֶחָד חֵלֶק אֶחָד מֵחֲבֵירוֹ,
וּכְשֶׁחוֹטֵא הָאֶחָד פּוֹגֵם עַצְמוֹ וּפוֹגֵם חֵלֶק אֲשֶׁר לַחֲבֵירוֹ בּוֹ, נִמְצָא
מִצַּד הַחֵלֶק הַהוּא, חֲבֵירוֹ עָרֵב עָלָיו, אִם כֵּן הֵם שְׁאָר זֶה עִם זֶה.

וּלְכָךְ רָאוּי לָאָדָם לִהְיוֹת חָפֵץ בְּטוֹבָתוֹ שֶׁל חֲבֵירוֹ וְעֵינוֹ טוֹבָה
עַל טוֹבַת חֲבֵירוֹ וּכְבוֹדוֹ יִהְיֶה חָבִיב עָלָיו כְּשֶׁלּוֹ, שֶׁהֲרֵי הוּא —
הוּא מַמָּשׁ. וּמִטַּעַם זֶה נִצְטַוֵּינוּ (ויקרא י״ט, י״ח): "וְאָהַבְתָּ לְרֵעֲךָ
כָּמוֹךָ". וְרָאוּי שֶׁיִּרְצֶה בְּכַשְׁרוּת חֲבֵירוֹ וְלֹא יְדַבֵּר בִּגְנוּתוֹ כְּלָל וְלֹא
יִרְצֶה בּוֹ. כְּדֶרֶךְ שֶׁאֵין הַקָּבָּ״ה רוֹצֶה בִּגְנוּתֵנוּ וְלֹא בְּצַעֲרֵנוּ, מִטַּעַם
הַקּוּרְבָה, אַף הוּא לֹא יִרְצֶה בִּגְנוּת חֲבֵירוֹ וְלֹא בְּצַעֲרוֹ וְלֹא בְּקִלְקוּלוֹ

or downfall. Rather, a person should be pained by it as if he himself were the victim. The reverse applies to his fellow's good fortune.

5. *He does not maintain His anger forever:*

This attribute is different from those mentioned above, for even though a person persists in sinning, the Holy One, Blessed Be He, does not persist in His anger. And even when He does become angry, it is not forever. Rather, He assuages His anger even if a person does not repent, as we find in the days of Yaravam ben Yoash, when the Holy One, Blessed Be He, restored the borders of the Land of Israel (*II Melachim* 14): Even though the people were unrepentant worshippers of calf idols, He had compassion for them. Why? Because of this attribute of not maintaining His anger forever. On the contrary, He deliberately mitigates His anger, even though the sin still exists. And He does not exact punishment; rather, He waits hopefully and compassionately for sinners to repent. This is the intention of the verse "Not forever will He do battle, nor will He bear a grudge for eternity" (*Tehillim* 103:9). Rather, the Holy One, Blessed Be He, conducts Himself with both tenderness and severity, as Israel's benefit requires.

This is a fitting attribute for a person to acquire in his conduct towards his fellow. Even if one is permitted to chastise his friend or his children severely, and they would accept the rebuke, this is no reason to harshen his chastisement and persist in his wrath, even if he is natu-

וְיֵרַע לוֹ מִמֶּנּוּ כְּאִלּוּ הוּא מַמָּשׁ הָיָה שָׁרוּי בְּאוֹתוֹ צַעַר אוֹ בְּאוֹתָהּ טוֹבָה.

הה' — לֹא הֶחֱזִיק לָעַד אַפּוֹ.

זוֹ מִדָּה אַחֶרֶת, שֶׁאֲפִילוּ הָאָדָם מַחֲזִיק בְּחֵטְא, אֵין הַקָּבָּ"ה מַחֲזִיק אַף. וְאִם מַחֲזִיק, לֹא לָעַד, אֶלָּא יְבַטֵּל כַּעֲסוֹ אֲפִילוּ שֶׁלֹּא יָשׁוּב הָאָדָם, כְּמוֹ שֶׁמָּצִינוּ בִּימֵי יָרָבְעָם בֶּן יוֹאָשׁ (מלכים ב' י"ד, כ"ו), שֶׁהֶחֱזִיר הַקָּבָּ"ה גְּבוּל יִשְׂרָאֵל, וְהֵם הָיוּ עוֹבְדֵי עֲגָלִים, וְרִחֵם עֲלֵיהֶם וְלֹא שָׁבוּ, אִם כֵּן לָמָה רִחֵם. בִּשְׁבִיל מִדָּה זוֹ, שֶׁלֹּא הֶחֱזִיק לָעַד אַפּוֹ, אַדְּרַבָּה, מַחֲלִישׁ אַפּוֹ, עִם הֱיוֹת שֶׁעֲדַיִן הַחֵטְא קַיָּים, אֵינוֹ מַעֲנִישׁ, אֶלָּא מְצַפֶּה וּמְרַחֵם אוּלַי יָשׁוּבוּ, וְהַיְינוּ (תהלים ק"ג, ט') "לֹא לָנֶצַח יָרִיב וְלֹא לְעוֹלָם יִטּוֹר", אֶלָּא הַקָּבָּ"ה מִתְנַהֵג בְּרַכּוּת וּבְקָשׁוּת, הַכֹּל לְטוֹבַת יִשְׂרָאֵל.

וְזוֹ מִדָּה רְאוּיָה לָאָדָם לְהִתְנַהֵג בָּהּ עִם חֲבֵירוֹ. אֲפִילוּ שֶׁהוּא רַשַּׁאי לְהוֹכִיחַ אֶת חֲבֵירוֹ אוֹ אֶת בָּנָיו, וְהֵם מִתְיַסְּרִים, לֹא מִפְּנֵי זֶה יַרְבֶּה תוֹכַחְתּוֹ וְלֹא יַחֲזִיק כַּעֲסוֹ אֲפִילוּ שֶׁכָּעַס, אֶלָּא יְבַטְּלֶנּוּ וְלֹא יַחֲזִיק לָעַד אַפּוֹ, גַּם אִם אַף הוּא הַמּוּתָּר לָאָדָם, כְּעֵין שֶׁפֵּירְשׁוּ

rally angry. Instead, he should assuage his anger and not linger over it, even where it would be permissible to do so.

This idea is comparable to our sages' explanation of the verse "When you see the donkey of your hated enemy struggling under his load..., עזוב תעזוב עמו — you shall surely help him" (*Shemot* 23:5). They explain the cause of the hatred mentioned in the verse as being that he saw his enemy transgressing, and, being a lone witness, he cannot testify in the rabbinical court. Thus, he is permitted to hate the fellow as regards his sin. Even so, the Torah demands, עזוב תעזוב עמו — "you shall surely help him," meaning, "abandon (עזוב) the anger in your heart." Indeed, it is a religious obligation to draw the person closer with love, for perhaps this method will succeed. This is exactly the attribute of "He does not maintain His anger forever."

6. *For He delights in kindness*:

We have already explained elsewhere that angels in a certain celestial chamber are appointed to receive the kind deeds man performs in this world. When the attribute of severity accuses Israel, these angels immediately exhibit those acts of kindness before the Heavenly Court, and the Holy One, Blessed Be He, shows compassion to Israel, since He delights in kindness. And even though [the people of Israel] may be guilty, He shows them mercy if they are kind to one another.

This can be compared to when the Holy Temple was destroyed, when G-d said to the angel Gavriel: "Go in

"כִּי תִרְאֶה חֲמוֹר שֹׂנַאֲךָ רוֹבֵץ תַּחַת מַשָּׂאוֹ" (שמות כ"ג, ה') וּפֵירְשׁוּ
(פסחים קי"ג, ב') מַה הִיא הַשִּׂנְאָה הַזֹּאת — שֶׁרָאָה אוֹתוֹ עוֹבֵר
עֲבֵירָה, וְהוּא יָחִיד אֵינוֹ יָכוֹל לְהָעִיד, וְשׂוֹנֵא אוֹתוֹ עַל דְּבַר עֲבֵירָה,
וַאֲפִילוּ הָכִי אָמְרָה תוֹרָה "עָזֹב תַּעֲזוֹב עִמּוֹ", שְׁבוֹק יָת דִּבְלִבָּךְ,
אֶלָּא מִצְוָה לְקָרֵב אוֹתוֹ בְּאַהֲבָה, אוּלַי יוֹעִיל בְּדֶרֶךְ זוֹ; וְהַיְנוּ מַמָּשׁ
מִדָּה זוֹ — "לֹא הֶחֱזִיק לָעַד אַפּוֹ".

הוּ' — כִּי חָפֵץ חֶסֶד הוּא

הֲלֹא פֵּירַשְׁנוּ בִּמְקוֹמוֹ (פרדס רימונים, שער ההיכלות, סוֹף
פרק ה') שֶׁיֵּשׁ בְּהֵיכָל יָדוּעַ מַלְאָכִים מְמוּנִּים לְקַבֵּל גְּמִילוּת חֲסָדִים
שֶׁאָדָם עוֹשֶׂה בָּעוֹלָם הַזֶּה, וְכַאֲשֶׁר מִדַּת הַדִּין מְקַטְרֶגֶת עַל יִשְׂרָאֵל,
מִיָּד אוֹתָם הַמַּלְאָכִים מַרְאִים הַחֶסֶד הַהוּא וְהַקָּבָּ"ה מְרַחֵם עַל יִשְׂרָאֵל,
מִפְּנֵי שֶׁהוּא חָפֵץ בְּחֶסֶד; וְעִם הֱיוֹת שֶׁהֵם חַיָּיבִים, אִם הֵם גּוֹמְלִים
חֶסֶד זֶה לָזֶה מְרַחֵם זֶה עֲלֵיהֶם.

וּכְמוֹ שֶׁהָיָה בִּזְמַן הַחֻרְבָּן, שֶׁנֶּאֱמַר לְגַבְרִיאֵל (יחזקאל י', ב'):
"בֹּא אֶל בֵּינוֹת לַגַּלְגַּל וְגוֹ'", כִּי הוּא שַׂר הַדִּין וְהַגְּבוּרָה וְנָתַן לוֹ
רְשׁוּת לְקַבֵּל כֹּחוֹת הַדִּין בֵּינוֹת לַגַּלְגַּל מִתַּחַת לַכְּרוּבִים מֵאֵשׁ הַמִּזְבֵּחַ,

between the *galgal*, beneath the *keruv*, and fill your hands with burning coals from among the *keruvim*, and throw them on the city..." (*Yechezkel* 10:2). For Gavriel is the angel of judgment and severity, and G-d gave him permission to receive the powers of severity from the fire on the Altar, which is between the *galgal*, below the *keruvim*. This is judgment according to the severities of *malchut*, which became so severe that it sought to destroy everything and annihilate the seed of Israel, which had incurred the penalty of destruction. However, the passage continues, "The form of a man's hand appeared under the wings of the *keruvim*" (ibid. 10:8). The meaning of this is that the Holy One, Blessed Be He, said to Gavriel, "Since they do kindness towards one another, even though they are guilty, they shall be saved, and a remnant of them will be left." The reason for this is the attribute of "He delights in kindness," that is, the kindness that one Jew shows another, for He remembers it in [the Jews'] favor, even though, from another point of view, they are unworthy.

Hence, a person should emulate this attribute in his own conduct. Even if one is aware that another person is doing him evil, and this angers him, if that person has some redeeming quality, e.g., he is kind to others, or he possesses some other virtue, this should be sufficient cause for one to dissipate his anger and find the other person pleasing, i.e., to delight in the kindness he does. One should say, "It is enough for me that he has this good quality." How much more so does all this apply to one's wife; as our sages have said: "It is enough that they raise our children and save us from sin." So, too, should a

דְּהַיְינוּ דִין גְּבוּרַת הַמַּלְכוּת, וְהָיָה הַדִּין מִתְחַזֵּק עַד שֶׁבִּקֵּשׁ לְכַלּוֹת
אֶת הַכֹּל, לְקַעֲקֵעַ בֵּיצָתָן שֶׁל יִשְׂרָאֵל, מִפְּנֵי שֶׁנִּתְחַיְּיבוּ כְּלָיָה, וּכְתִיב
(שָׁם, שָׁם, ח'): "וַיֵּרָא לַכְּרוּבִים תַּבְנִית יַד אָדָם תַּחַת כַּנְפֵיהֶם",
וְהַיְינוּ שֶׁאָמַר הַקָּבָּ"ה לְגַבְרִיאֵל, הֵם גּוֹמְלִים חֲסָדִים אֵלּוּ עִם אֵלּוּ
(וַיִּקְרָא רַבָּה סוֹף פֶּרֶק כ"ו); וְאַף אִם הֵם חַיָּיבִים, נִצּוֹלוּ וְהָיָה לָהֶם
שְׁאֵרִית. וְהַטַּעַם, מִפְּנֵי מִדָּה זוֹ, "כִּי חָפֵץ חֶסֶד הוּא", רוֹצֶה, בַּמֶּה
שֶׁיִּשְׂרָאֵל גּוֹמְלִים חֶסֶד, וְאוֹתוֹ צַד מַזְכִּיר לָהֶם, עִם הֱיוֹת שֶׁאֵינָם
כְּשֵׁרִים בְּצַד אֶחָד.

אִם כֵּן בְּמִדָּה זוֹ רָאוּי לָאָדָם לְהִתְנַהֵג, אַף אִם רָאָה שֶׁאָדָם עוֹשֶׂה
לוֹ רַע וּמַכְעִיסוֹ, אִם יֵשׁ בּוֹ צַד טוֹבָה, שֶׁמֵּטִיב לַאֲחֵרִים, אוֹ מִדָּה
טוֹבָה, שֶׁמִּתְנַהֵג כְּשׁוּרָה, יַסְפִּיק לוֹ צַד זֶה לְבַטֵּל כַּעֲסוֹ מֵעָלָיו וְיִרְצֶה
לִבּוֹ עִמּוֹ וְיַחְפֹּץ חֶסֶד, וְיֹאמַר, "דַּי לִי בְּטוֹבָה זוֹ שֶׁיֵּשׁ לוֹ". וְכָל
שֶׁכֵּן בְּאִשְׁתּוֹ, כִּדְפֵירְשׁוּ רַבּוֹתֵינוּ זִכְרָם לִבְרָכָה (יְבָמוֹת סג, א):
"דַּיֵּינוּ שֶׁמְּגַדְּלוֹת אֶת בָּנֵינוּ וּמַצִּילוֹת אוֹתָנוּ מִן הַחֵטְא".

person say to himself with regard to every man, "It is enough that he has been good to me or to someone else in such-and-such a way, or that he has such-and-such a positive quality." In this way, one should delight in kindness.

7. *He will again show us compassion*:

The Holy One, Blessed Be He, does not behave as man behaves. For when a person is provoked, he cannot bring himself to love the one who offended him to the same degree as before, even after he is appeased. But if a person sins and afterwards repents, his stature before the Holy One, Blessed Be He, is even greater than before.

This is the intention of a statement our sages made, "The perfectly righteous cannot stand where repentant sinners stand." They explain as follows:

"Why is the letter *hei* (ה) shaped like a porch? So that anyone who wants to go astray can do so!" The explanation of this is as follows: The physical world was created with the letter *hei*, for the Holy One, Blessed Be He, created the world in such a way that it is wide-open to evil and sin. There is no area where the opportunity to sin, the evil urge, and blemishes of the soul are absent! It is just like a wide-open, unfenced porch, which has no barriers against danger, as symbolized by the gap at the bottom of the *hei*. Anyone who desires to forgo the World to Come has many exits, since wherever he turns, he can find evil and sin through which he can enter the domain of the Outside Forces.

כָּךְ יֹאמַר עַל כָּל אָדָם, "דַּי לִי בְּטוֹבָה פְּלוֹנִית שֶׁעָשָׂה לִי אוֹ שֶׁעָשָׂה עִם פְּלוֹנִי אוֹ מִדָּה טוֹבָה פְּלוֹנִית שֶׁיֵּשׁ לוֹ" וְיִהְיֶה "חָפֵץ חֶסֶד".

הז' — יָשׁוּב יְרַחֲמֵנוּ.

אֵין הַקָּבָּ"ה מִתְנַהֵג כְּמִדַּת בָּשָׂר וָדָם, שֶׁאִם הִכְעִיסוֹ חֲבֵרוֹ כְּשֶׁהוּא מִתְרַצֶּה עִמּוֹ מִתְרַצֶּה מְעַט לֹא בְּאַהֲבָה הַקּוֹדֶמֶת; אֲבָל אִם חָטָא אָדָם וְעָשָׂה תְּשׁוּבָה, מַעֲלָתוֹ יוֹתֵר גְּדוֹלָה עִם הַקָּבָּ"ה.

וְהַיְינוּ (ברכות ל"ד, ב') "בַּמָּקוֹם שֶׁבַּעֲלֵי תְשׁוּבָה עוֹמְדִים אֵין צַדִּיקִים גְּמוּרִים יְכוֹלִין לַעֲמוֹד". וְהַטַּעַם כְּדְפֵירְשׁוּ בְּפֶרֶק "הַבּוֹנֶה" (בסיפרינו כתוב כך במנחות כ"ט, ב') בְּעִנְיַן ה, לָמָּה הִיא עֲשׂוּיָה כְּאַכְסַדְרָה, שֶׁכָּל הָרוֹצֶה לָצֵאת מֵעוֹלָמוֹ יֵצֵא, פֵּירוּשׁ הָעוֹלָם נִבְרָא בְה', וְהַקָּבָּ"ה בָּרָא הָעוֹלָם פָּתוּחַ לְצַד הָרַע וְהַחֵטְא לִרְוָוחָה, אֵין צַד שֶׁאֵין חוֹמֶר וְיֵצֶר הָרַע וּפְגָם, כְּמִין אַכְסַדְרָה, אֵינוֹ בַּעַל גְּדָרִים אֶלָּא פִּרְצָה גְּדוֹלָה פְּרוּצָה לְצַד הָרַע לְצַד מַטָּה, כָּל מִי שֶׁיִּרְצֶה לָצֵאת מֵעוֹלָמוֹ, כַּמָּה פְּתָחִין לוֹ, לֹא יִפְנֶה לְצַד שֶׁלֹּא יִמְצָא צַד חֵטְא וְעָוֹן לִיכָּנֵס אֶל הַחִיצוֹנִים.

And yet, the *hei* also has a gap in the top left corner, symbolizing repentance, which will be accepted by G-d. But why shouldn't a person reenter by the same path through which he left? Answer our sages: "Because this will have no effect!" For it is not enough for a repentant sinner to guard himself against sin the same way a perfectly righteous person does. A saint who has not sinned requires only a minor barrier, whereas for a repentant sinner, a small barrier is insufficient — he needs a number of tough restraints, since this frail defense was already smashed through once, and if he approaches the fence again, his evil urge might seduce him.

Therefore, he should not reenter via the same path by which he left, through the part of the porch he broke through. Rather, he should ascend to the narrow gap at the top of the *hei*, representing the restraints and penances he accepts upon himself in mending the broken fence, and he should enter through there.

For this reason, "The perfectly righteous cannot stand where repentant sinners stand" — for the latter did not enter through the same door as the righteous such that they should stand together. Instead, they mortified themselves in order to ascend through the upper door, and they inflicted penances on themselves and distanced themselves from sin much more than the righteous. They have therefore ascended and attained the level of the *hei* that is called "the Fifth Palace of Gan Eden," that is to say, the roof of the *hei*, whereas the righteous have entered only through the lower opening of the *hei* — the entrance to the porch.

וְהִיא פְּתוּחָה מִלְמַעְלָה שֶׁאִם יָשׁוּב יְקַבְּלוּהוּ. וְהִקְשׁוּ "וּלְהַדְרוּהוּ בְּהַאי" — "לֹא מִסְתַּיְיעָא מִלְתָא." רָצוּ בָּזֶה, שֶׁהַשָּׁב בִּתְשׁוּבָה לֹא יַסְפִּיק לוֹ שֶׁיִּהְיֶה נִגְדָּר בְּעָוֹן כִּגְדֵר הַצַּדִּיקִים, מִפְּנֵי שֶׁהַצַּדִּיקִים שֶׁלֹּא חָטְאוּ, גֶּדֶר מְעַט יַסְפִּיק אֲלֵיהֶם, אָמְנָם הַחוֹטֵא שֶׁחָטָא וְשָׁב לֹא יַסְפִּיק לוֹ גֶּדֶר מְעַט, אֶלָּא צָרִיךְ לְהַגְדִּיר עַצְמוֹ כַּמָּה גְּדָרִים קָשִׁים, מִפְּנֵי שֶׁאוֹתוֹ גֶּדֶר הַמְעַט כְּבָר נִפְרַץ פַּעַם אַחַת, אִם יִתְקָרֵב שָׁם, בְּקַל יְפַתֵּהוּ יִצְרוֹ, אֶלָּא צָרִיךְ לְהִתְרַחֵק הַרְחֵק גָּדוֹל מְאֹד.

וְלָזֶה לֹא יִכָּנֵס דֶּרֶךְ פֶּתַח הָאַכְסַדְרָה שֶׁהַפִּרְצָה שָׁם, אֶלָּא יִתְעַלֶּה וְיִכָּנֵס דֶּרֶךְ פֶּתַח צַר וְיַעֲשֶׂה כַּמָּה צָרוֹת וְסִגּוּפִים לְעַצְמוֹ וְיִסְתּוֹם הַפְּרָצוֹת.

וּמִטַּעַם זֶה "בַּמָּקוֹם שֶׁבַּעֲלֵי תְשׁוּבָה עוֹמְדִים וכו'", מִפְּנֵי שֶׁלֹּא נִכְנְסוּ דֶּרֶךְ פֶּתַח הַצַּדִּיקִים כְּדֵי שֶׁיִּהְיוּ עִם הַצַּדִּיקִים, אֶלָּא נִצְטַעֲרוּ וְעָלוּ דֶּרֶךְ פֶּתַח הָעֶלְיוֹן וְסִגְּפוּ עַצְמָם וְנִבְדְּלוּ מִן הַחֵטְא יוֹתֵר וְיוֹתֵר מִן הַצַּדִּיקִים, לְכָךְ עָלוּ וְעָמְדוּ בְּמַדְרֵגָה ה', הֵיכַל ה' שֶׁבְּגַן עֵדֶן, דְּהַיְינוּ גַּג הֵה"א, וְצַדִּיקִים בְּפֶתַח הֵה"א בִּכְנִיסַת הָאַכְסַדְרָה.

Therefore, when a person does *teshuvah* תשובה, that is to say, *tashuv hei* תשוב ה, when he returns the *hei* to its proper place, then the Holy One, Blessed Be He, will return his Shechinah to him. And the Holy One, Blessed Be He, will restore His love for the repentant person not only as it was originally but in an even greater measure. This is the explanation of the attribute "He will again show us compassion": He will increase His compassion for Israel, perfecting us and drawing us closer to Himself.

This is also how a person should behave towards his fellow. He should not nurse the hatred born of anger he once felt. Rather, when he sees that his fellow desires his friendship, he should show him even greater compassion and love than before, saying, "He is like the penitents in whose place even the perfectly righteous cannot stand." In this way, a person will draw his fellow very close to himself — much closer than he would draw those who have behaved perfectly righteously towards him, never wronging him.

8. *He will vanquish our iniquities:*

The relationship of the Holy One, Blessed Be He, to Israel is according to this attribute, namely, the secret of vanquishing iniquity. For the precepts are compared to a grapevine that's "budding, its blossoms bursting forth" (*Bereishit* 40:10) — it shoots upwards without limit, entering His blessed Presence. However, sins have no entrance there, G-d forbid. Rather, He suppresses them, denying them entry, as it is written: "...no harm will befall you

וְלָזֶה, כַּאֲשֶׁר הָאָדָם יַעֲשֶׂה תְּשׁוּבָה, דְּהַיְינוּ תָשׁוּב ה' אֶל מְקוֹמָהּ, וְיַחֲזִיר הַקָּבָּ"ה שְׁכִינָתוֹ עָלָיו, אֵינוּ שָׁב כְּאַהֲבָה הָרִאשׁוֹנָה בִּלְבַד, אֶלָּא יוֹתֵר וְיוֹתֵר. וְהַיְינוּ "יָשׁוּב יְרַחֲמֵנוּ", שֶׁיּוֹסִיף רַחֲמִים לְיִשְׂרָאֵל וִיתַקְּנֵם וִיקָרְבֵם יוֹתֵר.

כָּךְ הָאָדָם צָרִיךְ לְהִתְנַהֵג עִם חֲבֵרוֹ, לֹא יִהְיֶה נוֹטֵר אֵיבָה מֵהַכַּעַס הַקּוֹדֵם, אֶלָּא כְּשֶׁיִּרְאֶה שֶׁחֲבֵרוֹ מְבַקֵּשׁ אַהֲבָתוֹ יִהְיֶה לוֹ בְּמַדְרֵגַת רַחֲמִים וְאַהֲבָה יוֹתֵר וְיוֹתֵר מִקּוֹדֶם, וְיֹאמַר: "הֲרֵי הוּא לִי כְּבַעֲלֵי תְּשׁוּבָה, שֶׁאֵין צַדִּיקִים גְּמוּרִים יְכוֹלִים לַעֲמוֹד אֶצְלָם", וִיקָרְבֵהוּ תַּכְלִית קוּרְבָה יוֹתֵר מִמַּה שֶׁמְּקָרֵב אוֹתָם שֶׁהֵם צַדִּיקִים גְּמוּרִים עִמּוֹ, שֶׁלֹּא חָטְאוּ אֶצְלוֹ.

הח' — יְכְבּוֹשׁ עֲוֹנוֹתֵינוּ.

הֲרֵי הַקָּבָּ"ה מִתְנַהֵג עִם יִשְׂרָאֵל בְּמִדָּה זוֹ, וְהִיא סוֹד כְּבִישַׁת הֶעָוֹן. כִּי הִנֵּה הַמִּצְוָה הִיא כְּפוֹרַחַת עָלְתָה נִצָּהּ, וּבוֹקֵעַ וְעוֹלֶה עַד אֵין תַּכְלִית לִכְנוֹס לְפָנָיו יִתְבָּרֵךְ. אָמְנָם הָעֲוֹנוֹת אֵין לָהֶם כְּנִיסָה שָׁם, חַס וְשָׁלוֹם, אֶלָּא כּוֹבְשָׁם שֶׁלֹּא יִכָּנְסוּ, כְּדִכְתִיב (תהלים ה',

יגורך" (*Tehillim* 5:5), which our sages interpret as implying that "no harm will befall man in Your dwelling place מגורך." Thus, sin has no entry into the Inner Sanctum.

Since the precepts reside in His blessed Presence, they have no reward in this world. For how could G-d grant spiritual reward in the material world? Behold, the entire world is unworthy of a single precept and the spiritual bliss of His Presence.

For the same reason, G-d does not take the precepts as bribes. For instance, the Holy One, Blessed Be He, does not say, G-d forbid, "He has fulfilled forty commandments and committed ten transgressions; thus, thirty commandments remain, for ten are deducted in repayment for the ten transgressions!" Rather, if even a perfectly righteous individual commits a single sin, it is as if he has burnt the Torah. But when he pays his debt, he receives reward for all the precepts he has fulfilled. This is a great kindness that the Holy One, Blessed Be He, does for the righteous — He does not deduct from the precepts they fulfill, for these are very precious to Him and ascend directly to His blessed Presence. Indeed, how could transgressions, whose punishment is a portion of that which is most despicable — Gehinom — detract from precepts, whose reward is the radiance of the Shechinah, which is so highly valued? How could one be exchanged for the other? Instead, the Holy One, Blessed Be He, collects the debt due for transgressions, and then He bestows the reward for all the precepts a person has fulfilled.

This is the attribute of "vanquishing iniquity" — that is, transgressions do not prevail before G-d as the com-

ה'): "לֹא יְגוּרְךָ רָע", "לֹא יָגוּר בִּמְגוּרְךָ רָע" (שׁוֹחַר טוֹב שָׁם, שַׁבָּת קמ"ט, ב') אִם כֵּן אֵין הֶעָוֹן נִכְנָס פְּנִימָה.

וּמִטַּעַם זֶה "שְׂכַר מִצְוָה בְּהַאי עָלְמָא לֵיכָּא" (קִדּוּשִׁין ל"ט, ב'), מִפְּנֵי שֶׁהֵם לְפָנָיו יִתְבָּרֵךְ, וְהֵיאַךְ יִתֵּן לוֹ מִמַּה שֶּׁלְּפָנָיו שָׂכָר רוּחָנִי בָּעוֹלָם גַּשְׁמִי, וַהֲרֵי כָּל הָעוֹלָם אֵינוֹ כְּדַאי לְמִצְוָה אַחַת וְלִקוֹרַת רוּחַ אֲשֶׁר לְפָנָיו.

וּמִטַּעַם זֶה לֹא יִקַּח שׁוֹחַד שֶׁל מִצְוֹת. הַמָּשָׁל בָּזֶה, אֵין הַקָּדוֹשׁ בָּרוּךְ הוּא אוֹמֵר, "עָשָׂה אַרְבָּעִים מִצְוֹת וְאֶשֶׁר עֲבֵירוֹת נִשְׁאֲרוּ שְׁלֹשִׁים מִצְוֹת וְיֵלְכוּ עֶשֶׂר בְּעֶשֶׂר", חַס וְחָלִילָה, אֶלָּא אֲפִילוּ צַדִּיק גָּמוּר וְעָשָׂה עֲבֵירָה אַחַת, דּוֹמֶה לְפָנָיו כְּאִלּוּ שָׂרַף אֶת הַתּוֹרָה, עַד שֶׁיְּרַצֶּה חוֹבוֹ וְאַחַר כָּךְ יְקַבֵּל שָׂכָר כָּל מִצְוֹתָיו. וְזֶה חֶסֶד גָּדוֹל שֶׁעוֹשֶׂה הַקָּבָּ"ה עִם הַצַּדִּיקִים, שֶׁאֵינוֹ מְנַכֶּה, מִפְּנֵי שֶׁהַמִּצְווֹת חֲשׁוּבוֹת מְאֹד וּמִתְעַלּוֹת עַד לְפָנָיו יִתְבָּרֵךְ, וְהֵיאַךְ יְנַכֶּה מֵהֶן בִּשְׁבִיל הָעֲבֵירוֹת. כִּי שְׂכַר הָעֲבֵירָה הוּא מֵחֵלֶק הַגֵּיהִנּוֹם, מֵהַנִּבְזֶה, וְהַמִּצְווֹת שְׂכָרָן מֵהַנִּכְבָּד, זִיו הַשְּׁכִינָה, הֵיאַךְ יְנַכֶּה אֵלּוּ בְּצַד אֵלּוּ. אֶלָּא הַקָּבָּ"ה גּוֹבֶה חוֹב הָעֲבֵירוֹת וּמַשְׂכִּיר שְׂכַר כָּל הַמִּצְווֹת.

וְהַיְינוּ "יִכְבֹּשׁ עֲוֹנוֹתֵינוּ", שֶׁאֵין הָעֲווֹנוֹת מִתְגַּבְּרִין לְפָנָיו

mandments do. Rather, He suppresses transgressions, preventing them from ascending and entering His Presence. And although He watches all the ways of man, both bad and good, He does not suppress the good. Rather, it rises up, ascending to the very heights where all the precepts merge to build an edifice and form a precious garment. Transgressions, however, lack this special quality — instead, He vanquishes them, so they'll have no success and no entry into the Inner Sanctum.

A person should also conduct himself according to this attribute — he should not suppress his fellow's virtues but remember the evil he has done. On the contrary, he should vanquish the evil, erasing it from memory and abandoning it, so that he will find no evil in his fellow, and his good qualities will be spread out before him. Thus, a person should always remember the good, intensifying it over all the evil actions his fellow has done to him. He should not detract from this good in his heart, saying, "Although he did me a good turn, he also did bad to me," thereby forgetting his fellow's qualities. This one should not do. Rather, he should allow himself to be appeased in every possible way regarding his fellow's misdeeds, never overlooking his good qualities. And he should turn a blind eye to his faults as much as possible, just as the Holy One, Blessed Be He, does in vanquishing our iniquities.

כְּמִצְווֹת. אֶלָּא כּוֹבֵשׁ אוֹתָם שֶׁלֹּא יִתְעַלּוּ וְלֹא יִכָּנְסוּ עִם הֱיוֹת שֶׁהוּא מַשְׁגִּיחַ עַל דַּרְכֵי אִישׁ, הַטּוֹב וְהָרָע, עִם כָּל זֶה הַטּוֹב אֵינוֹ כּוֹבְשׁוֹ, אֶלָּא פּוֹרֵחַ וְעוֹלֶה עַד לִמְאֹד וְנִכְלָל מִצְוָה בְּמִצְוָה וְנִבְנֶה מִמֶּנּוּ בִּנְיָן וּלְבוּשׁ נִכְבָּד; וַעֲווֹנוֹת אֵין לָהֶם סְגֻלָּה זוֹ, אֶלָּא כּוֹבֵשׁ אוֹתָם, שֶׁלֹּא יַצְלִיחוּ הַצְלָחָה זוֹ וְלֹא יִכָּנְסוּ פְּנִימָה.

אַף מִדָּה זוֹ צָרִיךְ הָאָדָם לְהִתְנַהֵג בָּהּ, שֶׁלֹּא יִכְבֹּשׁ טוֹבַת חֲבֵרוֹ וְיִזְכּוֹר רָעָתוֹ שֶׁגְּמָלָהוּ, אֶלָּא אַדְּרַבָּה, יִכְבֹּשׁ הָרָע וְיִשְׁכָּחֵהוּ וְיַזְנִיחֵהוּ וְלֹא יָגוּר בִּמְגוּרוֹ רָע, וְתִהְיֶה הַטּוֹבָה סְדוּרָה תָמִיד לְפָנָיו, וְיִזְכּוֹר לוֹ הַטּוֹבָה וְיַגְבִּירָהּ לוֹ עַל כָּל הַמַּעֲשִׂים שֶׁעָשָׂה לוֹ, וְלֹא יְנַכֶּה בִּלְבּוֹ וְיֹאמַר, "אִם עָשָׂה לִי טוֹבָה הֲרֵי עָשָׂה לִי רָעָה" וְיִשְׁכַּח הַטּוֹבָה, לֹא יַעֲשֶׂה כֵן. אֶלָּא בָּרָעָה יִתְרַצֶּה כָּל דֶּרֶךְ רִיצּוּי שֶׁיּוּכַל, וְהַטּוֹבָה אַל יַזְנִיחָהּ לְעוֹלָם מִבֵּין עֵינָיו, וְיַעֲלִים עֵינוֹ מִן הָרָעָה כָּל מַה שֶּׁיּוּכַל, כְּדֶרֶךְ שֶׁהַקָּבָּ"ה כּוֹבֵשׁ עֲווֹנוֹת, כִּדְפֵירַשְׁתִּי.

9. And You will cast all their sins into the depths of the sea:

This attribute is the goodness of the Holy One, Blessed Be He. For when [the children of] Israel sinned, he delivered them into the hands of Pharoah. But when they repented, why should He have punished Pharoah, or Sancheriv, or Haman and others like them? Yet the Holy One, Blessed Be He, is not content with saying to [the children of] Israel, "Repent!" and then no further evil will befall them, for Haman, Pharoah, or Sancheriv will be removed from them. This is not enough; instead, the iniquity of Haman reverts onto his own head, and so, too, with Pharoah and Sancheriv.

The reason the Holy One, Blessed Be He, conducts Himself in this manner is to be found in the secret contained in the verse "The goat will bear all the sins of Israel upon it to the land of Gezerah..." (*VaYikra* 16:22). The explanation is that the goat itself bears the punishment for their sins! Now this is very hard to understand, for if Israel sinned, why should the goat be responsible?

This is understood as follows: When a person confesses with the intention of accepting upon himself the cleansing of his sin — as King David states: "Cleanse me thoroughly of my wrongdoing..." (*Tehillim* 51:4), and as we pray, "Erase my sin in Your great compassion" — he hopes his punishment will be light in order that it not interfere with his Torah study. As we say in our prayers: "...but not by way of severe suffering." This was also King David's intentions when he stated, "You are just with

הט׳ — וְתַשְׁלִיךְ בִּמְצוּלוֹת יָם כָּל חַטֹּאתָם.

זוֹ מִדָּה טוֹבָה לְהַקָּבָּ״ה. שֶׁהֲרֵי יִשְׂרָאֵל חָטְאוּ מְסָרָם בְּיַד פַּרְעֹה
וְשָׁבוּ בִּתְשׁוּבָה, לָמָּה יַעֲנִישׁ פַּרְעֹה. וְכֵן סַנְחֵרִיב וְכֵן הָמָן וְדוֹמֵיהֶם.
אֵין הַקָּבָּ״ה מִתְנַחֵם בִּלְבַד לוֹמַר: ״שָׁבוּ בִּתְשׁוּבָה, אִם כֵּן לֹא יִהְיֶה
לָהֶם עוֹד רָעָה, אִם כֵּן יִסְתַּלֵּק הָמָן מֵעֲלֵיהֶם, אוֹ פַּרְעֹה אוֹ סַנְחֵרִיב״,
זֶה לֹא יַסְפִּיק, אֶלָּא יָשׁוּב עֲמַל הָמָן עַל רֹאשׁוֹ וְכֵן פַּרְעֹה וְכֵן סַנְחֵרִיב.

וְהַטַּעַם לְהַנְהָגָה זוֹ הוּא בְּסוֹד ״וְנָשָׂא הַשָּׂעִיר עָלָיו אֶת כָּל
עֲוֹנֹתָם אֶל אֶרֶץ גְּזֵירָה״ (ויקרא ט״ז, כ״ב), וּפֵירוּשׁוֹ, שֶׁהַשָּׂעִיר נוֹשֵׂא
עֲוֹנוֹת מַמָּשׁ, וְזֶה קָשֶׁה מְאֹד, וְכִי יִשְׂרָאֵל חָטְאוּ וְהַשָּׂעִיר נוֹשֵׂא.

אֶלָּא הַמִּדָּה הִיא כָּךְ: הָאָדָם מִתְוַדֶּה וְכַוָּנָתוֹ בְּוִידּוּי לְקַבֵּל עָלָיו
טָהֳרָה, כְּעִנְיָן שֶׁאָמַר דָּוִד (תהלים נ״א, ד׳): ״הֶרֶב כַּבְּסֵנִי מֵעֲוֹנִי״,
וְכֵן הוּא אָמְרוּ ״מָחוֹק בְּרַחֲמֶיךָ הָרַבִּים״, אֵינוֹ מִתְפַּלֵּל אֶלָּא שֶׁיִּהְיוּ
יִסּוּרִים קַלִּים שֶׁלֹּא יִהְיֶה בָּהֶם בִּטּוּל תּוֹרָה, וְזֶה שֶׁאוֹמְרִים ״אֲבָל
לֹא עַל יְדֵי יִסּוּרִים רָעִים״, וְכָךְ הוּא מְכַוֵּן בִּהְיוֹתוֹ אוֹמֵר ״וְאַתָּה

regard to all that befalls me," expressing a willingness to accept suffering upon himself for those sins that can be purged only by means of severe affliction or death. And so it is — when a person confesses his wrongdoing in *vidduy*, the Holy One, Blessed Be He, immediately decrees severe suffering upon him for his sins. Then Samae-l appears to claim his due, for this is the portion allotted him, as the *Zohar* on *"Pikudei"* explains. But all the person's sins ultimately devolve upon his head. This way, Israel is purified. This is just like the goat that bore the sins of Israel to its death in Gezerah.

The reason for this is that the Holy One, Blessed Be He, decreed upon His world that all who punish Israel will be annihilated. That's why any animal that is party to a transgression must be killed. Similarly, the stones used to carry out the sentence of those condemned to death by stoning, and the sword used to carry out the sentence of those condemned to decapitation, must be buried in order to nullify their existence and power after they have carried out the judgment.

This is also the secret of the statue Nevuchadnetzar saw in his dream (*Daniel* 2:32-34): When the people of Israel were given into the hand of the Babylonian king, symbolized by "a head of gold," this same king was eventually subjugated by the king of Persia, symbolized by "a silver chest and arms," who was in turn expelled by another nation, and so on, until Israel descended to the "legs...of iron and clay." And what will be the final happy ending? Eventually, the Holy One, Blessed Be He, will execute favorable judgment upon Israel, as it is written:

צַדִּיק עַל כָּל הַבָּא עָלַי״, מַמָּשׁ הוּא מְקַבֵּל יִסּוּרִים בְּסֵבֶר פָּנִים יָפוֹת לְהִתְכַּפֵּר, מִפְּנֵי שֶׁיֵּשׁ עֲווֹנוֹת שֶׁיִּסּוּרִים מְמָרְקִים אוֹ מִיתָה מְמָרֶקֶת, וְכֵן הִיא הַמִּדָּה, מִיָּד שֶׁזֶּה מִתְוַדֶּה בִּתְפִלָּתוֹ, וּפֵירְשׁוּ בַּזּוֹהַר, בְּפָרָשַׁת פִּקּוּדֵי (רס״ב, ב'), שֶׁהוּא חֵלֶק סמאל כְּעֵין הַשָּׂעִיר, מַהוּ חֶלְקוֹ. שֶׁהַקָּבָּ״ה גּוֹזֵר עָלָיו יִסּוּרִים וּמִיָּד מְזַדְּמֵן שָׁם סמאל וְהוֹלֵךְ וְגוֹבֶה חוֹבוֹ, וַהֲרֵי נוֹשֵׂא הַשָּׂעִיר הָעֲווֹנוֹת, שֶׁהַקָּבָּ״ה נוֹתֵן לוֹ רְשׁוּת לִגְבּוֹת חוֹבָן, וְיִשְׂרָאֵל מִתְטַהֲרִין, וְהִנֵּה הַכֹּל יִתְגַּלְגֵּל עַל סמאל.

וְהַטַּעַם, שֶׁהַקָּבָּ״ה גָּזַר עַל עוֹלָמוֹ שֶׁכָּל מִי שֶׁיַּעֲשֶׂה כֵּן יִתְבַּטֵּל, וְזֶה טַעַם ״וְאֶת הַבְּהֵמָה תַּהֲרֹגוּ״ (ויקרא כ', ט״ו), וְכֵן הָאֶבֶן שֶׁל מִצְוַת הַנִּסְקָלִין וְהַסַּיִיף שֶׁל מִצְוַת הַנֶּהֱרָגִין טְעוּנִין קְבוּרָה, לְבַטֵּל מְצִאוּתָם וְכֹחָם כְּאַחַר שֶׁיִּגְמוֹר דִּינָם.

וַהֲרֵי בָּזֶה מַמָּשׁ סוֹד הַצֶּלֶם שֶׁל נְבוּכַדְנֶצַּר (דניאל ב', לב—לד), נִמְסְרוּ יִשְׂרָאֵל בְּיַד מֶלֶךְ בָּבֶל, ״רֵאשָׁה דִי דַהֲבָא״, נִכְנַע הַהוּא רֵישָׁא, וְנִמְסְרוּ בְּיַד פָּרַס שֶׁהֵן ״חֲדוֹהִי וּדְרָעוֹהִי דִי כְסַף״, וְכֵן הוֹדְחוּ אֵלּוּ מִפְּנֵי אֵלּוּ עַד שֶׁיֵּרְדוּ יִשְׂרָאֵל לְ״רַגְלוֹהִי מִנְהוֹן דִי פַרְזֶל וּמִנְהוֹן דִי חֲסַף״. וּמַה יִּהְיֶה תַּכְלִית הַטּוֹב. בְּסוֹף הקב״ה מַעֲמִידָם וְעוֹשֶׂה בָּהֶם דִּין, כְּדִכְתִיב (דברים ל״ב, כ״ג): ״חִצַּי אֲכַלֶּה בָּם״ — ״חִצַּי

"...I will spend My arrows upon them" (*Devarim* 32:23), meaning that the arrows will be spent but not on Israel. "And then the parts of iron, clay, brass, silver, and gold together will be crushed..." (*Daniel* 2:35). First, it is written, "And he smote the idol to its legs" (ibid. 2:34), implying that there was nothing left of the idol but its legs, the head, arms, and torso having lost all their power. Nevertheless, later it is written, "together [they] will be crushed" (ibid. 2:35), for in the future, the Holy One, Blessed Be He, will indict Samae-l and all his evil agents, who carry out his deeds, and He will execute justice upon them.

This is the attribute of "and You will cast all their sins into the depths of the sea," implying that the Holy One, Blessed Be He, will send forth the attribute of judgment to cast down those who are called "the depths of the sea," as the verse states: "The wicked are like the troubled sea, for it cannot rest, and its waters cast up mud and mire" (*Yeshayahu* 57:20). This refers to those who execute judgment on Israel: He will return their recompense upon their own heads, for after the people of Israel receive their judgment, the Holy One, Blessed Be He, regrets His original demand that they be shamed. And this is not all, for "...I was only a little angry, and [the nations of the world] helped make it worse" (*Zechariah* 1:15).

A person also ought to behave this way with his fellow. Even if the latter is wicked and crushed through suffering, he should not despise him, for "having been whipped, he is like your brother." On the contrary, he should draw close the downcast and those who are pun-

כֵּלִים וְיִשְׂרָאֵל אֵינָם כֵּלִים" (סוטה ט', א'). "בֵּאדַיִן דָּקוּ כַחֲדָה וגו'
נְחָשָׁא כַּסְפָּא וְדַהֲבָא וגו'" (דניאל ב', ל"ב). הִנֵּה בְּהַתְחָלָה כְּתִיב
(שם, שם, ל"ד): "וּמְחָת לְצַלְמָא עַל רַגְלוֹהִי". אֵין מִכָּל הַצֶּלֶם אֶלָּא
רַגְלַיִם, שֶׁכְּבָר נִתְבַּטֵּל כֹּחָם וְעָבְרוּ רֹאשָׁה וּדְרָעוֹהִי וּמְעוֹהִי, וְעִם
כָּל זֶה בְּסוֹף "דָּקוּ כַחֲדָה", עָתִיד הקב"ה לְהַעֲמִיד סמאל וְהָרְשָׁעִים
עוֹשֵׂי מַעֲשָׂיו וּפְעוּלוֹתָיו וְיַעֲשֶׂה בָּהֶם הַדִּין.

וְהַיְינוּ — "וְתַשְׁלִיךְ בִּמְצוּלוֹת יָם כָּל חַטֹּאתָם", יִרְצֶה, הַשְׁלִיךְ
כֹּחַ הַדִּין לְהַפִּיל עַל יְדֵי אֵלּוּ שֶׁהֵם מְצוּלוֹת יָם; "וְהָרְשָׁעִים כַּיָּם
נִגְרָשׁ כִּי הַשְׁקֵט לֹא יוּכָל וַיִּגְרְשׁוּ מֵימָיו רֶפֶשׁ וָטִיט" (ישעיהו נ"ז,
כ'), אֵלּוּ הֵם הָעוֹשִׂים דִּין בְּיִשְׂרָאֵל, שֶׁיָּשִׁיב אַחַר כָּךְ אֶת כָּל גְּמוּלָם
בְּרֹאשָׁם. וְהַטַּעַם, מִפְּנֵי שֶׁאַחַר שֶׁיִּשְׂרָאֵל קִבְּלוּ הַדִּין, הקב"ה מִתְנַחֵם
אֲפִילּוּ עַל מַה שֶּׁקָּדַם, וְתוֹבֵעַ עֶלְבּוֹנָם, וְלֹא דַי, אֶלָּא "אֲנִי קָצַפְתִּי
מְעָט וְהֵמָּה עָזְרוּ לְרָעָה" (זכריה א', ט"ו).

גַּם בְּמִדָּה זוֹ צָרִיךְ לְהִתְנַהֵג הָאָדָם עִם חֲבֵרוֹ: אֲפִילּוּ שֶׁיִּהְיֶה רָשָׁע
מְדוּכָּא בְּיִסּוּרִין אַל יִשְׂנָאֵהוּ, שֶׁאַחַר שֶׁנִּקְלָה הֲרֵי הוּא כְּאָחִיךְ: וִיקָרֵב

ished, have compassion for them, and save them from their enemies. He should not say, "His sin caused his suffering," but he should have compassion upon him in accordance with this attribute.

10. *Show faithfulness to Ya'akov*:

The name *Israel* refers to a higher level than the name *Ya'akov*. This attribute, "show faithfulness to *Ya'akov*," applies to those individuals of average spiritual stature, who do not know how to go beyond what the Law requires. They are called 'Ya'akov,' for they adhere faithfully only to the strict requirements of the Law. The Holy One, Blessed Be He, also has this aspect of faithfulness regarding correctness in judgment. Towards those whose conduct in this world is correct, the Holy One, Blessed Be He, also conducts Himself with this quality of faithfulness, having compassion for them in executing justice and fairness.

So, too, a person should act towards his fellow with fairness and faithfulness, and he should not pervert the justice due his friend. He should have compassion for his fellow and be faithful, just as the Holy One, Blessed Be He, shows compassion for His creatures of average stature, according to this quality of faithfulness, in order to perfect them.

הַמּוֹרְדִים וְהַפּוֹשְׁעִים וִירַחֵם עֲלֵיהֶם, וְאַדְּרַבָּה יַצִּילֵם מִיַּד אוֹיֵב, וְאַל

יֹאמַר: "עֲווֹנוֹ גָּרַם לוֹ", אֶלָּא יְרַחֲמֵהוּ בְּמִדָּה זוֹ, כִּדְפֵירַשְׁתִּי.

הי' — תִּתֵּן אֱמֶת לְיַעֲקֹב

מִדָּה זוֹ הִיא, שֶׁיֵּשׁ לְיִשְׂרָאֵל מַעֲלָה: אוֹתָם הַבֵּינוֹנִים, שֶׁאֵינָם
יוֹדְעִים לְהִתְנַהֵג לִפְנִים מִשּׁוּרַת הַדִּין, וְהֵם נִקְרָאִים "יַעֲקֹב", מִפְּנֵי
שֶׁאֵינָם מִתְנַהֲגִים אֶלָּא עִם הַנְהָגוֹת אֲמִתִּיּוֹת, גַּם הַקָּבָּ"ה יֵשׁ לוֹ מִדַּת
"אֱמֶת", שֶׁהוּא עַל צַד מְצִיאוּת הַמִּשְׁפָּט וְהַיּוֹשֶׁר, וְאִילּוּ הֵם
הַמִּתְנַהֲגִים בָּעוֹלָם? בְּיוֹשֶׁר, הַקָּבָּ"ה מִתְנַהֵג עִמָּהֶם בֶּאֱמֶת, מְרַחֵם
עֲלֵיהֶם עַל צַד הַיּוֹשֶׁר וְהַמִּשְׁפָּט.

גַּם כֵּן הָאָדָם צָרִיךְ לְהִתְנַהֵג עִם חֲבֵירוֹ עַל צַד הַיּוֹשֶׁר וְהָאֱמֶת
בְּלִי לְהַטּוֹת מִשְׁפַּט חֲבֵרוֹ, לְרַחֵם עָלָיו בֶּאֱמֶת, כְּמוֹ שֶׁהַשֵׁ"י מְרַחֵם
עַל הַבְּרִיּוֹת הַבֵּינוֹנִים בְּמִדַּת אֱמֶת, וּלְתַקֵּן אוֹתָם.

11. *Kindness to Avraham*:

This attribute applies to those whose conduct goes beyond the requirements of the Law, like Avraham our Patriarch. Thus, the Holy One, Blessed Be He, also conducts Himself towards them in a way that goes beyond the requirements of the Law. That is, He does not demand the strict execution of justice, not even regarding correctness. Rather, He goes beyond the letter of the Law, just as they do. This is the aspect of "kindness to Avraham" — the Holy One, Blessed Be He, displays the attribute of kindness towards those whose conduct is like Avraham's.

So, too, with man: Although he conducts himself properly and correctly, with justness towards all men, towards those who are particularly righteous and pious, his conduct should go beyond the strict requirements of the Law. Wherever he displays patience towards all men, with the righteous and pious he should have much more patience, showing them compassion beyond what the Law requires in his dealings with others. They should be exceedingly important to him and especially beloved, and they should be among his friends.

12. *Which You have sworn to our fathers*:

Some people are unworthy, yet the Holy One, Blessed Be He, has compassion for all. On the verse "...I will have mercy and show kindness to whomever I desire" (*Shemot* 33:19), the Talmud comments:

היא׳ — חסד לאברהם.

הֵם הַמִּתְנַהֲגִים בָּעוֹלָם לִפְנִים מִשּׁוּרַת הַדִּין כְּאַבְרָהָם אָבִינוּ, גַּם הקב״ה מִתְנַהֵג עִמָּהֶם לִפְנִים מִשּׁוּרַת הַדִּין, אֵינוֹ מַעֲמִיד עִמָּהֶם הַדִּין עַל תּוֹקְפּוֹ אַף לֹא בְּדֶרֶךְ הַיּוֹשֶׁר, אֶלָּא נִכְנַס עִמָּהֶם לִפְנִים מִן הַיּוֹשֶׁר, כְּמוֹ שֶׁהֵם מִתְנַהֲגִים. וְהַיְינוּ ״חֶסֶד לְאַבְרָהָם״, הקב״ה מִתְנַהֵג בְּמִדַּת הַחֶסֶד עִם אוֹתָם שֶׁהֵם כְּמוֹ ״אַבְרָהָם״ בְּהִתְנַהֲגוּת.

גַּם הָאָדָם, עִם הֱיוֹת שֶׁעִם כָּל אָדָם יִהְיֶה מִתְנַהֵג בְּצֶדֶק וּבְיוֹשֶׁר וּבְמִשְׁפָּט, עִם הַטּוֹבִים וְהַחֲסִידִים תִּהְיֶה הַנְהָגָתוֹ לִפְנִים מִשּׁוּרַת הַדִּין; וְאִם לִשְׁאָר הָאָדָם הָיָה סַבְלָן קְצָת, לְאֵלּוּ יוֹתֵר וְיוֹתֵר; וִירַחֵם עֲלֵיהֶם לִיכָּנֵס עִמָּהֶם לִפְנִים מִשּׁוּרַת הַדִּין שֶׁהוּא מִתְנַהֵג בָּהּ עִם שְׁאָר הָאָדָם; וְצָרִיךְ שֶׁיִּהְיוּ אֵלּוּ חֲשׁוּבִים לְפָנָיו מְאֹד מְאֹד וַחֲבִיבִים לוֹ וְהֵם יִהְיוּ מֵאַנְשֵׁי חֶבְרָתוֹ.

הי״ב — אֲשֶׁר נִשְׁבַּעְתָּ לַאֲבוֹתֵינוּ.

יֵשׁ בְּנֵי אָדָם שֶׁאֵינָם הֲגוּנִים, והקב״ה מְרַחֵם עַל כּוּלָם. וּפֵירְשׁוּ

The Holy One, Blessed Be He, says, "This storehouse is for those who are unworthy." But there is another storehouse — of grace — from which the Holy One, Blessed Be He, bestows grace on the righteous as an unearned gift. For the Holy One, Blessed Be He, said, "Behold, they have the merit of their fathers. I made an oath to the Patriarchs, so even if they are unworthy, they will merit, because they are of the seed of the Patriarchs, to whom I swore. Therefore, I will lead them and guide them until they are perfected."

(*Berachot* 7a; *Shemot Rabbah* 45)

This is also how a person should conduct himself. Even if he meets wicked people, he should not behave cruelly towards them or abuse them and so on. Rather, he should show them compassion, saying, "Ultimately, they are the children of Avraham, Yitzchak, and Ya'akov. Although they may not behave properly, their fathers were upright and worthy. Hence, one who despises the sons despises the fathers, too. I do not wish their fathers to be despised because of me!" Thus, he should conceal their disgrace and improve them as much as he can.

13. *From days of old:*

This is the attribute with which the Holy One, Blessed Be He, conducts Himself towards the people of Israel when their merit and all else fail, and they are unworthy. What, then, does the Holy One, Blessed Be He,

בַּגְּמָרָא (ברכות ז', א'): "וְחַנּוֹתִי אֶת אֲשֶׁר אָחוֹן" (שמות ל"ג, י"ט)
— "אָמַר הקב"ה אוֹצָר זֶה לְאוֹתָם שֶׁאֵינָם הֲגוּנִים", יֵשׁ אוֹצָר
חֲנוּנִים, שֶׁהקב"ה חוֹנֵן וְנוֹתֵן לָהֶם מַתְּנַת חִנָּם, לְפִי שֶׁאָמַר הקב"ה:
"הֲרֵי יֵשׁ לָהֶם זְכוּת אָבוֹת, אֲנִי נִשְׁבַּעְתִּי לָאָבוֹת, אִם כֵּן, עִם הֱיוֹת
שֶׁאֵינָם הֲגוּנִים, יִזְכּוּ בִּשְׁבִיל שֶׁהֵם מִזֶּרַע הָאָבוֹת, שֶׁנִּשְׁבַּעְתִּי לָהֶם;
לְפִיכָךְ אֲנַהֲלֵם וְאֶנְהָגֵם עַד שֶׁיִּתּוּקְנוּ".

וְכָךְ יִהְיֶה הָאָדָם: אַף אִם יִפְגַּע בָּרְשָׁעִים אַל יִתְאַכְזֵר כְּנֶגְדָּם אוֹ
יְחָרְפֵם וְכַיּוֹצֵא, אֶלָּא יְרַחֵם עֲלֵיהֶם וְיֹאמַר: "סוֹף סוֹף הֵם בְּנֵי אַבְרָהָם
יִצְחָק וְיַעֲקֹב, אִם הֵכ אֵינָם כְּשֵׁרִים — אֲבוֹתֵיהֶם כְּשֵׁרִים וַהֲגוּנִים,
וְהַמְבַזֶּה הַבָּנִים מְבַזֶּה הָאָבוֹת, אֵין רְצוֹנִי שֶׁיִּתְבַּזּוּ אֲבוֹתֵיהֶם עַל
יָדִי", וּמְכַסֶּה עֶלְבּוֹנָם וּמְתַקְּנָם כְּפִי כֹחוֹ.

הי"ג — מִימֵי קֶדֶם.

הֲרֵי מִדָּה שֶׁיֵּשׁ לְהַקָּבָּ"ה עִם יִשְׂרָאֵל: כְּשֶׁתָּמָה זְכוּת אָבוֹת

do? The verse states: "I recall My kindness towards you in your youth, My love for you on the day of your marriage..." (*Yirmeyahu* 2:2). The Holy One, Blessed Be He, recalls the days of old and the love He felt towards the people of Israel, and His compassion is aroused. This way, He remembers all the commandments they have fulfilled since their birth and all the good qualities with which the Holy One, Blessed Be He, conducts His world. From all these, the Holy One, Blessed Be He, fashions a special treasure with which to show them compassion. This attribute includes all the others, as explained in the "*Idra*."

So, too, should a person improve his conduct towards others. For even if he cannot find a reason for showing love and compassion to his fellows from amongst those mentioned previously, he should say, "There was surely a time when they had not yet sinned, and in that time or in former days they were worthy." For their sake, he should recall the love of "...those just weaned from milk and torn away from the breast" (*Yeshayahu* 28:9). This way, he will not find a single person unworthy of kindness, prayers, or compassion.

Until now, we have explained the Thirteen Attributes in which a person should emulate his Creator. These are the Supernal Attributes of Mercy, and their special property is that just as a person conducts himself here below, so will he be worthy of opening up the channel of the same Supernal Attribute Above for himself. Exactly

וְכַיוֹצֵא, מַה יַּעֲשֶׂה, וַהֲרֵי מִצַּד עַצְמָם אֵינָם הֲגוּנִים. כְּתִיב (ירמיה
ב', א'): "זָכַרְתִּי לָךְ חֶסֶד נְעוּרַיִךְ אַהֲבַת כְּלוּלוֹתָיִךְ", מַמָּשׁ זוֹכֵר
הַקָּבָּ"ה יְמֵי קַדְמוֹנִים, אַהֲבָה שֶׁהָיָה מִקּוֹדֶם, וּמְרַחֵם עַל יִשְׂרָאֵל,
וּבָזֶה יַזְכִּיר לָהֶם כָּל הַמִּצְוֹת שֶׁעָשׂוּ מִיּוֹם שֶׁנּוֹלְדוּ וְכָל מִדּוֹת טוֹבוֹת
שֶׁהַקָּבָּ"ה מַנְהִיג בָּהֶם עוֹלָמוֹ, וּמִכּוּלָם עוֹשֶׂה סְגוּלָה לְרַחֵם בִּשְׁבִילָם.
וַהֲרֵי זֶה מִדָּה כּוֹלֶלֶת כָּל הַמִּדּוֹת כּוּלָם כִּדְפֵירְשׁוּ בְּאִדְּרָא (נשא קל"ד,
ב').

כָּךְ הָאָדָם יְתַקֵּן הַנְהָגָתוֹ עִם בְּנֵי אָדָם, שֶׁאֲפִילוּ לֹא יִמְצָא טַעֲנָה
מֵאֵלוּ הַנִּזְכָּרוֹת, יֹאמַר: "כְּבָר הָיָה שָׁעָה קוֹדֶם שֶׁלֹּא חָטְאוּ, וַהֲרֵי
אוֹתָהּ שָׁעָה, אוֹ בַּיָּמִים קַדְמוֹנִים, הָיוּ כְּשֵׁרִים", וְיִזְכּוֹר לָהֶם הַטּוֹבָה
שֶׁעָשׂוּ בְּקַטְנוּתָם, וְיִזְכּוֹר לָהֶם אַהֲבַת גְּמוּלֵי מֵחָלָב עַתִּיקֵי מִשָּׁדַיִם,
וּבָזֶה לֹא יִמְצָא אָדָם שֶׁאֵינוֹ רָאוּי לְהֵיטִיבוֹ וּלְהִתְפַּלֵּל עַל שְׁלוֹמוֹ
וּלְרַחֵם עָלָיו.

עַד כָּאן הִגִּיעוּ שְׁלֹשׁ עֶשְׂרֵה מִדּוֹת, שֶׁבָּהֶן יִהְיֶה הָאָדָם דּוֹמֶה
אֶל קוֹנוֹ, שֶׁהֵן מִדּוֹת שֶׁל רַחֲמִים עֶלְיוֹנוֹת. וּסְגוּלָתָן: כְּמוֹ שֶׁיִּהְיֶה
הָאָדָם מִתְנַהֵג לְמַטָּה כָּךְ יִזְכֶּה לִפְתּוֹחַ לוֹ מִדָּה עֶלְיוֹנָה מִלְמַעְלָה,
מַמָּשׁ כְּפִי מַה שֶׁיִּתְנַהֵג כָּךְ מַשְׁפִּיעַ מִלְמַעְלָה,

according to his behavior will the outflow of mercy be bestowed from Above, and he will cause this attribute to shine in the world. For this reason, he should not ignore these Thirteen Attributes or allow these verses to depart from his mouth. Rather, they should be a constant reminder to him when the occasion for making use of one of these attributes arises. He should remember and say to himself, "This situation requires this particular attribute. I will not budge from it, lest this attribute become concealed or disappear from the world."

וְגוֹרֵם שֶׁאוֹתָהּ הַמִּדָּה תָּאִיר בָּעוֹלָם. וּלְכָךְ אַל יָלוֹזוּ מֵעֵינֵי הַשֵּׂכֶל שְׁלֹשׁ עֶשְׂרֵה מִדּוֹת אֵלּוּ וְהַפָּסוּק לֹא יָסוּף מִפִּיו, כְּדֵי שֶׁיִּהְיֶה לוֹ לְמַזְכֶּרֶת. כַּאֲשֶׁר יָבוֹא לוֹ מַעֲשֶׂה שֶׁיִּצְטָרֵךְ לְהִשְׁתַּמֵּשׁ בְּמִדָּה אַחַת מֵהֶן, יִזְכּוֹר וְיֹאמַר: "הֲרֵי דָּבָר זֶה תָּלוּי בְּמִדָּה פְּלוֹנִית, אֵינִי רוֹצֶה לָזוּז מִמֶּנָּה, שֶׁלֹּא תִּתְעַלֵּם וְתִסְתַּלֵּק הַמִּדָּה הַהִיא מִן הָעוֹלָם".

Chapter 2

For a person to emulate his Creator according to the secret of the attributes of *keter*, he must possess several qualities, which characterize the way G-d conducts His world:

1) He must be humble. The quality of humility is all-encompassing, for it derives from *keter*. It is the most sublime of all attributes; nevertheless, it does not exalt or glorify itself over the other attributes. On the contrary, it always descends, gazing downwards. There are two reasons for this: One reason is that *keter* is ashamed to gaze at its Cause; instead, He Who emanated *keter* watches over it at all times in order to bestow goodness upon it, while *keter* gazes at those below it. Similarly, a person should be ashamed to gaze upward and glorify himself. Rather, he should lower his gaze, minimizing his worth. This quality depends mainly on the head — for a person glorifies himself by raising his head upwards haughtily,

פֶּרֶק שֵׁנִי

עוֹד, לִהְיוֹת הָאָדָם דּוֹמֶה לְקוֹנוֹ, בְּסוֹד מִדַּת הַכֶּתֶר, צָרִיךְ שֶׁיִּהְיוּ
בּוֹ כַּמָּה גוּפֵי פְּעוּלוֹת, שֶׁהֵם עִיקַר הַהַנְהָגָה.

הָרִאשׁוֹנָה. הַכּוֹלֶלֶת הַכֹּל, הִיא מִדַּת הָעֲנָוָה, מִפְּנֵי שֶׁהִיא תְּלוּיָה
בַּכֶּתֶר, שֶׁהֲרֵי הִיא מִדָּה עַל כָּל הַמִּדּוֹת וְאֵינָהּ מִתְעַלָּה וּמִתְגָּאָה
לְמַעְלָה, אָמְנָם יוֹרֶדֶת וּמִסְתַּכֶּלֶת לְמַטָּה תָּדִיר. וְזֶה מִשְּׁנֵי טְעָמִים,
הָאֶחָד — שֶׁהוּא בּוֹשׁ לְהִסְתַּכֵּל בְּסִיבָּתוֹ, אֶלָּא מַאֲצִילוֹ מַבִּיט בּוֹ
תָּמִיד לְהֵיטִיבוֹ, וְהוּא מַבִּיט בַּתַּחְתּוֹנִים. כָּךְ הָאָדָם צָרִיךְ שֶׁיֵּבוֹשׁ
מִלְּהִסְתַּכֵּל לְצַד מַעְלָה, לְהִתְגָּאוֹת, אֶלָּא תָּדִיר יִסְתַּכֵּל לְצַד מַטָּה
לְהַפְחִית עַצְמוֹ כָּל מַה שֶּׁיּוּכַל. וַהֲרֵי הַמִּדָּה הַזֹּאת הִיא תְּלוּיָה דֶּרֶךְ
כְּלָל בָּרֹאשׁ, שֶׁאֵין הָאָדָם מִתְגָּאֶה אֶלָּא בַּהֲרָמַת רֹאשׁוֹ כְּלַפֵּי מַעְלָה,
וְהֶעָנִי מַשְׁפִּיל רֹאשׁוֹ לְמַטָּה.

whereas a poor person lowers his head.

Now, there is none so patient and humble as our G-d in His attribute of *keter*, for He is absolute compassion, and before Him no flaw or transgression, no severe judgment or other quality can prevent Him from watching over man and bestowing bounty and goodness upon him constantly. So, too, should man conduct himself. No reason whatsoever should prevent him from doing good to others always and at every moment, and no transgressions or misdeeds of unworthy people should stop him from bestowing good on those in need. And just as G-d sustains all creatures, from the highest to the lowest, despising none of them (for if He despised any creatures because of their insignificance, they could not exist for even a moment), watching over them and showing compassion to all, so, too, should man do good to all, not despising any creature. Even the lowliest beings should be very important in his eyes, and he should show concern for them, doing good to all who require his goodness. This quality, too, depends on *keter*, the secret of the head in general.

2) A person's thoughts should emulate the thought process of *keter*. Just as the *chochmah* (wisdom) of *keter* never stops thinking good thoughts, and, because it is absolute compassion, it allows no evil to enter, severity and harshness having no place there, so, too, should a person's thoughts be void of anything unseemly. And just as the *chochmah* of *keter* is the secret of the Primal Torah, where all the secrets of Torah are contained, so, too, should a person's mind contain nothing other than Torah

וַהֲרֵי אֵין סַבְלָן וְעָנָיו כֵּאלֹהֵינוּ בְּמִדַּת הַכֶּתֶר, שֶׁהִיא תַּכְלִית הָרַחֲמִים, וְלֹא יִכָּנֵס לְפָנָיו שׁוּם פְּגָם, וְלֹא עָוֹן, וְלֹא דִין, וְלֹא שׁוּם מִדָּה מוֹנַעַת מִלְּהַשְׁגִּיחַ וּלְהַשְׁפִּיעַ וּלְהֵיטִיב תָּדִיר. כָּךְ צָרִיךְ הָאָדָם שֶׁשּׁוּם סִבָּה שֶׁבָּעוֹלָם לֹא תִמְנָעֵהוּ מִלְּהֵיטִיב, וְשׁוּם עָוֹן אוֹ מַעֲשֵׂה בְּנֵי אָדָם בִּלְתִּי הָגוּן לֹא יִכָּנֵס לְפָנָיו כְּדֵי שֶׁיְּעַכְּבֵהוּ מִלְּהֵיטִיב לְאוֹתָם הַצְּרִיכִים טוֹבָתוֹ בְּכָל עֵת וּבְכָל רֶגַע. וּכְמוֹ שֶׁהוּא יוֹשֵׁב וְזָן מִקַּרְנֵי רְאֵמִים וְעַד בֵּיצֵי כִנִּים וְאֵינוֹ מְבַזֶּה שׁוּם בְּרִיָּה, שֶׁאִילּוּ יְבַזֶּה הַבְּרוּאִים מִפְּנֵי פְּחִתוּתָם לֹא יִתְקַיְּימוּ אֲפִילּוּ רֶגַע, אֶלָּא מַשְׁגִּיחַ וְנוֹתֵן רַחֲמִים עַל כּוּלָּם, כָּךְ צָרִיךְ שֶׁיִּהְיֶה הָאָדָם מֵיטִיב לַכֹּל, וְלֹא יִתְבַּזֶּה שׁוּם נִבְרָא לְפָנָיו, אֲפִילּוּ בְּרִיָּה קַלָּה שֶׁבַּקַּלִּים תִּהְיֶה מְאֹד חֲשׁוּבָה בְּעֵינָיו וְיִתֵּן דַּעְתּוֹ עָלֶיהָ, וְיֵיטִיב לְכָל הַמִּצְטָרֵךְ אֶל טוֹבָתוֹ. וְזוֹ מִדָּה תְּלוּיָה בְּכֶתֶר בְּסוֹד הָרֹאשׁ דֶּרֶךְ כְּלָל.

הַשְּׁנִיָּה — מַחֲשַׁבְתּוֹ תִּדְמֶה לְמַחֲשֶׁבֶת הַכֶּתֶר. כְּמוֹ שֶׁאוֹתָהּ חָכְמָה לֹא תִפְסוֹק תָּמִיד לַחְשׁוֹב מַחֲשָׁבוֹת טוֹבוֹת, וְהָרַע לֹא יִכָּנֵס בָּהּ, מִפְּנֵי שֶׁהִיא רַחֲמִים גְּמוּרִים, וְאֵין שָׁם דִּין לֹא שׁוּם קוֹשִׁי כְּלָל, כָּךְ הָאָדָם תָּמִיד תִּהְיֶה מַחֲשַׁבְתּוֹ פְּנוּיָה מִכָּל דָּבָר מְכוֹעָר. וּכְמוֹ שֶׁהִיא סוֹד חָכְמָה תּוֹרָה קְדוּמָה, וְלֹא יֶחְסַר שׁוּם סוֹד תּוֹרָה, כָּךְ לֹא יִפְנֶה אֶל שׁוּם פְּנִיָּה חוּץ מִמַּחֲשֶׁבֶת הַתּוֹרָה, וְלַחְשׁוֹב בְּגַדְלוּת הָאֵל

thoughts, meditation on the greatness of G-d and His acts of kindness and benevolence, and so forth. As a rule, no strange or irrelevant thoughts should enter one's mind. Such was the elevated level of Rabbi Shimon bar Yochai and his comrades, and when Rabbi Yose's thoughts once strayed a little from the Torah, note how Rabbi Shimon rebuked him, as retold in the *Zohar* on "*VaYakhel.*"

3) A person's forehead (*metzach*) should display no harshness. Rather, one should emulate the display of Divine Willingness, accepting everything. Even though certain people arouse one's anger, he should conciliate them and placate them with good will, for this is what G-d does, placating the powers of severity that prevail in anger. He directs them in good will and washes over them with great wisdom, causing the anger to subside lest it break through its boundaries and cause damage, G-d forbid. Thus, one should follow the example of the Divine Will, which derives from the most elevated level of *chochmah* in the *metzach* of *Atik*, whence all severities are appeased. This example should also extend to constant pleasantness towards all creatures, for if a person is harsh towards others, he will not find favor Above. This is the meaning of the Mishnah: "Anyone with whom his fellow-men are pleased, G-d is pleased with him...."

4) A person's ears should always turn to hear good, while falsehood or despicable things should be denied entry. Just as the secret of Supernal 'Listening" does not receive any cry for severe judgment or any damaging, evil gossip, a person should not listen to anything but good and positive things. To other things, which arouse anger,

וּפְעוּלוֹתָיו הַטּוֹבוֹת, וּלְהֵיטִיב, וְכַיּוֹצֵא. כְּלָלוֹ שֶׁל דָּבָר — לֹא יִכָּנֵס זָר וּבָטֵל בְּמַחֲשַׁבְתּוֹ. וְזוֹ הָיְתָה מַעֲלַת רַבִּי שִׁמְעוֹן וַחֲבֵרָיו. וְהִנֵּה כְּשֶׁהִפְרִיד רַבִּי יוֹסֵי מַחֲשַׁבְתּוֹ מְעַט, כַּמָּה הוֹכִיחוֹ רַבִּי שִׁמְעוֹן (זוהר פרשת ויקהל, רי״ז, ב׳).

הַשְּׁלִישִׁית — מִצְחוֹ לֹא יִהְיֶה בּוֹ קֹשִׁי כְּלָל, אֶלָּא יִדְמֶה תָּמִיד לְמֵצַח הָרָצוֹן, שֶׁיִּרְצֶה אֶת הַכֹּל. אֲפִילוּ שֶׁיִּמְצָא בְּנֵי אָדָם כּוֹעֲסִים, יְרַצֵּם וְיַשְׁקִיטֵם בִּרְצוֹנוֹ הַטּוֹב. שֶׁכֵּן מֵצַח הָרָצוֹן הוּא תָּמִיד רוֹצֶה וּמְרַצֶּה הַגְּבוּרוֹת וּמְתַקְּנָם, אַף הוּא יִרְצֶה הַגְּבוּרוֹת הַמִּתְגַּבְּרִים בְּכַעֲסָם, וְהוּא יְנַהֲלֵם בְּרָצוֹן טוֹב וְיִשְׁתַּתֵּף שָׁם חָכְמָה גְּדוֹלָה לְהַשְׁבִּית הַכַּעַס, שֶׁלֹּא יַעֲבוֹר הַגְּבוּל וִיקַלְקֵל חַס וְשָׁלוֹם, וְיַעֲשֶׂה דּוּגְמָא לָרָצוֹן הָעֶלְיוֹן שֶׁהוּא נִמְשָׁךְ מִן הַחָכְמָה הַנִּפְלָאָה בְּמִצְחָא דְעַתִּיקָא וּמִשָּׁם מְרַצֶּה הַכֹּל. וְגַם יַמְשִׁיךְ לִהְיוֹת תָּמִיד נוֹחַ לַבְּרִיּוֹת, שֶׁאִם מִדּוֹתָיו קָשׁוֹת מִצַּד אֶחָד עִם בְּנֵי אָדָם, לֹא יִתְרַצּוּ מִמֶּנּוּ. וְזֶה טַעַם הַמִּשְׁנָה (אבות פ״ג, מ״ג): ״כָּל שֶׁרוּחַ הַבְּרִיּוֹת נוֹחָה הֵימֶנּוּ רוּחַ הַמָּקוֹם נוֹחָה הֵימֶנּוּ״.

הָרְבִיעִית — שֶׁיִּהְיוּ אָזְנָיו נוֹטוֹת תָּמִיד לִשְׁמֹעַ הַטּוֹב, אָמְנָם שֵׁמַע שָׁוְא אוֹ הַמְגוּנֶּה לֹא יִכָּנֵס בָּהֶן כְּלָל, כְּדֶרֶךְ שֶׁסּוֹד הָאֲזָנָה הָעֶלְיוֹנָה אֵין שׁוּם צַעֲקַת דִּין וְלֹא פְּגַם לָשׁוֹן הָרַע נִכְנַס שָׁם, כָּךְ לֹא יַאֲזִין אֶלָּא טוֹבוֹת וְהַדְּבָרִים הַמּוֹעִילִים, וּשְׁאָר הַדְּבָרִים הַמַּגְבִּירִים

he should not listen at all. And just as the words and speech of the Serpent have no entry Above, no despicable thing should enter a person's ears. This is the meaning of the phrase "you shall not accept a false report" (*Shemot* 23:1). How much more so does this apply to other despicable things, which should not enter his ears; rather, he should listen only to good things.

5) A person's eyes should not gaze at anything despicable. Rather, his eyes should always be open to watch over unfortunates and have as much compassion for them as he can. He should not close his eyes to the suffering of the poor. Rather, he should give as much thought to their predicament as possible, arousing the compassion of both Heaven and man for them. He should distance himself from noticing evil, just as the Supernal 'Eye' is ever open, always looking at the good.

6) Regarding the nose, nary a breath of anger should ever be found in it. Rather, it should contain the breath of life and good will and patience, even toward those who are unworthy. One should always seek to fulfill the desire of others, to satisfy every request, and to revive the broken-spirited. He should always exhale forgiveness of sin and pardon of iniquity. He should not be angry with those who offend him; rather, he should constantly be willing to be appeased, and he should desire to do kindness, pleasing everyone.

7) A person's face should always shine, and he should receive all men with a cheerful countenance. For regarding the Supernal *keter*, it is written, "In the light of the King's countenance is life..." (*Mishlei* 16:15). And just

כַּעַס לֹא יַאֲזִין אֲלֵיהֶם כְּלָל. וּכְמוֹ שֶׁהַנַּחָשׁ וְדִבּוּרוֹ וּלְשׁוֹנוֹ אֵינוֹ נִכְנָס לְמַעֲלָה, כָּךְ לֹא יִכָּנֵס אֵלָיו שׁוּם דָּבָר מְגֻנֶּה, וְהַיְנוּ "לֹא תִשָּׂא שֵׁמַע שָׁוְא" (שמות כ"ג, א'). כָּל שֶׁכֵּן שְׁאָר דִּבּוּר הַמְגֻנֶּה שֶׁלֹּא יִכָּנֵס לְאָזְנוֹ כְּלָל וְלֹא תִהְיֶה קַשֶּׁבֶת אֶלָּא הַדְּבָרִים הַטּוֹבִים.

הַחֲמִישִׁית — עֵינָיו, לֹא יִסְתַּכֵּל בָּהֶן בְּשׁוּם דָּבָר מְגֻנֶּה, אָמְנָם תִּהְיֶינָה תָּמִיד פְּקוּחוֹת לְהַשְׁגִּיחַ וּלְרַחֵם עַל הָאֻמְלָלִים כְּפִי כֹחוֹ, וּכְשֶׁיִּרְאֶה בְּצָרַת עָנִי לֹא יַעֲצוֹם עֵינָיו כְּלָל, אֶלָּא יִתְבּוֹנֵן בְּדַעְתּוֹ עָלָיו כְּפִי כֹחוֹ וִיעוֹרֵר רַחֲמִים עָלָיו בִּפְנֵי שָׁמַיִם וּבִפְנֵי הַבְּרִיּוֹת, וְיִתְרַחֵק מִכָּל הַשְׁגָּחָה רָעָה, וּכְדֶרֶךְ שֶׁהָעַיִן הָעֶלְיוֹנָה פְּקוּחָה וּמִסְתַּכֶּלֶת תָּמִיד אֶל הַטּוֹב.

הַשִּׁשִּׁית — בְּחוֹטְמוֹ, מֵעוֹלָם לֹא יִמָּצֵא בּוֹ חֲרוֹן אַף כְּלָל, אֶלָּא תָּמִיד בְּאַפּוֹ חַיִּים וְרָצוֹן טוֹב וַאֲרִיכוּת אַף, אֲפִילוּ לְאוֹתָם שֶׁאֵינָם הֲגוּנִים, וְתָמִיד רוֹצֶה לְמַלְּאוֹת רָצוֹן וּלְהָפִיק כָּל שְׁאֵלָה וּלְהַחֲיוֹת כָּל נִדְכֶּה, וּמוֹצִיא מֵחוֹטְמוֹ תָּמִיד מְחִלַת עָוֹן וְהַעֲבָרַת פֶּשַׁע, וְאֵינוֹ כּוֹעֵס בְּחוֹטֵא לוֹ, אֶלָּא מִתְרַצֶּה תָּמִיד וְחָפֵץ חֶסֶד לַעֲשׂוֹת נַחַת רוּחַ לַכֹּל.

הַשְּׁבִיעִית — פָּנָיו תִּהְיֶינָה מְאִירוֹת תָּמִיד וִיקַבֵּל כָּל אָדָם בְּסֵבֶר פָּנִים יָפוֹת, שֶׁכֵּן בִּכְבוֹד עֶלְיוֹן נֶאֱמַר (משלי ט"ז, ט"ו): "בְּאוֹר פְּנֵי

as no flush of anger or severity enters there, the light of his countenance should be unchanging, so that all who look into his face will find nothing but joy and cheerfulness. Nothing should disturb him from this.

8) His mouth should express nothing but good, and the content of his words should be Torah and constant good will. No ugly words, curses, anger, or frivolous talk should escape his mouth. Rather, it should resemble the Supernal 'Mouth,' which is never sealed, never silent from uttering good at all times. Thus, one must speak well of everything, expressing benevolence and blessings constantly.

These are eight good qualities, all of which come under the banner of humility. They all correspond to the Supernal 'Limbs' of *keter*. Thus, when a person desires to draw near to the higher worlds and emulate G-d in order to open His sources to those below, he must be expert in these two chapters.

Of course, we know that it is not always possible to conduct oneself in accordance with these qualities, since there are other qualities one must master. (These are the lower severities, as we will explain.) Nevertheless, on certain days, either these severities are inactive, and man does not require them — for *keter* reigns — or the service pertaining to *keter* is needed. At these times, one must use all the qualities we've mentioned, and any others required in Divine service at their proper time should not be exercised, for the light of *keter* nullifies them. Similarly, at this time one should not draw on the qualities of severity.

מֶלֶךְ חַיִּים", וְאֵין שׁוּם אוֹדֶם וָדִין נִכְנָס שָׁם כְּלָל, כָּךְ אוֹר פָּנָיו לֹא
יִשׁוּנֶּה וְכָל הַמִּסְתַּכֵּל בָּהֶם לֹא יִמְצָא אֶלָּא שִׂמְחָה וְסֵבֶר פָּנִים, וְשׁוּם
סִיבָּה לֹא תַטְרִידֵהוּ מִזֶּה כְּלָל.

הַשְּׁמִינִית — פִּיו, לֹא יוֹצִיא אֶלָּא טוֹבָה וּגְזֵרַת אֲמָרָיו תּוֹרָה
וַהֲפָקַת רָצוֹן טוֹב תָּמִיד, וְלֹא יוֹצִיא מִפִּיו דָּבָר מְגוּנֶה וְלֹא קְלָלָה
וְלֹא רוֹגֶז וְכַעַס כְּלָל וְלֹא דְבָרִים בְּטֵלִים, וְיִהְיֶה דוֹמֶה לְאוֹתוֹ הַפֶּה
הָעֶלְיוֹן, שֶׁאֵינוֹ נִסְתָּם כְּלָל, שֶׁלֹּא יֶחֱשֶׁה וְלֹא יִמָּנַע טוֹב תָּמִיד, וְלָכֵן
צָרִיךְ לְדַבֵּר טוֹבָה עַל הַכֹּל וּלְהוֹצִיא מִפִּיו טוֹבָה וּבְרָכָה תָּמִיד.

הֲרֵי אֵלּוּ שְׁמוֹנֶה מִדּוֹת טוֹבוֹת, וְכוּלָן תַּחַת דֶּגֶל הָעֲנָוָה, שֶׁכּוּלָן
לְמַעְלָה בַּכֶּתֶר בְּאֵיבָרִים עֶלְיוֹנִים. וּבָעֵת שֶׁיִּרְצֶה הָאָדָם לְהִתְקָרֵב
לְמַעְלָה, לְהִדָּמוֹת אֵלָיו, לִפְתּוֹחַ מְקוֹרוֹתָיו אֶל הַתַּחְתּוֹנִים, צָרִיךְ
שֶׁיִּשְׁתַּלֵּם בִּשְׁנֵי פְּרָקִים אֵלּוּ.

אָמְנָם יָדַעְנוּ שֶׁאִי אֶפְשָׁר לְהִתְנַהֵג בְּאֵלּוּ הַמִּדּוֹת תָּמִיד, מִפְּנֵי
שֶׁיֵּשׁ מִדּוֹת אֲחֵרוֹת שֶׁהָאָדָם צָרִיךְ לְהִשְׁתַּלֵּם בָּהֶן, וְהֵן מֵהַגְּבוּרוֹת
הַתַּחְתּוֹנוֹת, כַּאֲשֶׁר נְבָאֵר. אֲבָל יֵשׁ יָמִים יְדוּעִים, שֶׁאֵין הַגְּבוּרוֹת
פּוֹעֲלוֹת וְאֵין בְּנֵי אָדָם צְרִיכִים אֲלֵיהֶן, לְפִי שֶׁהַכֶּתֶר שׁוֹלֵט בָּהֶם,
אוֹ שָׁעוֹת שֶׁהַכֶּתֶר מִתְבַּקֵּשׁ, אָז צָרִיךְ שֶׁיִּשְׁתַּמֵּשׁ בְּכָל אֵלֶּה הַמִּדּוֹת
שֶׁזָּכַרְנוּ. אָמְנָם שְׁאָר הַמִּדּוֹת, עִם הֱיוֹת שֶׁהֵן צוֹרֶךְ עֲבוֹדָה בִּשְׁעָתָן,
אֵין עֵת עַתָּה לְהִשְׁתַּמֵּשׁ בָּהֶן, מִפְּנֵי שֶׁאוֹר הַכֶּתֶר מְבַטְּלָן, וְכָךְ הוּא

On Shabbat, for example, when the world is sweetened according to the secret of the delight of the Shabbat (and therefore, the courts do not sit on Shabbat), one should activate all the qualities mentioned above in order to open the sources Above. For if a person concentrates on the lights of *keter* in his prayers, yet he behaves contrary to them in his actions, how can he open the sources of *keter*, which he repels with his deeds? Is it not all the more so that if *Keter* does not reside in the *sefirah* Above pertaining to the powers of severity and holy anger, *keter* will not rest upon a person who allows the external expression of anger to prevail, even though he does so for the sake of Heaven? This is particularly true since he intends to allow the external expression of anger to prevail over the Supernal qualities, which will say, "How arrogant this person is! The light of *keter* is not revealed in us, for we are the holy and pure severities, yet this person desires to reveal the light of *keter* when filled with anger and acting in an ugly, superficial way!"

Thus, on festivals, Shabbatot, and Yom Kippur, and at times of prayer and study — which are not times of severity but, on the contrary, times when the Supernal Will is revealed — he should direct his mind to all these qualities. At other times, a person may activate other qualities in his Divine service (but not negative ones, for whenever they are in control, it is to his disadvantage, as will be explained). Then, when he employs these qualities, he will surely open up the sources Above. Therefore, every person must accustom himself to these qualities little by little. The main quality he should acquire, the key

לֹא יִשְׁתַּמֵּשׁ בְּאוֹתָן הַמִּדּוֹת הַקָּשׁוֹת. כְּגוֹן בְּשַׁבָּת, שֶׁהָעוֹלָם מִתְמַתֵּק בְּסוֹד עוֹנֶג וְאֵין דָּנִין בְּשַׁבָּת. אָז יִשְׁתַּמֵּשׁ בְּמִדּוֹת אֵלּוּ כֻּלָּם, כְּדֵי לִפְתּוֹחַ הַמְּקוֹרוֹת הָעֶלְיוֹנִים, שֶׁאִלּוּ יְכַוֵּן בְּכַוָּנָתוֹ אֶל אוֹרוֹת הַכֶּתֶר בִּתְפִלּוֹתָיו וְהוּא יִפְעַל בִּפְעוּלוֹתָיו בְּהֶפֶךְ, הֵיאַךְ יִפְתַּח מְקוֹר הַכֶּתֶר, וַהֲרֵי הוּא דוֹחֵהוּ מַמָּשׁ בְּמַעֲשָׂיו. וַהֲרֵי הַדְּבָרִים קַל וָחוֹמֶר, אִם הַסְּפִירוֹת הָעֶלְיוֹנוֹת מִגְּבוּרוֹת הַדִּינִים הַקְּדוֹשִׁים וְהַכַּעַס הַקָּדוֹשׁ, לֹא יִשְׁרֶה הַכֶּתֶר בָּהֶן אִם הָאָדָם יַגְבִּיר הַכַּעַס הַחִיצוֹנִי, אֲפִילוּ יִהְיֶה לְשֵׁם שָׁמַיִם, כָּל שֶׁכֵּן שֶׁלֹּא יִשְׁרֶה הַכֶּתֶר מְאוֹרוֹ עָלָיו. וּמַה גַּם שֶׁהוּא בָּא לְעוֹרֵר עַל הַמִּדּוֹת הָעֶלְיוֹנוֹת, וְהֵן אוֹמְרוֹת: "כַּמָּה עַזּוּת פָּנִים יֵשׁ בּוֹ. אֵין אוֹר הַכֶּתֶר מִתְגַּלֶּה בָּנוּ מִפְּנֵי דִּינֵנוּ הַקָּדוֹשׁ וְהַטָּהוֹר, וְהוּא רוֹצֶה לְגַלּוֹתוֹ מָלֵא כַּעַס וּפְעוּלוֹת מְגוּנּוֹת חִצוֹנִיּוֹת".

לְכָךְ צָרִיךְ הָאָדָם בְּיָמִים טוֹבִים, בְּשַׁבָּתוֹת וְיוֹם הַכִּפּוּרִים, וּבִשְׁעוֹת הַתְּפִלָּה וּשְׁעוֹת עֵסֶק הַתּוֹרָה, שֶׁאֵינָן שְׁעוֹת הַגְּבוּרוֹת, אֶלָּא שְׁעוֹת גִּלּוּי הָרָצוֹן הָעֶלְיוֹן, לְכוֹנֵן דֵּעוֹתָיו בְּמִדּוֹת הָאֵלּוּ כֻּלָּן. וּשְׁאָר שְׁעוֹת יִשְׁתַּמֵּשׁ בַּמִּדּוֹת הַנִּשְׁאָרוֹת לַעֲבוֹדַת ד', לֹא הַמְגֻנָּה מֵהֶן, שֶׁאֵין לוֹ עֵת לִשְׁלוֹט בָּאָדָם אֶלָּא לְרַעְתוֹ, כַּאֲשֶׁר נְבָאֵר. וְאָז, כַּאֲשֶׁר יִשְׁתַּמֵּשׁ בְּמִדּוֹת אֵלּוּ, יִהְיֶה נָכוֹן וּבָטוּחַ שֶׁיִּפָּתַח הַמְּקוֹרוֹת הָעֶלְיוֹנִים. לְפִיכָךְ צָרִיךְ כָּל אָדָם לְהַרְגִּיל עַצְמוֹ בְּאֵלּוּ הַמִּדּוֹת מְעַט מְעַט, וְהָעִקָּרִית שֶׁיִּתְפּוֹס, שֶׁהִיא

to them all, is humility — for this is the highest and foremost aspect of *keter*, in which all are contained.

Now, the essence of humility is that a person does not see his value at all; rather, he considers himself nothing — as Moshe, the humblest one of all, said: "...what are we that you should complain against us?" (*Shemot* 16:7) — to the extent that one deems himself the lowliest of creatures, exceedingly despicable and loathsome. When a person strives to acquire this quality, all other qualities are drawn after it, for the primary quality of *keter* is to view itself as nothing before the One from Whom it emanates. Likewise, a person should consider himself nothing at all, thinking that it would have been better never to have been created. Consequently, he will act towards those who despise him as if they were correct and he were at fault. This will be a means of acquiring good qualities.

I have found a remedy whereby a person can accustom himself to these things little by little, possibly curing himself of the disease of arrogance and allowing himself to enter the gates of humility. This cure is composed of three 'medications':

First, a person should accustom himself to flee as far as possible from honor. For if he allows others to honor him, he will acquire the habit of pride, and by nature he will always desire honor. Then he will be able to be healed only with difficulty.

Second, a person should train himself to see his shameful side, saying to himself, "Although others are unaware of my lack of worth, what of it? Do I myself not

מַפְתֵּחַ הַכֹּל, הָעֲנָוָה, מִפְּנֵי שֶׁהִיא רֹאשׁ לְכֻלָּן, בְּחִינָה רִאשׁוֹנָה בַּכֶּתֶר, וְתַחְתֶּיהָ יֻכְלַל הַכֹּל.

וְהִנֵּה, עִקַּר הָעֲנָוָה הוּא, שֶׁלֹּא יִמְצָא בְּעַצְמוֹ עֵרֶךְ כְּלָל, אֶלָּא יַחֲשֹׁב שֶׁהוּא הָאַיִן, וּכְמַאֲמַר הֶעָנִי (שמות ט״ז, ז'): "וְנַחְנוּ מָה כִּי תַלִּינוּ עָלֵינוּ". עַד שֶׁיִּהְיֶה הוּא בְּעֵינָיו הַבְּרִיָּה הַשְּׁפֵלָה שֶׁבְּכָל הַנִּבְרָאִים וּבָזוּי וּמָאוּס מְאֹד. וְכַאֲשֶׁר יִגַּע תָּמִיד לְהַשִּׂיג הַמִּדָּה הַזֹּאת, כָּל שְׁאָר הַמִּדּוֹת נִגְרָרוֹת אַחֲרֶיהָ, שֶׁהֲרֵי הַכֶּתֶר, הַמִּדָּה הָרִאשׁוֹנָה אֲשֶׁר בּוֹ, שֶׁנִּרְאָה עַצְמוֹ לְאַיִן לִפְנֵי מַאֲצִילוֹ, כָּךְ יָשִׂים הָאָדָם עַצְמוֹ אַיִן מַמָּשׁ וְיַחֲשֹׁב הֶעְדֵּרוֹ טוֹב מְאֹד מִן הַמְּצִיאוּת, וּבָזֶה יִהְיֶה לְנוֹכַח הַמְבַזִּים אוֹתוֹ כְּאִלּוּ הַדִּין עִמָּהֶם, וְהוּא הַנִּבְזֶה אֲשֶׁר עָלָיו הָאָשָׁם, וְזוֹ תִּהְיֶה סִבַּת קִנְיַן הַמִּדּוֹת הַטּוֹבוֹת.

וַאֲנִי מָצָאתִי תְרוּפָה לְהַרְגִּיל הָאָדָם עַצְמוֹ בִּדְבָרִים אֵלּוּ מְעַט מְעַט, אֶפְשָׁר שֶׁיִּתְרַפֵּא בָּהּ מֵחוֹלִי הַגַּאֲוָה וְיִכָּנֵס בְּשַׁעֲרֵי הָעֲנָוָה. וְהוּא תַחְבֹּשֶׁת הַנַּעֲשָׂה מִשְּׁלֹשָׁה סַמִּים:

הָרִאשׁוֹנָה — שֶׁיַּרְגִּיל עַצְמוֹ לִהְיוֹת בּוֹרֵחַ מֵהַכָּבוֹד כָּל מַה שֶּׁיּוּכַל. שֶׁאִם יִתְנַהֵג שֶׁיְּכַבְּדוּהוּ בְּנֵי אָדָם, יִתְלַמֵּד בָּהֶם עַל צַד הַגַּאֲוָה וְיִתְרַצֶּה הַטֶּבַע תָּמִיד בְּכָךְ, וּבְקוֹשִׁי יוּכַל לְהֵרָפֵא.

הַשְּׁנִיָּה — שֶׁיַּרְגִּיל מַחֲשַׁבְתּוֹ לִרְאוֹת בְּבִזְיוֹנוֹ, וְיֹאמַר "עִם הֱיוֹת שֶׁבְּנֵי אָדָם אֵינָם יוֹדְעִים אֶת גְּרִיעוּתִי, מַה לִּי מִזֶּה, וְכִי אֲנִי אֵינִי

know that I am despicable in such-and-such a way, whether in lack of knowledge or ability or in eating and excreting?" and so on, until he becomes despised in his eyes.

Third, a person should constantly recall his sins and desire purification, rebuke, and suffering, asking himself, "Which type of suffering is the best in the world and will not distract me from Divine service? Surely, there is none better than these — to be scorned and despised and insulted," for these will not weaken his strength and vitality with illness, nor will they rob him of his food and clothing, his life, or his children's lives. Hence, a person should actually desire this form of suffering, saying to himself, "Why should I fast and torment myself with sackcloth and self-affliction, which weaken my strength for G-d's service? Why should I desire these for myself? It is far better for me to be afflicted with contempt and shame while my strength does not depart or weaken." Thus, when insults are meted out to him, he should rejoice in them. Contrary to the typical reaction to them, he should desire them.

From these three ingredients, one can make a balm for his heart. He should accustom himself to this approach all his days.

I have found another excellent potion, although it is not as effective as the aforementioned remedy. A person should accustom himself to two things:

First, he should respect all creatures, recognizing in them the greatness of the Creator, Who formed man in His wisdom and Whose wisdom is contained in all crea-

מַכִּיר בְּעַצְמִי שֶׁאֲנִי נִבְזֶה בְּכָךְ וְכָךְ, אִם בְּהֶעְדֵּר הַיְדִיעָה וְחוּלְשַׁת הַיְּכוֹלֶת וּבִזְיוֹן הַמַּאֲכָל וְהַפֶּרֶשׁ הַיּוֹצֵא מִמֶּנִּי וְכַיּוֹצֵא" עַד שֶׁיִּהְיֶה נִבְזֶה בְּעֵינָיו נִמְאָס.

הַשְּׁלִישִׁית — שֶׁיַּחֲשׁוֹב עַל עֲווֹנוֹתָיו תָּמִיד וְיִרְצֶה בְּטָהֳרָה וְתוֹכַחַת וְיִסּוּרִים, וְיֹאמַר "מָה הֵם הַיִּסּוּרִין הַיּוֹתֵר טוֹבִים שֶׁבָּעוֹלָם שֶׁלֹּא יַטְרִידוּנִי מֵעֲבוֹדַת ד'", אֵין חָבִיב בְּכוּלָּם מֵאֵלּוּ שֶׁיְּחָרְפוּהוּ וִיבַזּוּהוּ וִיגַדְּפוּהוּ, שֶׁהֲרֵי לֹא יִמְנְעוּ מִמֶּנּוּ כֹּחוֹ וְאוֹנוֹ בַּחֲלָאִים וְלֹא יִמְנְעוּ אֲכִילָתוֹ וּמַלְבּוּשׁוֹ וְלֹא יִמְנְעוּ חַיָּיו וְחַיֵּי בָּנָיו בְּמִיתָה, אִם כֵּן מַמָּשׁ יַחְפּוֹץ בָּהֶם, וְיֹאמַר "מַה לִי לְהִתְעַנּוֹת וּלְהִסְתַּגֵּף בְּשַׂקִּים וּמַלְקִיּוֹת, הַמַּחֲלִישִׁים כֹּחִי מֵעֲבוֹדַת ד', וַאֲנִי לוֹקֵחַ אוֹתָם בְּיָדִי. יוֹתֵר טוֹב אֶסְתַּגֵּף בְּבִזְיוֹן בְּנֵי אָדָם וְחֶרְפָּתָם לִי וְלֹא יָסוּר כֹּחִי וְלֹא יֶחְלַשׁ", וּבָזֶה כְּשֶׁיָּבוֹאוּ הָעֶלְבּוֹנוֹת עָלָיו יִשְׂמַח בָּהֶם וְאַדְּרַבָּה יַחְפּוֹץ בָּהֶם.

וְיַעֲשֶׂה מִשְּׁלוֹשֶׁת הַמִּינִים אֵלּוּ תַּחְבּוֹשֶׁת לְלִבּוֹ וְיִתְלַמֵּד כָּל יָמָיו.

וְעוֹד מָצָאתִי מַשְׁקֶה טוֹב מְאֹד, אֲבָל לֹא יוֹעִיל הַמַּשְׁקֶה כָּל כָּךְ כְּמוֹ שֶׁיּוֹעִיל אַחַר תַּחְבּוֹשֶׁת הַנִּזְכֶּרֶת לְעֵיל. וְהוּא: שֶׁיַּרְגִּיל עַצְמוֹ בִּשְׁנֵי דְּבָרִים:

הָרִאשׁוֹן הוּא, לְכַבֵּד הַנִּבְרָאִים כּוּלָּם, אַחַר שֶׁיַּכִּיר בָּהֶם מַעֲלַת הַבּוֹרֵא אֲשֶׁר יָצַר הָאָדָם בְּחָכְמָה, וְכֵן כָּל הַנִּבְרָאִים חָכְמַת הַיּוֹצֵר

tures. He should realize that all creatures are to be greatly honored, since He Who fashioned all things — the Wise and Exalted One — has busied Himself with creating them, and if he despises them, G-d forbid, it affects the honor of their Creator.

This is comparable to an expert craftsman who fashions a vessel with great skill, but when he displays his work to people, one of them mocks and derides it. How angry that craftsman will be, since, by scorning the work of his hands, the critic is belittling his very skill. So, too, the Holy One, Blessed Be He, is grieved if any of His creatures is despised. This is the meaning of the verse "How many are Your works, O L-rd..." (*Tehillim* 104:24) — not "how great" (*mah gadlu*) but "how many" (*mah rabbu*), suggesting great importance, as in the phrase "*rav beito*" (*Esther* 1:8), meaning "head or senior of the house." The verse continues, "You have made them all with wisdom." Thus, since Your Wisdom is involved with them, Your works are great and many, and it is proper for man to seek the wisdom in them and not despise them.

Second, one should accustom himself to loving his fellowmen in his heart. Even the wicked should be viewed as if they were his brothers. What's more, he should continue until love for all people is fixed in his heart. He should come to love even the wicked in his heart, saying, "I only wish they were righteous, returning in repentance, so that all of them would be great men desired by the Omnipresent One." As Moshe, the faithful lover of all Israel, said: "I wish all the people of G-d were prophets" (*BeMidbar* 11:29). And how should he love

בָּהֶם, וְיִרְאֶה בְּעַצְמוֹ שֶׁהֲרֵי הֵם נִכְבָּדִים מְאֹד מְאֹד, שֶׁנִּטְפַּל יוֹצֵר הַכֹּל הֶחָכָם הַנַּעֲלֶה עַל כָּל בִּבְרִיאָתָם, וְאִילּוּ יְבַזֶּה אוֹתָם, חַס וְשָׁלוֹם נוֹגֵעַ בִּכְבוֹד יוֹצְרָם.

וַהֲרֵי זֶה יִדְמֶה אֶל חָכָם צוֹרֵף, עָשָׂה כְּלִי בְּחָכְמָה גְדוֹלָה וְהֶרְאָה מַעֲשֵׂהוּ אֶל בְּנֵי אָדָם, וְהִתְחִיל אֶחָד מֵהֶם לְגַנּוֹתוֹ וּלְבַזּוֹתוֹ, כַּמָּה יַגִּיעַ מֵהַכַּעַס אֶל הֶחָכָם הַהוּא מִפְּנֵי שֶׁמְּבַזִּין חָכְמָתוֹ בִּהְיוֹתָם מְבִזִּים מַעֲשֵׂה יָדָיו, וְאַף הַקָּבָּ"ה יֵרַע בְּעֵינָיו אִם יְבַזּוּ שׁוּם בְּרִיָּה מִבְּרִיּוֹתָיו. וְזֶה שֶׁכָּתוּב (תהלים ק"ד, כ"ד): "מָה רַבּוּ מַעֲשֶׂיךָ ה'", לֹא אָמַר "גָּדְלוּ" אֶלָּא "רַבּוּ", לָשׁוֹן "רַב בֵּיתוֹ" (אסתר א', ח'), חֲשׁוּבִים מְאֹד, "כֻּלָּם בְּחָכְמָה עָשִׂיתָ", וְאַחַר שֶׁנִּטְפְּלָה חָכְמָתְךָ בָּהֶם רַבּוּ וְגָדְלוּ מַעֲשֶׂיךָ, וְרָאוּי לָאָדָם לְהִתְבּוֹנֵן מִתּוֹכָם חָכְמָה וְלֹא בִּזָּיוֹן.

הַשֵּׁנִי — יַרְגִּיל עַצְמוֹ לְהַכְנִיס אַהֲבַת בְּנֵי אָדָם בְּלִבּוֹ, וַאֲפִילּוּ הָרְשָׁעִים, כְּאִילּוּ הָיוּ אֶחָיו, וְיוֹתֵר מִזֶּה, עַד שֶׁיִּקָּבַע בְּלִבּוֹ אַהֲבַת בְּנֵי אָדָם כֻּלָּם. וַאֲפִילּוּ הָרְשָׁעִים יֶאֱהַב אוֹתָם בְּלִבּוֹ, וְיֹאמַר: "מִי יִתֵּן וְיִהְיוּ אֵלּוּ צַדִּיקִים שָׁבִים בִּתְשׁוּבָה וְיִהְיוּ כֻּלָּם גְּדוֹלִים וּרְצוּיִים לַמָּקוֹם", כְּמַאֲמַר אוֹהֵב נֶאֱמָן לְכָל יִשְׂרָאֵל, שֶׁאָמַר (במדבר יא, מט): "וּמִי יִתֵּן כָּל עַם ד' נְבִיאִים וגו'". וּבַמֶּה יֶאֱהַב. בִּהְיוֹתוֹ מַזְכִּיר

them? By recalling in his thoughts their good qualities, and by covering up their flaws and refusing to see their defects; rather, he should look for their good qualities. He should say to himself: "If this poor, loathsome fellow were very rich, how much would I delight in his company, as I delight in the company of so-and-so. And if he were dressed in handsome garments like so-and-so, there would be no difference between them. If so, why should he lack honor in my eyes, being that he is superior to me in G-d's eyes, since he is plagued and crushed with poverty and suffering, which cleanse one of sin? Why, then, should I hate him whom the Holy One, Blessed Be He, loves?"

This way, his heart will turn to the positive side of things, and he will accustom himself to ponder the good qualities we have mentioned.

בְּמַחֲשַׁבְתּוֹ טוֹבוֹת אֲשֶׁר בָּהֶם, וִיכַסֶּה מוּמָם, וְלֹא יִסְתַּכֵּל בְּנִגְעֵיהֶם אֶלָּא בַּמִּדּוֹת הַטּוֹבוֹת אֲשֶׁר בָּהֶם. וְיֹאמַר בְּלִבּוֹ: "אִילּוּ הָיָה הֶעָנִי הַמָּאוּס הַזֶּה בַּעַל מָמוֹן רַב, כַּמָּה הָיִיתִי שָׂמֵחַ בְּחֶבְרָתוֹ, כְּמוֹ שֶׁאֲנִי שָׂמֵחַ בְּחֶבְרַת פְּלוֹנִי, וַהֲרֵי זֶה, אִילּוּ יַלְבִּישׁוּהוּ הַלְּבוּשִׁים הַנָּאִים כְּמוֹ פְּלוֹנִי, הֲרֵי אֵין בֵּינוֹ לְבֵינוֹ הֶבְדֵּל, אִם כֵּן לָמָּה יֶעְדַּר כְּבוֹדוֹ בְּעֵינַי. וַהֲרֵי בְּעֵינֵי ד' חָשׁוּב מִמֶּנִּי, שֶׁהוּא נָגוּעַ מְדוּכָּא בְּעוֹנִי וְיִסּוּרִים וּמְנוּקֶּה מֵעָוֹן, וְלָמָּה אֶשְׂנָא מִי שֶׁהַקָּבָּ"ה אוֹהֵב". וּבָזֶה יִהְיֶה לְבָבוֹ פּוֹנֶה אֶל צַד הַטּוֹב וּמַרְגִּיל עַצְמוֹ לַחֲשׁוֹב בְּכָל מִדּוֹת טוֹבוֹת שֶׁזָּכַרְנוּ.)

Chapter 3

How should a person train himself in the attribute of *chochmah*? Although it is hidden and exceedingly exalted, the attribute of *chochmah* Above is spread out over all creation. As it is written, "How many are Your works, O L-rd; You have made them all in *chochmah*..." (*Tehillim* 104:24). Similarly, a person's *chochmah* should pervade all his actions, and he should be ready to benefit and influence others with his *chochmah* — according to their capacity — letting nothing prevent him.

Now, the attribute of *chochmah* Above has two aspects: The higher aspect faces *keter* and does not face downwards; rather, it receives from above. The lower aspect faces downwards, overseeing the other *sefirot*, to which the attribute of *chochmah* extends.

Likewise, a person should have two aspects: The first aspect should be communion in solitude with his Creator in order to increase and perfect his *chochmah*; the

פֶּרֶק שְׁלִישִׁי

הֵיאַךְ יַרְגִּיל הָאָדָם עַצְמוֹ בְּמִדַּת הַחָכְמָה. הִנֵּה, הַחָכְמָה הָעֶלְיוֹנָה פְּרוּסָה עַל כָּל הַנִּמְצָאִים כֻּלָּם, עִם הֱיוֹתָהּ נֶעְלֶמֶת וְנִשְׂגָּבָה מְאֹד, וְעָלֶיהָ נֶאֱמַר (תהלים ק"ד, כ"ד): "מָה רַבּוּ מַעֲשֶׂיךָ ד' כֻּלָּם בְּחָכְמָה עָשִׂיתָ". כָּךְ רָאוּי לָאָדָם שֶׁתִּהְיֶה חָכְמָתוֹ מְצוּיָה בַּכֹּל, וְיִהְיֶה מְלַמֵּד לְהוֹעִיל לִבְנֵי אָדָם לְכָל אֶחָד וְאֶחָד כְּפִי כֹחוֹ, כָּל מַה שֶּׁיּוּכַל לְהַשְׁפִּיעַ עָלָיו מֵחָכְמָתוֹ יַשְׁפִּיעֵהוּ, וְלֹא תַטְרִידֵהוּ שׁוּם סִבָּה כְּלָל.

וְהִנֵּה, אֶל הַחָכְמָה שְׁנֵי פָנִים, הַפָּן הָעֶלְיוֹן הַפּוֹנֶה אֶל הַכֶּתֶר, וְאֵין אוֹתָם הַפָּנִים מִסְתַּכְּלִים לְמַטָּה, אֶלָּא מְקַבְּלִים מִלְמַעְלָה; הַפָּן הַשֵּׁנִי, הַתַּחְתּוֹן, פּוֹנֶה לְמַטָּה, לְהַשְׁגִּיחַ בַּסְּפִירָה שֶׁהִיא מִתְפַּשֶּׁטֶת בְּחָכְמָתָהּ אֲלֵיהֶם.

כָּךְ יִהְיֶה אֶל הָאָדָם שְׁנֵי פָנִים, הַפָּן הָרִאשׁוֹן הוּא הִתְבּוֹדְדוּתוֹ

second should be to teach others the *chochmah* with which the Holy One, Blessed Be He, has endowed him. And just as the attribute of *chochmah* Above extends to each *sefirah* according to its measure and needs, one should disseminate his *chochmah* to each person in the measure his intellect can grasp, according to what is proper for him and his needs. One should take care not to give more than the mind of the recipient can contain, lest harm result, for the Supernal *sefirah* does not go beyond the limits of the recipient.

Moreover, it is the nature of *chochmah* to oversee all of existence, for it is the Supernal Thought, which contemplates everything that exists. Of *chochmah* it is said: "For My thoughts are not your thoughts..." (*Yeshayahu* 55:8), "...and He gives thought so that he who is exiled is not banished forever" (*II Shemuel* 14:14), and " 'For I know the thoughts I think of you [the House of Israel],' says the L-rd, 'thoughts of peace and not evil, to give you hope for the future' " (*Yirmeyahu* 29:11).

In the same way, man should keep a watchful eye on the conduct of the nation of G-d in order to benefit it. His thoughts should be concerned with bringing near those who have strayed and thinking well of them. Just as the Divine Mind contemplates the benefit of all existence, he should contemplate the benefit of his fellows, taking counsel with G-d and His people regarding both individual and communal matters. And concerning one who has strayed from the good path, he should guide him to proper conduct, serving as his advisor and counselor and directing and leading him to good and forthright

בְּקוֹנוֹ, כְּדֵי לְהוֹסִיף בְּחָכְמָה וּלְתַקְּנָהּ; הַשֵּׁנִי — לְלַמֵּד בְּנֵי אָדָם מֵאוֹתָהּ חָכְמָה שֶׁהַקָּבָּ"ה הִשְׁפִּיעַ עָלָיו. וּכְמוֹ שֶׁהַחָכְמָה מֻשְׁפַּעַת אֶל כָּל סְפִירָה וּסְפִירָה כְּפִי שִׁעוּרָהּ וְצָרְכָּהּ, כֵּן יַשְׁפִּיעַ בְּכָל אָדָם כְּפִי שִׁעוּר שֶׂכְלוֹ אֲשֶׁר יוּכַל שְׂאֵת וְהַנָּאוּת אֵלָיו לְצָרְכּוֹ, וְיִשָּׁמֵר מִלָּתֵת יוֹתֵר מִשִּׁעוּר שֵׂכֶל הַמּוּשְׁפָּע, שֶׁלֹּא תִמָּשֵׁךְ מִמֶּנּוּ תַּקָלָה, שֶׁכֵּן הַסְּפִירָה הָעֶלְיוֹנָה אֵינָהּ מוֹסֶפֶת עַל הַשִּׁעוּר הַמּוּגְבָּל בַּמְקַבֵּל.

וְעוֹד, שֶׁדֶּרֶךְ הַחָכְמָה לִהְיוֹתָהּ מַשְׁגַּחַת עַל כָּל הַמְּצִיאוּת, מִפְּנֵי שֶׁהִיא הַמַּחֲשָׁבָה הַחוֹשֶׁבֶת עַל כָּל הַנִּמְצָאוֹת, וְעָלֶיהָ נֶאֱמַר (ישעיה נ"ה, ח') "כִּי לֹא מַחְשְׁבוֹתַי מַחְשְׁבוֹתֵיכֶם", וּכְתִיב (שמואל ב' י"ד, י"ד): "וְחָשַׁב מַחֲשָׁבוֹת לְבִלְתִּי יִדַּח מִמֶּנּוּ נִדָּח", וּכְתִיב (ירמיה כ"ט, י"א): "כִּי אָנֹכִי יָדַעְתִּי אֶת הַמַּחֲשָׁבוֹת אֲשֶׁר אֲנִי חֹשֵׁב עֲלֵיכֶם נְאוּם ד' מַחְשְׁבוֹת שָׁלוֹם וְלֹא רָעָה לָתֵת לָכֶם אַחֲרִית וְתִקְוָה".

כָּךְ צָרִיךְ הָאָדָם לִהְיוֹת עֵינָיו פְּקוּחוֹת עַל הַנְהָגַת עַם ד' לְהוֹעִילָם, וּמַחְשְׁבוֹתָיו תִּהְיֶינָה לְקָרֵב הַנִּדָּחִים וְלַחֲשֹׁב עֲלֵיהֶם מַחֲשָׁבוֹת טוֹבוֹת; כְּמוֹ שֶׁהַשֵּׂכֶל חוֹשֵׁב לְתוֹעֶלֶת הַנִּמְצָא כֻּלּוֹ, כָּךְ יַחֲשֹׁב הוּא תּוֹעֶלֶת הַחֲבֵרִים, וְיִתְיָעֵץ עֵצוֹת טוֹבוֹת עִם ד' וְעִם עַמּוֹ בִּפְרָט וּבִכְלָל, וְהַיּוֹצֵא מֵהַהַנְהָגָה הַטּוֹבָה יְנַהֲלֵהוּ אֶל הַהַנְהָגָה הַיְשָׁרָה, וְיִהְיֶה לוֹ כְּמוֹ שֵׂכֶל וּמַחֲשָׁבָה לְנַהֲגוֹ וּלְנַהֲלוֹ אֶל הַמִּנְהָג הַטּוֹב וְהַיּוֹשֶׁר, כְּמַחֲשָׁבָה הָעֶלְיוֹנָה הַמְיַשֶּׁרֶת הָאָדָם הָעֶלְיוֹן.

behavior, just as the Supernal Thought guides the highest worlds.

Furthermore, *chochmah* gives life to all things. As it is written: "...*chochmah* gives life to those who possess it" (*Kohelet* 7:12). Likewise, one should instruct the entire world in the ways of life, helping others attain life in this world and in the World to Come and providing them with the means to live. In general, one should give life to all beings.

In addition, *chochmah* is the source of all existence. As the verse states: "How many are Your works, O L-rd; You have made them all with *chochmah*..." (*Tehillim* 104:24). Thus, everything lives and exists due to that source.

In the same way, a person should act as father to all G-d's creatures, particularly Israel, for its holy souls emanate from that source. At all times, he should pray for mercy and blessing for the world, being like our Father Above, Who has compassion for His creatures. And regarding those afflicted with suffering, he should constantly pray for them as if they were his own children and he had formed them himself, for this is what the Holy One, Blessed Be He, desires. As Moshe, the faithful shepherd, said: "Did I conceive this nation...that You say to me, 'Carry it in your bosom...'?" (*BeMidbar* 11:12). In this way, a person should carry all of G-d's people "as a nurse carries an infant" (ibid.). He should "...gather the lambs in his arm, lifting them to his bosom, and lead the little ones" (*Yeshayahu* 40:11). He should take care of the desolate, seek out the young, heal the broken, nourish the

וְעוֹד, הַחָכְמָה תְּחַיֶּה הַכֹּל, כְּדִכְתִיב (קהלת ז', יב): "וְהַחָכְמָה
תְּחַיֶּה בְעָלֶיהָ". כָּךְ יִהְיֶה הוּא מוֹרֶה חַיִּים לְכָל הָעוֹלָם וְגוֹרֵם לָהֶם
חַיֵּי הָעוֹלָם הַזֶּה וְחַיֵּי הָעוֹלָם הַבָּא וּמַמְצִיא לָהֶם חַיִּים. זֶה הַכְּלָל:
יִהְיֶה נוֹבֵעַ חַיִּים לַכֹּל.

וְעוֹד, הַחָכְמָה אָב לְכָל הַנִּמְצָאוֹת, כְּדִכְתִיב (תהלים ק"ד, כ"ד):
"מָה רַבּוּ מַעֲשֶׂיךָ ד' כֻּלָּם בְּחָכְמָה עָשִׂיתָ". וְהֵן חַיִּים וּמִתְקַיְּימִים
מִשָּׁם.

כָּךְ יִהְיֶה הוּא אָב לְכָל יְצוּרָיו שֶׁל הַקָּבָּ"ה, וּלְיִשְׂרָאֵל עִיקָר,
שֶׁהֵן הַנְּשָׁמוֹת הַקְּדוֹשׁוֹת הָאֲצוּלוֹת מִשָּׁם, וִיבַקֵּשׁ תָּמִיד רַחֲמִים וּבְרָכָה
לָעוֹלָם, כְּדֶרֶךְ שֶׁהָאָב הָעֶלְיוֹן רַחֲמָן עַל בְּרוּאָיו, וְיִהְיֶה תָּמִיד מִתְפַּלֵּל
בְּצָרַת הַמִּצְרִים כְּאִילּוּ הָיוּ בָּנָיו מַמָּשׁ וּכְאִילּוּ הוּא יְצָרָם, שֶׁזֶּהוּ
רְצוֹנוֹ שֶׁל הַקָּבָּ"ה, כְּדֶרֶךְ שֶׁאָמַר הָרוֹעֶה הַנֶּאֱמָן (במדבר יא, לב):
"הֶאָנֹכִי הָרִיתִי אֵת כָּל הָעָם הַזֶּה וגו' כִּי תֹאמַר אֵלַי שָׂאֵהוּ בְחֵיקֶךָ",
וּבָזֶה יִשָּׂא אֶת כָּל עַם ד' כַּאֲשֶׁר יִשָּׂא הָאוֹמֵן אֶת הַיּוֹנֵק, בִּזְרֹעוֹ יְקַבֵּץ
טְלָאִים וּבְחֵיקוֹ יִשָּׂא, עָלוֹת יְנַהֵל, הַנִּכְחָדוֹת יִפְקוֹד, הַנֶּעֱדָר יְבַקֵּשׁ,

needy, and return the lost. One should have compassion for Israel, bearing its burdens cheerfully, just as the Merciful Father bears all. One should not tire or hide or despair, leading each person according to his needs. These are the qualities of *chochmah*: a father who is merciful to his children.

Furthermore, one's compassion should extend to all creatures, and he should neither despise nor destroy them, for the *chochmah* Above extends to all of creation — inanimate objects, plants, animals, and humans. For this reason, our sages have warned us against treating food disrespectfully. Just as the Supernal *chochmah* despises nothing, since everything is created from there — as the verse states, "You have made them all with *chochmah*" (*Tehillim* 104:24) — a person should show compassion to all the works of the Holy One, Blessed Be He. That's why Rabbi Yehudah the Prince was punished: He had no pity on a calf that tried to evade slaughter by hiding behind him, and he said to it, "Go! For this purpose, you were created," suffering — which derives from the aspect of severity — came upon him, for compassion shields against severity. Thus, when Rabbi Yehudah the Prince had mercy on a weasel, quoting the verse "...His mercies extend to all His deeds" (*Tehillim* 145:9), he was delivered from severity, for the light of *chochmah* spread over him, and his suffering disappeared.

Similarly, one should not disparage any creature, for all of them were created with *chochmah*. Nor should one uproot plants unless they are needed or kill animals unless they are needed. And one should choose a noble

הַנִּשְׁבֶּרֶת יְרַפֵּא, הַנִּצְרָכָה יְכַלְכֵּל, הָאוֹבְדוֹת יַחֲזִיר, וִירַחֵם עַל יִשְׂרָאֵל
וְיִשָּׂא בְּסֵבֶר פָּנִים יָפוֹת מַשָּׂאָם, כְּאָב הָרַחֲמָן הָעֶלְיוֹן הַסּוֹבֵל כֹּל,
וְלֹא יָבוֹל וְלֹא יִתְעַלֵּם וְלֹא יָקוּץ וִינַהֵל לְכָל אֶחָד כְּפִי צָרְכּוֹ אֵלּוּ הֵן
מִדּוֹת הַחָכְמָה, אָב רַחֲמָן עַל בָּנִים.

עוֹד צָרִיךְ לִהְיוֹת רַחֲמָיו פְּרוּסִים עַל כָּל הַנִּבְרָאִים, לֹא יְבַזֵּם
וְלֹא יְאַבְּדֵם. שֶׁהֲרֵי הַחָכְמָה הָעֶלְיוֹנָה הִיא פְּרוּסָה עַל כָּל הַנִּבְרָאִים,
דּוֹמֵם וְצוֹמֵחַ וְחַי וּמְדַבֵּר, וּמִטַּעַם זֶה הוּזְהַרְנוּ מִבִּזּוּי אוֹכָלִים. וְעַל
דָּבָר זֶה רָאוּי, שֶׁכְּמוֹ שֶׁהַחָכְמָה הָעֶלְיוֹנָה אֵינָהּ מְבַזָּה שׁוּם נִמְצָא
וְהַכֹּל נַעֲשָׂה מִשָּׁם, דִּכְתִיב (תהלים ק"ד, כ"ד) "כֻּלָּם בְּחָכְמָה
עָשִׂיתָ", כֵּן יִהְיֶה רַחֲמֵי הָאָדָם עַל כָּל מַעֲשָׂיו יִתְבָּרֵךְ. וּמִטַּעַם זֶה
הָיָה עוֹנֶשׁ רַבֵּינוּ הַקָּדוֹשׁ, עַל יְדֵי שֶׁלֹּא חָס עַל בֶּן הַבָּקָר שֶׁהָיָה
מִתְחַבֵּא אֶצְלוֹ וְאָמַר לוֹ "זִיל, לְכָךְ נוֹצַרְתָּ" (בבא מציעא פ"ה, א),
בָּאוּ לוֹ יִסּוּרִין, שֶׁהֵם מִצַּד הַדִּין, שֶׁהֲרֵי הָרַחֲמִים מְגִינִים עַל הַדִּין,
וְכַאֲשֶׁר רִיחַם עַל הַחוּלְדָּה וְאָמַר "וְרַחֲמָיו עַל כָּל מַעֲשָׂיו כְּתִיב",
נִיצַל מִן הַדִּין, מִפְּנֵי שֶׁפֵּרַשׂ אוֹר הַחָכְמָה עָלָיו, וְנִסְתַּלְּקוּ הַיִּסּוּרִים.

וְעַל דֶּרֶךְ זֶה לֹא יְבַזֶּה שׁוּם נִמְצָא מִן הַנִּמְצָאִים, שֶׁכּוּלָּם בְּחָכְמָה,
וְלֹא יַעֲקוֹר הַצּוֹמֵחַ אֶלָּא לְצוֹרֶךְ, וְלֹא יָמִית הַבַּעַל חַי אֶלָּא לְצוֹרֶךְ,

death for them, using a carefully inspected knife, in order to maximize his compassion.

This is the general principle: Having pity on all beings and not hurting them depends on *chochmah*. However, if one intends to raise them higher and higher — from plant to animal, and from animal to human — then it is permissible to uproot a plant and slaughter an animal, taking away from them in order to benefit them.

וְיִבְרוֹר לָהֶם מִיתָה יָפָה בְּסַכִּין בְּדוּקָה, לְרַחֵם כָּל מַה שֶּׁאֶפְשָׁר.

זֶה הַכְּלָל, הַחֶמְלָה עַל כָּל הַנִּמְצָאִים שֶׁלֹּא לְחַבְּלָם, תְּלוּיָה בְּחָכְמָה. זוּלָתִי לְהַעֲלוֹתָם אֶל מַעֲלָה. מְצוֹמֵחַ לְחַי, מֵחַי לִמְדַבֵּר — שֶׁאָז מוּתָּר לַעֲקוֹר הַצּוֹמֵחַ וּלְהָמִית הַחַי, לָחוֹב עַל מְנָת לִזְכּוֹת.

Chapter 4

How should a person train himself in the attribute of *binah* (understanding)? This is achieved by returning in complete repentance, for there is nothing as important as repentance, in that it rectifies every flaw. And just as *binah* sweetens all severities and neutralizes their bitterness, one should repent and rectify all flaws. A person who calls repentance to mind all the days of his life causes *binah* to illuminate all his days, the result being that all his days are spent in repentance. That is, he merges himself with *binah*, which is repentance, so that all the days of his life are crowned with the secret of the higher level of repentance.

Note that all existence is rooted in repentance, according to the secret of the Jubilee. In addition, the root of the external forces — expounded in the mystical teachings as the secret of the River Dinur — is also rooted therein and flows therefrom. (However, the River Dinur

פֶּרֶק רְבִיעִי

הֵיאַךְ יַרְגִּיל הָאָדָם עַצְמוֹ בְּמִדַּת הַבִּינָה, וְהוּא — לָשׁוּב בִּתְשׁוּבָה, שֶׁאֵין דָּבָר חָשׁוּב כָּמוֹהָ, מִפְּנֵי שֶׁהִיא מְתַקֶּנֶת כָּל פְּגַם. וּכְמוֹ שֶׁדֶּרֶךְ הַבִּינָה לְמַתֵּק כָּל הַדִּינִים וּלְבַטֵּל מְרִירוּתָם, כָּךְ הָאָדָם יָשׁוּב בִּתְשׁוּבָה וִיתַקֵּן כָּל פְּגַם. וּמִי שֶׁמְּהַרְהֵר בִּתְשׁוּבָה כָּל יָמָיו, גּוֹרֵם שֶׁתָּאִיר הַבִּינָה בְּכָל יָמָיו, וְנִמְצְאוּ כָּל יָמָיו בִּתְשׁוּבָה, דְּהַיְינוּ לִכְלוֹל עַצְמוֹ בְּבִינָה, שֶׁהִיא תְּשׁוּבָה, וִימֵי חַיָּיו מְעוּטָּרִים בְּסוֹד הַתְּשׁוּבָה הָעֶלְיוֹנָה.

וּרְאֵה, כִּי כְמוֹ שֶׁהַתְּשׁוּבָה יֵשׁ בָּהּ שׁוֹרֶשׁ כָּל הַנִּמְצָאוֹת, בְּסוֹד הַיּוֹבֵל, וַהֲרֵי שׁוֹרֶשׁ הַחִיצוֹנִים, סוֹד נְהַר דִּינוּר, הַנִּכְלָל בִּקְדוּשָׁה

itself is included in Holiness, according to the mystical teachings regarding the severities.) This is called 'the outflow of Divine Anger.' But by means of the mystical teaching regarding the verse "G-d smelled the pleasing scent of the sacrifices..." (*Bereishit* 8:21), that 'outflow' returns to its source, the severities become sweetened, the anger ceases, and "G-d refrain[s] from the evil..." (*Shemot* 32:14). Likewise, by means of the mystery of repentance, man also achieves this effect. Therefore, one should not say that repentance benefits only the aspects of holiness in man. For his evil aspects are rectified as well, just as the severities are sweetened by this attribute.

Know that Kayin himself was evil, and he derived from evil, yet he was told, "If you do good, will you not be uplifted...?" (*Bereishit* 4:7), meaning, "Do not think that, because you derive from evil, you have no hope. This is false. For 'if you do good,' anchoring yourself firmly in repentance, you will be 'uplifted,' i.e., you can enter into the good implanted there, via the root of your soul, and do yourself good." For everything bitter has a sweet Supernal root, as the mystical teachings explain. Thus, a person's evil actions may be turned into good, and his deliberate transgressions may be turned into merits. For when one returns in complete repentance, these selfsame evil deeds from the 'Left Side,' which were prosecutors against him, enter the higher worlds and become rooted in holiness there, transforming themselves into good rather than becoming nullified. This is just what Kayin was told regarding his own self-betterment.

Thus, had Kayin repented, thereby becoming recti-

בְּסוֹד הַגְּבוּרוֹת, נִשְׁרָשׁ שָׁם וְיִתְפַּשֵּׁט מִשָּׁם וְיִקָּרֵא הִתְפַּשְּׁטוּת חֲרוֹן אַף, וּבְסוֹד "וַיָּרַח ד' אֶת רֵיחַ הַנִּיחֹחַ" (בראשית ח', כא) יַחֲזוֹר הַהִתְפַּשְּׁטוּת הַהוּא אֶל מְקוֹרוֹ וְיוּמְתְּקוּ הַדִּינִים וְיִשְׁקוֹט הַחֲרוֹן וְיִנָּחֵם ד' עַל הָרָעָה, כָּךְ הָאָדָם בְּסוֹד תְּשׁוּבָתוֹ עוֹשֶׂה סוֹד זֶה. שֶׁלֹּא תֹאמַר שֶׁהַתְּשׁוּבָה טוֹבָה לַחֵלֶק הַקְּדוֹשָׁה שֶׁבָּאָדָם, אֶלָּא גַּם לַחֵלֶק הָרַע, שֶׁבּוֹ מִתְמַתֵּק, כְּעֵין הַמִּדָּה הַזֹּאת.

תֵּדַע, שֶׁהֲרֵי קַיִן רַע הָיָה וּמְנֻחָשׁ הָיָה, וְנֶאֱמַר לוֹ (בראשית ד', ז'): "הֲלֹא אִם תֵּיטִיב שְׂאֵת" — אַל תַּחֲשׁוֹב מִפְּנֵי שֶׁאַתָּה מִצַּד הָרָע שֶׁאֵין לְךָ תַּקָּנָה, זֶה שֶׁקֶר. "הֲלֹא אִם תֵּיטִיב" וְתַשְׁרִישׁ עַצְמְךָ בְּסוֹד הַתְּשׁוּבָה, — "שְׂאֵת", תִּסְתַּלֵּק שָׁם בְּסוֹד הַטּוֹב הַמּוּשְׁרָשׁ שָׁם, שֶׁכָּל מַר עֶלְיוֹן שָׁרְשׁוֹ מָתוֹק, וְיָכוֹל לִכָּנֵס דֶּרֶךְ שָׁרְשׁוֹ לְהֵיטִיב עַצְמוֹ. וְלָזֶה, הַפְּעוּלּוֹת עַצְמָן מֵיטִיב הָאָדָם וּזְדוֹנוֹת נַעֲשׂוּ לוֹ כִּזְכֻיּוֹת, כִּי הִנֵּה אוֹתָן הַפְּעוּלּוֹת שֶׁעָשָׂה הָיוּ מְקַטְרְגִים מִסִּטְרָא דִשְׂמָאלָא, שָׁב בִּתְשׁוּבָה שְׁלֵימָה הֲרֵי מַכְנִיס וּמַשְׁרִישׁ אוֹתָן הַפְּעוּלּוֹת לְמַעְלָה, וְכָל אוֹתָם הַמְקַטְרְגִים אֵינָם מִתְבַּטְּלִין אֶלָּא מְטִיבִין עַצְמָן וּמִשְׁתָּרְשִׁים בַּקְּדוֹשָׁה כְּעֵין הֲטָבַת קַיִן.

fied, then the state of Adam's sin — in which Kayin was conceived (the name Kayin deriving from the words *kina demisavuta*, meaning 'contaminated nest') — would have been to his credit, according to the mystical interpretation of the concept of 'the Son Brings Merit to His Father.' However, Kayin did not desire to repent, and therefore the entire Left Side derives from there, but all its branches will eventually become sweetened, returning to perfection. The reason for this is exactly as we have explained — a person who caused evil to become rooted in himself can sweeten it and restore it to good.

Therefore, when a person purifies his evil inclination and transforms it into good, it becomes rooted in holiness. This is the elevated level of repentance that a person who wishes to conduct himself in this manner should contemplate every day, and he should also repent in some way, so that all his days will be spent in repentance.

וַהֲרֵי אִם קַיִן שָׁב בִּתְשׁוּבָה וְנִתְקַן, הִנֵּה זְדוֹן אָדָם הָרִאשׁוֹן, שֶׁבּוֹ הוֹלִיד אֶת קַיִן, קִינָא דִּמְסָאֲבוּתָא, הָיָה נֶחְשָׁב לוֹ זְכוּת, בְּסוֹד "בְּרָא מְזַכֶּה אַבָּא" (סנהדרין ק״ד, א׳). אָמְנָם לֹא רָצָה לָשׁוּב, וּלְכָךְ כָּל סִטְרָא דִּשְׂמָאלָא נִמְשָׁךְ מִשָּׁם, וְכָל עֲנָפָיו עֲתִידִין לְהִתְמַתֵּק וְהֵם שָׁבִים וּמִתְמַתְּקִים. וְהַיְנוּ מַמָּשׁ מִן הַטַּעַם שֶׁפֵּירַשְׁתִּי, שֶׁהָאָדָם מַשְׁרִישׁ בְּעַצְמוֹ סוֹד הָרַע וּמַמְתִּיקוֹ וּמַכְנִיסוֹ אֶל הַטּוֹב.

לְפִיכָךְ הָאָדָם מְטַהֵר יֵצֶר הָרָע וּמַכְנִיסוֹ אֶל הַטּוֹב וְהוּא מִשְׁתָּרֵשׁ בַּקְּדוּשָׁה לְמַעְלָה. וְזוֹ הִיא מַעֲלַת הַתְּשׁוּבָה, שֶׁהָאָדָם יִתְנַהֵג בָּהּ, צָרִיךְ שֶׁבְּכָל יוֹם וָיוֹם יְהַרְהֵר בָּהּ וְיַעֲשֶׂה תְּשׁוּבָה בְּצַד מָה, כְּדֵי שֶׁיִּהְיוּ כָּל יָמָיו בִּתְשׁוּבָה.

Chapter 5

How should a person train himself in the attribute of *chesed* (kindness)? The main way to enter into the secret of *chesed* is to love G-d so absolutely that one will never forsake His service for any reason; for, compared with the love of God, Blessed Be He, no other love has any worth. Therefore, he should first attend to the requirements of his Divine service; then, the remainder of his time may be used for other needs.

This love should be fixed firmly in his heart, whether he receives good from the Holy One, Blessed Be He, or suffering and chastisement — both should be considered expressions of G-d's love for him. As the verse states, "Faithful are the wounds inflicted by a loving friend..." (*Mishlei* 27:6). Furthermore, it is written, "...and with all your might" (*Devarim* 6:5), which our sages interpret as meaning, "With whatever measure He metes out to you" (*Berachot* 9:5), thereby including all attributes in the attrib-

פֶּרֶק חֲמִישִׁי

כֵּיצַד יַרְגִּיל הָאָדָם עַצְמוֹ בְּמִדַּת הַחֶסֶד. עִיקַּר כְּנִיסַת הָאָדָם אֶל
סוֹד הַחֶסֶד הוּא, לֶאֱהוֹב אֶת ד' תַּכְלִית אַהֲבָה, שֶׁלֹּא יַנִּיחַ עֲבוֹדָתוֹ
לְשׁוּם סִיבָּה. מִפְּנֵי שֶׁאֵין דָּבָר נֶאֱהָב אֶצְלוֹ כְּלָל לְעֶרֶךְ אַהֲבָתוֹ
יִתְבָּרַךְ. וְלָזֶה יְתַקֵּן תְּחִילָּה צָרְכֵי עֲבוֹדָתוֹ, וְאַחַר כָּךְ הַמּוֹתָר יִהְיֶה
לִשְׁאָר הַצְּרָכִים.

וְתִהְיֶה הָאַהֲבָה הַזֹּאת תְּקוּעָה בְּלִבּוֹ, בֵּין יְקַבֵּל טוֹבוֹת מֵאֵת
הַקָּבָּ"ה וּבֵין יְקַבֵּל יִסּוּרִין וְתוֹכָחוֹת, יַחְשְׁבֵם לְאַהֲבָה לוֹ, כְּדִכְתִיב
(מִשְׁלֵי כ"ז, ו'): "נֶאֱמָנִים פִּצְעֵי אוֹהֵב", וּכְדִכְתִיב (דְּבָרִים ו', ה'):
"וּבְכָל מְאֹדֶךָ" וּפֵירְשׁוּ (בְּרָכוֹת נ"ד, א'): "בְּכָל מִדָּה וּמִדָּה וְגוֹ'",

ute of *chesed*. Thus, although the secret of Divine conduct, which stems from the attribute of *malchut* (sovereignty), may be expressed as severity, it is connected to *chesed*.

Such was the habit of Nachum Ish Gamzu, who would always say: "This, too, is for the good!" He always sought to connect everything to the side of *chesed*, which is called 'good,' so he would say that even what appeared to be on the left, bound to the side of *gevurah* (severity), was in reality only for good, bound to *chesed*. This way, he would concentrate on the goodness of the attribute of *malchut*, concealing its severity. This is a great method of constantly binding oneself to *chesed*.

The *Tikkunim* states: "Who is a pious, kindhearted person? One who does kindness (*chesed*) to his Creator!" For when a person does kindness in this world, he should intend to reinstate its parallel Supernal quality — this is called "doing kindness to his Creator." Therefore, it is necessary to know the types of deeds practiced among men, all of which a person must fulfill towards his Creator if he wants to acquire the attribute of *chesed*. For this reason, it is stated that the following are acts of kindness:

1) At the moment of a child's birth, one should provide him with all the necessities of his sustenance. Thus, he should have in mind the birth of *tiferet* from *binah*. For if "her labor is difficult" (*Bereishit* 35:17) because of the aspect of judgment, G-d forbid, *tiferet* will tend toward the aspect of *gevurah*, and its birth will be difficult. Therefore, it is necessary to ease the birth as much as possible so that *tiferet* will emerge on the right, and the child will be born without blemish. As we pray, "And

כְּדֵי לִכְלֹל כָּל הַמִּדּוֹת בְּחֶסֶד. וְנִמְצָא סוֹד הַנְהָגָתוֹ מֵהַמַּלְכוּת. וְעִם
הֱיוֹת שֶׁהִיא פּוֹעֶלֶת דִּין, הִיא קְשׁוּרָה בְּחֶסֶד.

וְהַיְינוּ מִדַּת נַחוּם אִישׁ גַּם זוֹ, שֶׁהָיָה אוֹמֵר (תענית כ"א, א'):
"גַּם זוֹ לְטוֹבָה", רָצָה לְקַשְׁרָה תָּמִיד בְּצַד הַחֶסֶד הַנִּקְרָא טוֹב (זוהר
תרומה קס"ח, ב'), וְהָיָה אוֹמֵר: "גַּם זוֹ", שֶׁנִּרְאָה שֶׁהִיא בִּשְׂמֹאל,
קְשׁוּרָה בִּגְבוּרָה, אֵינוּ אֶלָּא "לְטוֹבָה", הִיא קְשׁוּרָה בְּחֶסֶד, וְהָיָה
שָׁם דַּעְתּוֹ אֶל צַד הַטּוֹב בַּמִּדָּה הַהִיא וּמַסְתִּיר דִּינֶיהָ. וְזוֹ הִיא הַנְהָגָה
גְדוֹלָה לְהַקְשֵׁר בְּחֶסֶד תָּמִיד.

וּבַתִּקוּנִים (בִּתְחִלַּת הַהַקְדָּמָה) פֵּירְשׁוּ "אֵיזֶה חָסִיד, הַמִּתְחַסֵּד
עִם קוֹנוֹ". לְפִי שֶׁגְּמִילוּת חֲסָדִים שֶׁאָדָם עוֹשֶׂה בַּתַּחְתּוֹנִים, צָרִיךְ
שֶׁיְּכַוֵּן בָּהּ הַתִּקּוּן הָעֶלְיוֹן דֻּגְמָתוֹ, וְהוּא שֶׁגוֹמֵל חֶסֶד עִם קוֹנוֹ.
וְעַתָּה צָרִיךְ לָדַעַת כַּמָּה הֵן מִדּוֹת גְּמִילוּת חֲסָדִים בִּבְנֵי אָדָם, וְכוּלָּם
יַעֲשֶׂה עִם קוֹנוֹ לְמַעְלָה, אִם יִרְצֶה לִקְנוֹת מִדַּת הַחֶסֶד. וְלָזֶה נֶאֱמַר
כִּי מִדּוֹת גְּמִילוּת חֲסָדִים הֵם אֵלּוּ:

רִאשׁוֹנָה — בְּלֵידַת הָאָדָם צָרִיךְ לִגְמֹל עִמּוֹ כָּל תִּקּוּן לִמְזוֹנוֹ.
אִם כֵּן יַעֲלֶה בְּדַעְתּוֹ עֵת לֵידַת הַבִּינָה הַתִּפְאֶרֶת. וְיִהְיֶה בְּהַקְשׁוֹתָהּ
בְּלִדְתָּהּ מִצַּד הַדִּין, חַס וְשָׁלוֹם, יֵצֵא הַתִּפְאֶרֶת לְצַד הַגְּבוּרוֹת וְלֵידָתָהּ
בְּקוֹשִׁי, צָרִיךְ לְתַקֵּן שָׁם כָּל הָאֶפְשָׁר שֶׁתִּהְיֶה לֵידַת הַתִּפְאֶרֶת לְצַד
הַיָּמִין, כְּדֵי שֶׁיֵּצֵא הַוָּלָד בְּלִי מוּם כְּלָל, כִּדְאָמְרִינַן "וַתּוֹצִיא כָאוֹר

bring forth the radiance of our judgment, O Awesome, Holy One." That is to say, we pray that the judgment of *tiferet* will be on the side of light, which is to the right, and will thus be sanctified and separated from the severities. This includes one's intention that his deeds constantly bind *tiferet* to *chesed*, bringing *tiferet* forth from *binah* to the side of *chesed*. Then the child born will be eager to fulfill the commandments, and he will be cleansed of imperfections. Almost all the prohibitions in the Torah are included in this idea that the severities should not awaken overpowering harshness there, making the birth difficult, G-d forbid.

2) Circumcising the child, i.e., fulfilling the commandments perfectly, circumcising every aspect of 'husk' or 'foreskin' that attaches itself to *yesod*. One should pursue all those who cause the foreskin to grow on *yesod*, bringing them back in repentance in such a way that, by circumcising the foreskins of their hearts, he renders the Supernal Tzaddik 'without a foreskin.' He must maintain a firm stance in rectifying all those things that bring about the foreskin there. For this reason, by circumcising the foreskin of the Jewish people, Pinchas became worthy of the priesthood, for he did kindness to his Creator according to the mystical explanation of circumcision — by removing the foreskin from *yesod*, he became worthy of the quality of *chesed*. From this, one can learn all the other qualities of *chesed*.

3) Visiting the ill and healing them. As is known, the Shechinah is lovesick for unification. As the verse states, "...for I am sick with love" (*Shir HaShirim* 2:5). Her cure is

מִשְׁפָּטֵנוּ אָיֹם קָדוֹשׁ", דְּהַיְינוּ שֶׁיּוֹצִיא הַתִּפְאֶרֶת מִשְׁפָּט לְצַד הָאוֹר שֶׁהוּא הַיָּמִין וְיִהְיֶה קָדוֹשׁ וְנִבְדָּל מִן הַגְּבוּרוֹת. וּבָזֶה נִכְלָל הֱיוֹתוֹ מְכַוֵּין בְּמַעֲשָׂיו לְקֻשְּׁרוּ תָּמִיד בְּחֶסֶד וּלְהוֹצִיא מִן הַבִּינָה בְּצַד הַחֶסֶד, וְאָז יֵצֵא הַוָּלָד מְזוֹרָז. וּמְלוּבָּן. וְכִמְעַט בָּזֶה נִכְלָל אַזְהָרָה שֶׁבַּתּוֹרָה, כְּדֵי שֶׁלֹּא יְעוֹרְרוּ הַגְּבוּרוֹת תִּגְבּוֹרֶת הַדִּינִים שָׁם וְיִהְיֶה קֹשִׁי בְּלֵדָתָהּ חַס וְחָלִילָה.

שְׁנִיָּה — לָמוּל אֶת הַוָּלָד, הַיְינוּ לַעֲשׂוֹת כְּתִקּוּנוֹ וּמִצְוֹתָיו, שֶׁכָּל אֵיזֶה צַד קְלִיפָּה וְעָרְלָה הַמְטַפֶּלֶת אֶל הַיְסוֹד יָמוּל אוֹתָהּ, וְיִרְדּוֹף אַחַר כָּל אוֹתָם הַגּוֹרְמִים שָׁם עָרְלָה וְיַחֲזִירֵם בִּתְשׁוּבָה, בְּאוֹפֶן שֶׁבִּהְיוֹתוֹ מָל אֶת עָרְלַת לְבָבָם גּוֹרֵם שֶׁיִּהְיֶה הַצַּדִּיק הָעֶלְיוֹן בְּלִי עָרְלָה וְיַעֲמוֹד בְּחָזְקָה לְתַקֵּן כָּל הַדְּבָרִים הַגּוֹרְמִים שָׁם עָרְלָה. וְלָזֶה פִּינְחָס כְּשֶׁמָּל עָרְלַת בְּנֵי יִשְׂרָאֵל זָכָה אֶל הַכְּהוּנָה, מִפְּנֵי שֶׁגָּמַל חֶסֶד עִם קוֹנוֹ בְּסוֹד הַמִּילָה, שֶׁמָּל הַיְסוֹד מֵאוֹתָהּ עָרְלָה, זָכָה אֶל הַחֶסֶד. וְכֵן מִזֶּה יִלְמוֹד אֶל כָּל שְׁאָר מִדּוֹת הַחֶסֶד.

שְׁלִישִׁית — לְבַקֵּר חוֹלִים וּלְרַפְּאוֹתָם. כָּךְ יָדוּעַ, שֶׁהַשְּׁכִינָה הִיא חוֹלַת אַהֲבָה מֵהַיְּחוּד, כְּדִכְתִיב (שִׁיר הַשִּׁירִים ב׳, ה): "כִּי חוֹלַת

in the hands of man, who is able to bring her pleasant remedies. As it is written, "Sustain me with dainty cakes (*ashishot*), spread apples before me..." (ibid.). The *Tikkunim* expounds this verse according to the mystical explanation of the word אשישות — which implies everything bound to the attribute of *malchut* — the word being composed of איש (man), and אישה (woman), representing *gevurah*, which are the 'two arms' supporting *malchut*. Thus, a person who visits the sick sustains them in their illness.

Alternatively, "spread apples before me" means binding *malchut* between *netzach* and *hod*, for this is the proper place of *malchut*, being that she is red and white, like those apples whose colors are blended from the side of *chesed*. Thus, one must visit her, keep her in mind, and entreat her to accept food and drink from the flow of Supernal benevolence from which she abstains, because she is sick with the sins of Israel.

Just as one behaves toward ill people, so must he behave toward the 'ill' of the higher worlds. For she (*malchut*) is 'ill,' as we have just mentioned, and he (*tiferet*) is also 'ill,' for he is restless in the World to Come and isolated from her in this world. As it is written, "Like a bird who wanders far from her nest [the "bird" referring to the Shechinah], so is a man who wanders from his place" (*Mishlei* 27:8). He waits for her and swears that he will not return to his place until returning her to her place. Thus, he, too, is "ill because of our transgressions, crushed [willingly] because of our sins" (*Yeshayahu* 53:5). The healing of both lies in our hands. Therefore, it is

אַהֲבָה אָנִי", וּרְפוּאָתָהּ בְּיַד אָדָם לְהָבִיא לָהּ סַמָּנִים יָפִים, כְּדִכְתִיב
(שָׁם,): "סַמְּכוּנִי בָּאֲשִׁישׁוֹת", וּפֵירְשׁוּ בַּתִּיקוּנִים (תִּיקוּן י"ט): בְּסוֹד
אֲשִׁישׁוֹת הָיְינוּ כָּל הַדְּבָרִים הַנִּקְשָׁרִים בַּמַּלְכוּת, בְּאִישׁ י' חֶסֶד
וּבְאִשָּׁה ה' גְּבוּרָה בִּשְׁנֵי זְרוֹעוֹת, וְשָׁם הִיא נִסְמֶכֶת עֲלֵיהֶם, וּמִי
שֶׁעוֹשֶׂה זֶה סוֹמֵךְ בְּחָלְיוֹ.

הב' — "רַפְּדוּנִי בַּתַּפּוּחִים" (שָׁם,), פֵּירוּשׁ לְקַשְּׁרָהּ בֵּין נֵצַח
וְהוֹד, שֶׁשָּׁם הִיא רְפִידָתָהּ, בִּהְיוֹתָהּ חִיוֵּר וְסוֹמֶק, כַּתַּפּוּחִים הַלָּלוּ
שֶׁגּוֹנֵיהֶם מְזוּגִים מִצַּד הַחֶסֶד, וְצָרִיךְ לְבַקְּרָהּ וְלִזְכּוֹר אוֹתָהּ וּלְחַלּוֹת
פָּנֶיהָ שֶׁתִּתְקַבֵּל מַאֲכָל וּמַשְׁקֶה מֵהַשֶּׁפַע הָעֶלְיוֹן שֶׁהִיא מוֹנַעַת עַצְמָהּ
מִמֶּנּוּ וְתִקְצַר נַפְשָׁהּ בַּעֲמַל יִשְׂרָאֵל.

כְּדֶרֶךְ שֶׁהוּא בְּחוֹלִים הַגַּשְׁמִיִּים, כָּךְ צָרִיךְ בְּחוֹלִים הָעֶלְיוֹנִים
שֶׁהִיא חוֹלָה, כְּדַאֲמָרָן, וְהוּא חוֹלֶה דְּנָע מֵאַתְרֵיהּ בְּעָלְמָא דְּאָתֵי וְנָד
אֲבַתְרָהּ בְּעָלְמָא דֵּין, כְּדִכְתִיב (מִשְׁלֵי כ"ז, ח') "כְּצִפּוֹר נוֹדֶדֶת מִן
קִנָּהּ", שֶׁהִיא הַשְּׁכִינָה "כֵּן אִישׁ נוֹדֵד מִמְּקוֹמוֹ", וְנָטִיר לְהוּא וְאוֹמֵי
דְּלָא יָתִיב לְאַתְרֵיהּ עַד דְּיַחֲזִיר לָהּ לְאַתְרָהּ (זוֹהַר כִּי תֵצֵא
רע"ח, א'). הִנֵּה גַם הוּא מְחוֹלָל מִפְּשָׁעֵינוּ מְדוּכֶּה לִרְצוֹנוֹ מֵעֲוֹנוֹתֵינוּ,
וּרְפוּאַת שְׁנֵיהֶם בְּיָדֵינוּ. וְרָאוּי לְבַקְּרָם וּלְהַזְמִין צָרְכֵיהֶם בַּתּוֹרָה
וּבַמִּצְוֹת.

proper to visit them and attend to their needs by studying Torah and carrying out the precepts.

4) Giving charity to the poor. The parallel above refers to *yesod* and *malchut*. The *Tikkunim* explains that the charity (צדקה befitting them is to say "amen" ninety (צ) times during the daily prayers, recite *Kedushah* four (ד) times daily, utter one hundred (ק) blessings daily, and learn from the five (ה) books of the Torah daily.

In addition, every person should draw down 'charity' from *tiferet* for these 'poor ones' — each according to his ability — providing them with *leket* (gleanings) from all the *sefirot*; *shichechah* (forgotten sheaves), according to the mystical explanation of the Supernal 'sheaf,' which is *binah*; and *pe'ah* (field corners), which derives from *malchut* itself, being that it is the 'corner of the field' in relation to the other *sefirot*. It is written, "you shall leave them for the poor and the stranger" (*VaYikra* 19:10, 23:22), for even *tiferet* is a stranger to *malchut* below, so one must perform these precepts, which rectify *tiferet*. Similarly, *ma'aser ani* — the tithe to the poor — raises up *malchut* (called *'ma'aser,'* the tithe), which is given to *yesod*, which is called 'poor.' And if one binds *malchut* to *tiferet*, he give the tithe to 'the stranger.' Many rectifications are included in this.

5) Offering hospitality to strangers. This refers to *tiferet* and *yesod*, which should be given a guest house in which to rest, namely, in *malchut*. For according to the mystical explanation of exile, they are wayfarers searching for what they have lost; therefore, they must be brought into that place. According to the explanation in the *Zohar*, this refers to the commandment fulfilled by

רְבִיעִית — לָתֵת צְדָקָה לָעֲנִיִּים, וְדוּגְמַת יְסוֹד וּמַלְכוּת. וְהַצְּדָקָה הָרְאוּיָה אֲלֵיהֶם פֵּירְשׁוּ בְּתִיקוּנִים (תיקון י״ח), לְקַיֵּים צ׳ אָמֵנִים, ד׳ קְדוּשּׁוֹת, ק׳ בְּרָכוֹת ה׳ חוּמְשֵׁי תוֹרָה, בְּכָל יוֹם.

וְעוֹד כָּל אֶחָד כְּפִי כֹּחוֹ יַמְשִׁיךְ צְדָקָה מִתְפָּאֶרֶת לָעֲנִיִּים הַלָּלוּ, וְיַזְמִין אֲלֵיהֶם לֶקֶט מֵהַסְּפִירוֹת כּוּלָם, שֶׁכָּחָה מְסוֹד הָעוֹמֶר הָעֶלְיוֹן שֶׁהִיא בִּינָה, וּפֵאָה מִבְּחִינַת הַמַּלְכוּת עַצְמָהּ, שֶׁהִיא פֵּאָה לִשְׁאָר הַמִּדּוֹת, וּכְתִיב (ויקרא י״ט, י׳): ״לֶעָנִי וְלַגֵּר תַּעֲזוֹב אוֹתָם״, שֶׁאֲפִילוּ הַתִּפְאֶרֶת גֵּר לְמַטָּה בַּמַּלְכוּת. וְצָרִיךְ לָתֵת לוֹ מֵאֵלוּ הַתִּקּוּנִים, וְכֵן מַעֲשַׂר עָנִי, לְהַעֲלוֹת הַמַּלְכוּת שֶׁהִיא מַעֲשֵׂר אֶל הַיְסוֹד הַנִּקְרָא עָנִי, וְאִם יְקַשְׁרֶנָּה בְּתִפְאֶרֶת יִתֵּן מִן הַמַּעֲשֵׂר אֶל הַגֵּר. וְכַמָּה תִיקוּנִים נִכְלָלִים בָּזֶה.

חֲמִישִׁית — הַכְנָסַת אוֹרְחִים, הֵם הַתִּפְאֶרֶת וְהַיְסוֹד, לָתֵת לָהֶם בֵּית מְנוּחָה שֶׁיָּנוּחוּ בוֹ, דְּהַיְינוּ הַמַּלְכוּת, כֵּיוָן שֶׁהֵם הוֹלְכֵי דְרָכִים, בְּסוֹד הַגָּלוּת, לַחֲזוֹר עַל אֲבֵדָתָם, צָרִיךְ לְהַכְנִיסָם שָׁם. וּלְפִי הַמִּתְבָּאֵר

"those who traveled talked" (*Shofetim* 5:10), that is, those who are exiled from home in order to study Torah. They cause 'the guests' to busy themselves with the needs of *malchut*.

Similarly, all those who bring about the unification of *tiferet* and *malchut* some other way, and fix times for Torah study, cause *tiferet* to lodge with *malchut*, as explained in the *Tikkunim*. It is necessary to prepare food and drink for the 'guests' and accompany them on their way — that is, a person must bring *tiferet* and *yesod* into *malchut* and provide them with food there.

This is analogous to the mystical explanation of the verse "I came to My garden...I have eaten My honeycomb with My honey..." (*Shir HaShirim* 5:1), referring to the outflow of spiritual bounty suited to the level of Divine rulership of the lower worlds as it spreads forth from sweetened severities. One must also provide them with drink, according to the mystical interpretation of the continuation of the verse, "I have drunk My wine with My milk." This verse refers to the inner spiritual flow from the guarded wine and the sweetened milk, as explained in the mystical teachings: to bind *tiferet* to *malchut*, Ya'akov to Rachel, and *gevurah* to *netzach* or *hod*. This is the explanation given in "*Ra'aya Mehemna*."

As for the precept of 'accompanying them,' this means that a person and his soul should go there together with *tiferet* and *yesod* in their Supernal form, accompanying them there. In addition, this implies bringing the

בַּזּוֹהַר (וַיֵּרָא קט"ז, ב'), שֶׁזּוֹ מִצְוָה מִתְקַיֶּמֶת בְּהוֹלְכֵי עַל דֶּרֶךְ שִׂיחוּ, שֶׁהֵם הַמִּתְגָּרְשִׁים מִבָּתֵּיהֶם לַעֲסוֹק בַּתּוֹרָה, שֶׁגּוֹרְמִים שֶׁיִּהְיוּ הָאוֹרְחִים עוֹסְקִים בְּצָרְכֵי הַמַּלְכוּת.

וְכֵן כָּל הָעוֹשֶׂה יִחוּד אֶל הַתִּפְאֶרֶת בַּמַּלְכוּת מִבְּחִינָה אַחֶרֶת וְקוֹבֵעַ מָקוֹם לְתוֹרָתוֹ, גּוֹרֵם שֶׁהַתִּפְאֶרֶת יַעֲשֶׂה מְלוֹנוֹ בַּמַּלְכוּת. וְכֵן פֵּירֵשׁ בַּתִּיקוּנִים (בהקדמה). וְאֶל הָאוֹרְחִים צָרִיךְ לְהָכִין אֲכִילָה, שְׁתִיָּיה, לְוָיָה, דְּהַיְינוּ שֶׁצָּרִיךְ לְהַכְנִיס הַתִּפְאֶרֶת וְהַיְסוֹד אֶל הַמַּלְכוּת וְלָתֵת לָהֶם שָׁם אֲכִילָה, מֵעֵין "בָּאתִי לְגַנִּי וְכוּ' אָכַלְתִּי יַעְרִי עִם דִּבְשִׁי" (שיר השירים ה', א') שֶׁהוּא שֶׁפַע רָאוּי לְהַנְהָגָה הַתַּחְתּוֹנָה הַמִּתְפַּשֶּׁטֶת מִצַּד הַגְּבוּרָה הַמְּתוּקָה, וּשְׁתִיָּה, מֵעֵין "שָׁתִיתִי יֵינִי עִם חֲלָבִי" (שם), שֶׁהוּא שֶׁפַע פְּנִימִי מִן הַיַּיִן הַמְשׁוּמָר וּמִסּוֹד הֶחָלָב הַמִּתְמַתֵּק לְקַשֵּׁר הַתִּפְאֶרֶת בַּמַּלְכוּת יַעֲקֹב וְרָחֵל וְהַגְּבוּרָה בְּנֶצַח אוֹ בְהוֹד, כִּי כֵן פֵּירְשׁוּ בָּרַעְיָא מְהֵימְנָא (ויקרא דף ג' ב).

וְהַלְוָיָה, לְהָבִיא עַצְמוֹ וְנִשְׁמָתוֹ שָׁם עִמָּהֶם בְּדִיּוֹקָן עֶלְיוֹן, לְלַוּוֹתָם

other *sefirot* there to be with them, giving them a good send-off. Many things are included in this rectification. In general, a person should make an effort to do whatever is necessary for the performance of the mundane act, simultaneously concentrating on the things to which it alludes. This way, he is sure to achieve its parallel Above, once he has become accomplished in the mystical secrets. It is even better to verbalize the secrets on which he concentrates when performing the precept, thereby fulfilling the verse "...in your mouth and in your heart to do it" (*Devarim* 30:14).

6) Attending to the dead. How this relates to the higher worlds is very difficult to explain, for this is the secret of the *sefirot*, which conceal themselves and disappear into their sheaths Above. How necessary it is to correct and cleanse them of all disease of sin and to enclothe them in white — which is the purification of the *sefirot* in the crucible of good deeds — elevating them in the mystical secret of Unity, binding them Above. And carrying them on one's shoulders is the secret of the elevation of the *sefirot*, one by one, until they ascend beyond the level of the 'shoulder,' which connects arm and torso. Above this level is the hidden secret, which is incomprehensible. During burial, one should concentrate on the mystical secret of the verse "[Hashem] buried [Moshe] in the valley..." (ibid. 34:6), בגי (in the valley) being rendered in the *Tikkunim* as "with the Thirteen Attributes of Mercy," which are rooted in *keter*, in those aspects that face downwards to have mercy on the beings of the lower worlds. From there, he is who is buried

שָׁם, עוֹד לְהָבִיא שְׁאָר הַסְּפִירוֹת שָׁם עִמָּהֶם לַעֲשׂוֹת לָהֶם לְוָיָה טוֹבָה. וְכַמָּה דְבָרִים נִכְלָלִים בְּתִיקוּן זֶה. כְּלָל שֶׁל דָּבָר, יִשְׁתַּדֵּל בְּצוֹרֶךְ הֶדְיוֹט וִיכַוֵּן בִּרְמִיזוֹתוֹ וּמוּבְטָח הוּא שֶׁיַּעֲשֶׂה לְמַעְלָה כַּיּוֹצֵא בּוֹ, אַחַר שֶׁיִּהְיֶה בָּקִי בַּסּוֹדוֹת. וּמַה טּוֹב לְהַזְכִּיר בְּפִיו רְמִיזַת כַּוָּנָתוֹ הַנְּכוֹנָה בִּשְׁעַת מַעֲשֶׂה, לְקַיֵּם "בְּפִיךָ וּבִלְבָבְךָ לַעֲשׂוֹתוֹ" (דברים ל', י"ד).

שִׁשִּׁית — עֵסֶק הַחַי עִם הַמֵּת. וְדָבָר זֶה הֵיאַךְ יִתְיַחֵס לְמַעְלָה קָשֶׁה מְאֹד, כִּי הוּא סוֹד הַסְּפִירוֹת, שֶׁהֵם מִתְעַלְּמוֹת וּמִסְתַּלְּקוֹת אֶל נְרְתִיקָן לְמַעְלָה, כַּמָּה צָרִיךְ לְתַקְּנָן וּלְהַרְחִיצָן מִכָּל חֶלְאַת עָוֹן וּלְהַלְבִּישָׁן לְבָנִים, לְבוֹנֵי הַסְּפִירוֹת, בְּאוֹר הַמַּעֲשֶׂה הַטּוֹב, לְהִתְעַלּוֹת בְּסוֹד אֶחָד, לְקַשְּׁרָם לְמַעְלָה, וְלָשֵׂאת אוֹתָם עַל הַכָּתֵף, סוֹד עִילּוּי הַסְּפִירוֹת אֶחָד אֶל אֶחָד, עַד שֶׁיִּתְעַלּוּ לְמַעְלָה מֵהַכָּתֵף, שֶׁהוּא תְּחִלַּת חִבּוּר הַזְּרוֹעַ בַּגּוּף, וּלְמַעְלָה מִזֶּה הוּא סוֹד הַנֶּעְלָם שֶׁאֵין הַשָּׂגָה בּוֹ. וִיכַוֵּן בְּסוֹד הַקְּבוּרָה הַפָּסוּק (דברים ל"ד, ו'): "וַיִּקְבּוֹר אוֹתוֹ בַגַּי", דְּמְתַרְגְּמִינָן "בִּתְלֵיסַר מְכִילִין דְּרַחֲמֵי" (תקונים מזוהר חדש), שֶׁהֵן נוֹבְעוֹת בַּכֶּתֶר בִּבְחִינוֹתָיו הַפּוֹנוֹת לְמַטָּה, לְרַחֵם בַּתַּחְתּוֹנִים, וּמִשָּׁם יַעֲלֶה הַנִּקְבָּר אֶל הָעֵדֶן הָעֶלְיוֹן, חָכְמָה שֶׁבַּכֶּתֶר, וְצָרִיךְ הַתְיַשְּׁבוּת הַדַּעַת בָּזֶה מְאֹד.

ascends to the upper level of Eden, which is the *chochmah* of *keter*. Understanding this concept requires much methodical deliberation.

7) Bringing a bride to the *chuppah*. This includes all the necessities of Unification, for all prayers and spiritual unifications are contained in the mystical explanation of bringing a bride to the *chuppah*. The essence of Unification lies in the secret of Prayer, which includes several levels, each higher than the next: those sections dealing with the sacrifices; then the verses of praise; then the prayers recited while sitting, including the Shema and the blessings beforehand and afterwards; then the *Amidah* and the remainder of the liturgy. All these are acts of benevolence to the groom and bride, attending to their needs and the requirements of their union.

8) Making peace between a man and his fellow. This refers to *tiferet* and *yesod*, which sometimes become separated from one another. A person must make peace between them and restore them to equal stature, so that they will be bound together in love and friendship. This is brought about through the power of good deeds. For when *yesod* leans to the Left and *tiferet* to the Right, they stand in opposition to one another until *yesod* is adjusted to lean to the Right, like *tiferet*. And if, G-d forbid, there is any blemish of sin in the world, then there is hatred and controversy between the two of them, with no unity or bond between the *sefirot* at all.

Similarly, the same thing might occur between any two *sefirot*, one of which is on the Right and the other on the Left — between *chochmah* and *binah*, *chesed* and

שְׁבִיעִית — הַכְנָסַת כַּלָּה לַחוּפָּה. וּבָזֶה נִכְלָלִים כָּל צָרְכֵי
הַיִּחוּד. שֶׁכָּל הַתְּפִלּוֹת וְהַיִּחוּדִים הֵם סוֹד הַכְנָסַת כַּלָּה לַחוּפָּה,
וְעִיקָרָהּ בְּסוֹד הַתְּפִלָּה מִכַּמָּה מַדְרֵגוֹת זוֹ אַחַר זוֹ, קָרְבָּנוֹת, זְמִירוֹת,
תְּפִלָּה מְיוּשָׁב שֶׁבָּהּ קְרִיאַת שְׁמַע וּבִרְכוֹתֶיהָ. אַחַר כָּךְ תְּפִלָּה מְעוֹמָד
וּשְׁאָר תִּקּוּנִים הַבָּאִים אַחֲרֵיהֶם, הַכֹּל גְּמִילוּת חֶסֶד אֶל הֶחָתָן וְהַכַּלָּה
לְפַקֵּחַ עַל צָרְכֵיהֶם וְתִקּוּנֵי זִיוּוּגָם.

שְׁמִינִית — הֲבָאַת שָׁלוֹם בֵּין אָדָם לַחֲבֵרוֹ, שֶׁהֵם הַתִּפְאֶרֶת
וְהַיְסוֹד, לִפְעָמִים יִתְרַחֲקוּ זֶה מִזֶּה וְצָרִיךְ לְהַשְׁלִימָם וּלְתַקְּנָם שֶׁיִּהְיוּ
שָׁוִים וְנִקְשָׁרִים יַחַד בְּאַהֲבָה וְחִיבָּה, וְזֶה עַל יְדֵי כִּשְׁרוֹן הַמַּעֲשֶׂה
הַטּוֹב, שֶׁכַּאֲשֶׁר יִהְיֶה הַיְסוֹד נוֹטֶה אֶל הַשְּׂמֹאל וְהַתִּפְאֶרֶת אֶל הַיָּמִין
אָז הֵם נְגְדִּיִּים זֶה לָזֶה, עַד שֶׁהַיְסוֹד יַטֶּה אֶל הַיָּמִין כָּמוֹהוּ, וְכַאֲשֶׁר
חַס וְשָׁלוֹם יֵשׁ אֵיזֶה פְּגָם שֶׁל עָוֹן בָּעוֹלָם אָז יֵשׁ שִׂנְאָה נֶגְדִּית בֵּין
שְׁנֵיהֶם וְאֵין יִחוּד וְקֶשֶׁר בֵּין הַסְּפִירוֹת כְּלָל.

וְעַל דֶּרֶךְ זֶה יִהְיֶה גַּם כֵּן בֵּין כָּל שְׁתֵּי סְפִירוֹת, שֶׁהֵם יָמִין
וּשְׂמֹאל, בֵּין הַחָכְמָה וְהַבִּינָה אוֹ בֵּין הַחֶסֶד וְהַגְּבוּרָה אוֹ בֵּין הַנֶּצַח

gevurah, or *netzach* and *hod*. Then one must make peace between them. This means making peace between a man and his fellow. The same explanation applies regarding making peace between a man and his wife — that is, between *tiferet* and *malchut*. All similar ways of making peace are also acts of benevolence in the higher worlds.

וְהַהוֹד, צָרִיךְ לְהַכְנִיס שָׁלוֹם בֵּינֵיהֶם, וְהַיְינוּ הֲבָאַת שָׁלוֹם בֵּין אָדָם לַחֲבֵירוֹ וְכֵן בֵּין אִישׁ לְאִישְׁתּוֹ, דְּהַיְינוּ הַיְסוֹד שָׁלוֹם בֵּין הַתִּפְאֶרֶת וּמַלְכוּת, וְכָל כַּיּוֹצֵא בָּזֶה מִדַּרְכֵי שָׁלוֹם הוּא גְּמִילוּת חֶסֶד לְמַעְלָה.

Chapter 6

How should a person train himself in the attribute of *gevurah* (might, power, severity)? Know that any arousal of the *yetzer hara* actually arouses powerful *gevurot*. Therefore, one should not stir up the *yetzer hara*, lest *gevurah* be aroused. The explanation of this idea is as follows:

Man was created with two inclinations — the *yetzer hatov* and the *yetzer hara*, or the good inclination and the evil inclination, of which the former is *chesed*, and the latter, *gevurah*. However, the *Zohar* on *Bereishit* explains that the *yetzer hatov* was created for the needs of the person himself, whereas the *yetzer hara* was created for the sake of his wife. See how delightful these words are: *Tiferet* — which contains the quality of *chesed* — tends to the Right, and all its activity is on the Right, which is the *yetzer tov*. But *malchut* tends to the Left, and all its activity is with *gevurah*. Consequently, it is proper and beneficial

פֶּרֶק שִׁשִּׁי

הֵיאַךְ יַרְגִּיל הָאָדָם עַצְמוֹ בְּמִדַּת הַגְּבוּרָה. דַּע, כִּי כָל פְּעוּלוֹת הִתְעוֹרְרוּת יֵצֶר הָרָע, הֵן מַמָּשׁ מְעוֹרְרוֹת הַגְּבוּרוֹת הַחֲזָקוֹת. לְכָךְ לֹא יִתְנוֹעֵעַ לַיֵּצֶר הָרָע, שֶׁלֹּא יְעוֹרֵר גְּבוּרָה.

וְהַטַּעַם, שֶׁהָאָדָם נוֹצַר בִּשְׁתֵּי יְצִירוֹת, יֵצֶר טוֹב וְיֵצֶר הָרָע, זֶה חֶסֶד וְזֶה גְּבוּרָה. אָמְנָם פֵּירְשׁוּ בַּזֹּהַר פָּרָשַׁת בְּרֵאשִׁית (מ"ט, א'), שֶׁיֵּצֶר טוֹב נִבְרָא לָאָדָם עַצְמוֹ, לְצָרְכּוֹ, וְיֵצֶר הָרָע לְצוֹרֶךְ אִשְׁתּוֹ. רְאֵה כַּמָּה מְתוּקִים דְּבָרָיו. הֲרֵי הַתִּפְאֶרֶת, בַּעַל הַחֶסֶד, נוֹטֶה אֶל הַיָּמִין, וְכָל הַנְהָגוֹתָיו בִּימִין יֵצֶר טוֹב, וְהַנְּקֵבָה שְׂמָאלִית וְכָל הַנְהָגוֹתֶיהָ בִּגְבוּרָה, אִם כֵּן רָאוּי שֶׁלֹּא יְעוֹרֵר יֵצֶר הָרָע לְתוֹעֶלֶת

not to arouse the *yetzer hara*, lest it arouse *gevurah* in the higher worlds and destroy this world. Any arousal of the aspect of *gevurah* and the *yetzer hara* a person bestirs in himself creates a corresponding flaw in the higher worlds. Based on this idea, one should note how disgraceful anger and the like are, for they cause harsh *gevurot* to prevail.

Indeed, the *yetzer hara* should be bound and tied so that it cannot be activated in any physical activity — neither in desiring intercourse nor in desiring money, neither for anger nor for honor in any way. However, for the sake of his wife, a man should gently arouse his inclination toward sweetened *gevurot*, providing her with clothing and a house, for example. He should say: "By providing my wife with clothes, I am restoring the Shechinah," for the Shechinah is adorned by *binah*, which is also an aspect of *gevurah*, since *binah* includes all severities. (Yet *binah*'s abundant compassion sweetens those severities.) Therefore, all household necessities restore the Shechinah, which is sweetened by way of the *yetzer hara*, which was created solely to fulfill the Will of its Creator.

For this reason, a man should not intend to derive pleasure of any sort from the evil inclination. Rather, when his wife adorns herself and delights in their fine home in his presence, he should contemplate the restoration of the Shechinah, which is rectified by way of the beneficial powers of the Left, whence wealth and honor derive. For the sake of this [restoration], one should arouse the *yetzer hara* to love the Shechinah. Then he

עַצְמוֹ, שֶׁהֲרֵי מְעוֹרֵר אָדָם הָעֶלְיוֹן בִּגְבוּרָה וּמְאַבֵּד הָעוֹלָם, אִם כֵּן, כָּל הֶעָרוֹת שֶׁיְּעוֹרֵר הָאָדָם לְעַצְמוֹ לְצַד הַגְּבוּרָה וְיֵצֶר הָרָע, פּוֹגֵם הָאָדָם הָעֶלְיוֹן. וּמִכָּאן יִרְאֶה כַּמָּה מְגוּנֶּה הַכַּעַס וְכָל כַּיּוֹצֵא בוֹ, שֶׁהוּא מַגְבִּיר הַגְּבוּרוֹת הַקָּשׁוֹת.

אָמְנָם יֵצֶר הָרָע צָרִיךְ לִהְיוֹת קָשׁוּר וְאָסוּר, לְבִלְתִּי יִתְעוֹרֵר לְשׁוּם פְּעוּלָה שֶׁבָּעוֹלָם מִפְּעוּלוֹת גּוּפוֹ, לֹא לְחִימוּד בִּיאָה וְלֹא לְחֶמְדַּת מָמוֹן וְלֹא לְצַד כַּעַס וְלֹא לְצַד כָּבוֹד כְּלָל. אָמְנָם לְצוֹרֶךְ אִשְׁתּוֹ יְעוֹרֵר יִצְרוֹ בְּנַחַת לְצַד הַגְּבוּרוֹת הַמְּתוּקוֹת, כְּגוֹן לְהַלְבִּישָׁהּ, לְתַקֵּן לָהּ בַּיִת, וְיֹאמַר, ״בָּזֶה שֶׁאֲנִי מַלְבִּישָׁהּ אֲנִי מְתַקֵּן הַשְּׁכִינָה״, שֶׁהִיא מִתְקַשֶּׁטֶת בַּבִּינָה, שֶׁהִיא גְבוּרָה דְּכָלִיל כּוּלְּהוּ גְּבוּרוֹת, וְהֵן מִתְמַתְּקוֹת בַּהֲמוֹן רַחֲמִים, לְפִיכָךְ כָּל תִּיקוּנֵי הַבַּיִת הֵם תִּיקוּנֵי הַשְּׁכִינָה, שֶׁהִיא מִתְמַתֶּקֶת מִצַּד יֵצֶר הָרָע, הַגִּבְרָא לַעֲשׂוֹת רְצוֹן קוֹנוֹ לֹא זוּלַת.

לְפִיכָךְ לֹא יְכַוֵּן הָאָדָם בּוֹ שׁוּם הֲנָאָה שֶׁל כְּלוּם, אֶלָּא כְּשֶׁאִשְׁתּוֹ מִתְנָאָה לְפָנָיו בְּדִירָה נָאָה יְכַוֵּן לְתַקּוּנֵי שְׁכִינָה, שֶׁהִיא מִתְתַּקֶּנֶת בִּגְבוּרוֹת הַשְּׂמָאלִיּוֹת הַטּוֹבוֹת, שֶׁמִּשָּׁם הָעוֹשֶׁר וְהַכָּבוֹד. מִצַּד זֶה יְעוֹרֵר הַיֵּצֶר הָרָע לְאַהֲבָתָהּ, וְאָז יְכַוֵּן אֶל הַשְּׂמֹאל הַמִּתְעוֹרֵר לְקָרְבָהּ

should concentrate on drawing the Shechinah near through the aroused aspects of the Left, according to the mystical explanation of the verse "His left arm is under my head..." (*Shir HaShirim* 2:6), for the Shechinah is connected initially only by way of the Left. After this — as the verse continues, "...and his right arm embraces me" he should concentrate on sweetening all those acts of restoring the Shechinah with his *yetzer tov*, literally reinstating the Shechinah and causing her to rejoice by performing this precept for the sake of the Supernal Union. Thus, he sweetens all the severities and rectifies them through the Right.

This method applies to all types of desire deriving from the *yetzer hara* — they should be used mainly for the benefit of the wife G-d has chosen as his "compatible helper" (*Bereishit* 2:18). Afterwards, he should redirect all of them to his service of G-d, binding them to the Right.

בְּסוֹד "שְׂמֹאלוֹ תַּחַת לְרֹאשִׁי" (שיר השירים ח׳, ג׳). שֶׁאֵינָהּ מִתְקַשֶּׁרֶת תְּחִלָּה אֶלָּא מִצַּד הַשְּׂמֹאל, וְאַחַר כָּךְ "וִימִינוֹ תְּחַבְּקֵנִי" (שם), יְכַוֵּין לְמַתֵּק כָּל אוֹתָם הַתִּיקוּנִים בְּיִצְרוֹ הַטּוֹב, וּלְתַקֵּן אוֹתָהּ מַמָּשׁ, לְשַׂמְּחָהּ בִּדְבַר מִצְוָה לְשֵׁם יִחוּד עֶלְיוֹן, הֲרֵי הִמְתִּיק כָּל הַגְּבוּרוֹת וְתִיקְנָם בַּיָּמִין.

וְדֶרֶךְ זֶה יִהְיֶה לְכָל מִינֵי חֶמְדָּה הַבָּאִים מִצַּד יֵצֶר הָרַע, יִהְיֶה עִקָּרָם לְתִיקּוּנֵי הָאִשָּׁה אֲשֶׁר הוֹכִיחַ ד׳ לוֹ לְעֵזֶר כְּנֶגְדּוֹ, וְיַהֲפוֹךְ כּוּלָם אַחַר כָּךְ לַעֲבוֹדַת ד׳, לְקַשְּׁרָם בַּיָּמִין.

Chapter 7

How should a person train himself in the attribute of *tiferet* (truth)? Clearly, the attribute of *tiferet* is found in Torah study. However, great caution must be exercised to avoid becoming aloof through one's learning, which could cause great harm. For when a man holds himself proudly aloof [because of his learning], he causes the attribute of *tiferet*, which is Torah, to become aloof and withdrawn to a higher plane, G-d forbid. In contrast, he who humbles himself through words of Torah causes *tiferet* to descend and lower itself to flow forth to *malchut*.

Now, below the *sefirah* of *tiferet* are four *sefirot* and three corresponding qualities:

1) A teacher who exalts himself above his students causes *tiferet* to exalt itself, too, and rise above *netzach* and *hod*, which are called "students of [the Torah of] the L-rd" (*Yeshayahu* 54:13), that is, the students of *tiferet*. Thus, one who humbles himself and teaches his students with love

פֶּרֶק שְׁבִיעִי

הֵיאַךְ יַרְגִּיל הָאָדָם עַצְמוֹ בְּמִדַּת הַתִּפְאֶרֶת. אֵין סָפֵק שֶׁמִּדַּת הַתִּפְאֶרֶת הִיא הָעֵסֶק בַּתּוֹרָה. אָמְנָם צָרִיךְ זְהִירוּת גְּדוֹלָה שֶׁלֹּא יִתְגָּאֶה אָדָם בְּדִבְרֵי תוֹרָה, שֶׁלֹּא יִגְרוֹם רָעָה גְדוֹלָה, שֶׁהֲרֵי כְּמוֹ שֶׁהוּא מִתְגָּאֶה, רַק גּוֹרֵם שֶׁמִּדַּת הַתִּפְאֶרֶת, שֶׁהִיא הַתּוֹרָה, תִּתְגָּאֶה וְתִסְתַּלֵּק לְמַעֲלָה, ח"ו. אֶלָּא כָּל הַמַּשְׁפִּיל עַצְמוֹ בְּדִבְרֵי תוֹרָה גּוֹרֵם אֶל הַתִּפְאֶרֶת שֶׁיֵּרֵד וּמַשְׁפִּיל עַצְמוֹ לְהַשְׁפִּיעַ לְמַטָּה.

וַהֲרֵי לְמַטָּה מֵהַתִּפְאֶרֶת אַרְבַּע סְפִירוֹת וְלָהֶן שָׁלֹשׁ מִדּוֹת,

רִאשׁוֹנָה — הַמִּתְגָּאֶה עַל תַּלְמִידָיו גּוֹרֵם שֶׁהַתִּפְאֶרֶת יִתְגָּאֶה וְיִתְעַלֶּה מֵעַל נֵצַח וְהוֹד, שֶׁהֵם לְמוּדֵי ד' תַּלְמִידֵי הַתִּפְאֶרֶת, וְהַמַּשְׁפִּיל עַצְמוֹ (וּמְלַמְּדָה) [וּמְלַמְּדָם] בְּאַהֲבָה, גַּם הַתִּפְאֶרֶת יַשְׁפִּיל עַצְמוֹ אֶל תַּלְמִידָיו וְיַשְׁפִּיעֵם. לְפִיכָךְ יִהְיֶה הָאָדָם נוֹחַ לְתַלְמִידָיו וִילַמְּדֵם כַּאֲשֶׁר

causes *tiferet* to lower itself to its 'students' and flow forth to them. A teacher should therefore be pleasant to his students and teach them according to their ability to absorb. In this merit, *tiferet* will pour forth to 'the students of [the Torah of] the L-rd,' to the degree appropriate for them.

2) By virtue of his Torah learning, one might hold himself proudly aloof over the poor person and despise him. Thus, Eliyahu the Prophet appeared to Rabbi Shimon ben Elazar as an ugly, despicably, loathsome pauper in order to enlighten him. For in his elation with his learning, he insulted the poor fellow, who then rebuked Rabbi Shimon profusely for this character defect. Such a man, who exalts himself over the poor, causes *tiferet* to remain aloof from *yesod* rather than flowing forth to it. But if a sage pays attention to the poor, *tiferet* will flow into *yesod*. For this reason, sages should highly esteem the poor and draw them closer. This way, *tiferet* will greatly value *yesod* and bind itself to it.

3) A man who, by virtue of his Torah knowledge, holds himself haughtily aloof over the ignorant — that is, the people of the L-rd in general — causes *tiferet* to soar above *malchut* rather than flowing into it. Instead, a person should be of pleasant disposition towards G-d's creatures, and all civilized people should be worthy in his estimation, since they correspond to the secret of 'the Land.' If he calls them donkeys, G-d forbid, he casts them down to the external forces; as a result, he will not merit a son imbued with the light of Torah, as stated in the Gemara.

יוּכְלוּן שְׂאֵת, וְהַתִּפְאֶרֶת בִּזְכוּתוֹ יַשְׁפִּיעַ בְּלִמּוּדֵי ד' כְּפִי בְחִינָתָם הָרְאוּיָה אֲלֵיהֶם.

שֵׁנִית — הַמִּתְגָּאֶה בְּתוֹרָתוֹ עַל הֶעָנִי וּמְבַזֶּה אוֹתוֹ, כְּהַהוּא עוּבָדָא עִם אֵלִיָּהוּ, שֶׁנִּדְמָה לְרַבִּי שִׁמְעוֹן בֶּן אֶלְעָזָר כְּעָנִי מְכוֹעָר, נִבְזֶה וְנִמְאָס, לְהַכְשִׁילוֹ, שֶׁזָּחָה דַעְתּוֹ עָלָיו וְגִינָה אֶת הֶעָנִי, וְהוּא הוֹכִיחַ עַל פָּנָיו מוּמוֹ (תענית כ', א'). כִּי הַמִּתְגָּאֶה עַל הֶעָנִי גּוֹרֵם שֶׁהַתִּפְאֶרֶת יִתְגָּאֶה עַל הַיְסוֹד וְלֹא יַשְׁפִּיעַ בּוֹ. וְאִם תִּהְיֶה דַעְתּוֹ שֶׁל חָכָם מְיוּשֶּׁבֶת עָלָיו עִם הֶעָנִי, אָז הַתִּפְאֶרֶת יַשְׁפִּיעַ בַּיְסוֹד, לְפִיכָךְ יֵיחָשֵׁב הֶעָנִי מְאֹד אֵצֶל הֶחָכָם וִיקָרְבֵהוּ וְכָךְ יֵחָשֵׁב לְמַעְלָה הַיְסוֹד אֵצֶל הַתִּפְאֶרֶת וְיִתְקַשֵּׁר בּוֹ.

שְׁלִישִׁית — הַמִּתְגָּאֶה בְּתוֹרָתוֹ עַל עַמָּא דְאַרְעָה, שֶׁהוּא כְּלַל עַם ד', גּוֹרֵם שֶׁהַתִּפְאֶרֶת יִתְגָּאֶה מֵעַל הַמַּלְכוּת וְלֹא יַשְׁפִּיעַ בָּהּ. אֶלָּא יִהְיֶה דַעְתּוֹ מְעוֹרֶבֶת עִם הַבְּרִיּוֹת וְכָל עַם הַיִּשּׁוּב חֲשׁוּבִים לְפָנָיו, מִפְּנֵי שֶׁהֵם לְמַטָּה בְּסוֹד הָאָרֶץ, וְחַס וְחָלִילָה אִם קוֹרֵא אוֹתָם "חֲמוֹרִים", מוֹרִידֵם אֶל הַקְּלִיפוֹת, לְכָךְ לֹא יִזְכֶּה לְבֵן שֶׁיִּהְיֶה בּוֹ אוֹר תּוֹרָה, כִּדְאִיתָא בִּגְמָרָא (נדרים פא, א').

Rather, he should act pleasantly towards them, according to their manner, just as *tiferet* flows forth to *malchut* and directs it according to its intellectual immaturity, for "women are of unstable temperament." Included in this conduct is not being haughty towards anyone feeble-minded, for such a person is in the category of 'the dust of the earth.' For this reason, the earlier generations never exalted themselves in their Torah learning, as indicated by the incidents related in the *Zohar*, "*Bereishit*," regarding Rav Hamnuna and Rav Chaggai. The *Tikkunim* also tells of a venerable sage who fled when Rabbi Shimon bar Yochai sought to kiss him, lest he become proud in his learning.

Furthermore, in debating words of Torah, a man should accustom himself to the restitution of the Shechinah, preparing and beautifying her for *tiferet*. This means deciding the halachah according to the truth. This is the meaning of 'controversy for the sake of Heaven,' that is, controversy between the two opposing powers, *chesed* and *gevurah*, for the sake of Heaven (*tiferet*), in deciding the halachah (*malchut*) according to the truth (*tiferet*). But one should distance himself from any controversy that departs from this norm, for *tiferet* has no desire to be trapped in extraneous matters, even if they involve Torah learning. If they are for the purpose of dispute, their end is Gehinom, G-d forbid. The only controversy that does not blemish *tiferet* is one in Torah matters for the sake of Heaven, for "...all its paths are peace" (*Mishlei* 3:17), and "its end is love."

However, he who derives benefit from words of

אֶלָּא יִתְנַהֵג עִמָּהֶם בְּנַחַת עַל פִּי דַרְכָּם, כְּעֵין הַתִּפְאֶרֶת, שֶׁהוּא
מַשְׁפִּיעַ לְמַלְכוּת וּמַנְהִיגָהּ כְּפִי עֲנִיוּת דַעְתָּהּ, כִּי "דַעְתָּן שֶׁל נָשִׁים
קַלּוֹת", (שבת ל"ג, ב). וּבִכְלַל זֶה, שֶׁלֹּא יִתְגָּאֶה עַל כָּל חֲלוּשֵׁי
הַדַעַת, שֶׁהֵם בִּכְלַל "עֲפַר הָאָרֶץ". וּמִפְּנֵי זֶה הַקַּדְמוֹנִים לֹא הָיוּ
מִתְגָּאִים בַּתּוֹרָה, כְּעוּבְדָא דְרַב הַמְנוּנָא בְּפָרָשַׁת בְּרֵאשִׁית (הקדמת
הזוהר ז', א') וּכְעוּבְדָא דְאַדְרַב חַגַּאי (זוהר שלח קנ"ח, א'), וּבְתִיקּוּנִים (סוף
תקון כ"ו): "הַהוּא סָבָא דְּבָעֵי לְנַשְׁקָא לֵיהּ פַּרְח", שֶׁלֹּא הָיָה רוֹצֶה
לְהִתְגָּאוֹת בְּדִבְרֵי תּוֹרָה.

עוֹד יִהְיֶה רָגִיל בְּהֱיוֹתוֹ נוֹשֵׂא וְנוֹתֵן בְּדִבְרֵי תּוֹרָה לְכַוֵּן אֶל
תִּקּוּנֵי שְׁכִינָה, לְתַקְּנָהּ וּלְקַשְּׁטָהּ אֶל הַתִּפְאֶרֶת, דְּהַיְינוּ הֲלָכָה אֶל
הָאֱמֶת. וְזֶהוּ "מַחֲלוּקֶת לְשֵׁם שָׁמַיִם", דְּהַיְינוּ חֶסֶד וּגְבוּרָה לָבוֹא אֶל
הַתִּפְאֶרֶת שָׁוִים לְהַסְכִּים הֲלָכָה עִמּוֹ. וְכָל מַחֲלוּקֶת שֶׁיֵּצֵא מִן הַשּׁוּרָה
הַזֹּאת יִבָּדֵל מִמֶּנּוּ, כִּי לֹא יִרְצֶה הַתִּפְאֶרֶת לְהִתְאַחֵז בַּחוּץ אֲפִילוּ
שֶׁיִּהְיֶה בְּדִבְרֵי תּוֹרָה, אִם הוּא לְקַנְטֵר סוֹפָהּ גֵּיהִנָּם, חַס וְחָלִילָה.
וְאֵין לְךָ מַחֲלוּקֶת שֶׁלֹּא יִפְגּוֹם הַתִּפְאֶרֶת, אֶלָּא מַחֲלוּקֶת הַתּוֹרָה לְשֵׁם
שָׁמַיִם, שֶׁכָּל נְתִיבוֹתֶיהָ שָׁלוֹם וְאַהֲבָה בְּסוֹפָהּ.

Torah blemishes this attribute, for it is holy, and he profanes it with secular matters. Happy is the portion of the person who strives in Torah to delight the Most Exalted One.

The most important thing of all is to purify one's mind by scrutinizing his thoughts and examining himself in the course of debate. If he finds even a trace of impure thought, he must retract his words and always admit the truth in order that *tiferet*, the quality of truth, be found therein.

וְאִם יְכַוֵּין לְהִנָּאוֹת מִדִּבְרֵי תּוֹרָה, פּוֹגֵם בְּמִדָּה הַזֹּאת, שֶׁהִיא קוֹדֶשׁ וּמוֹצִיאָהּ אֶל דִּבְרֵי חֹל. וְכַאֲשֶׁר יַעֲסֹק בַּתּוֹרָה לַהֲנָאַת גָּבוֹהַּ אַשְׁרֵי חֶלְקוֹ.

וְעִיקַּר הַכֹּל הוּא, לְצָרֵף דַּעְתּוֹ בְּמִבְחַן הַמַּחֲשָׁבָה וּלְפַשְׁפֵּשׁ בְּעַצְמוֹ דֶּרֶךְ מַשָּׂא וּמַתָּן, אִם יִמָּצֵא שֶׁמֶץ עֶרְוַת דָּבָר יַחֲזֹר בּוֹ, וּלְעוֹלָם יוֹדֶה עַל הָאֱמֶת, כְּדֵי שֶׁיִּמָּצֵא שָׁם הַתִּפְאֶרֶת מִדַּת אֱמֶת.

Chapter 8

How should a person train himself in the attributes of *netzach*, *hod*, and *yesod*? In fact, the rectifications of *netzach* and *hod* have some aspects in common and others that are unique to each of them.

First of all, one should help students of the Torah and support them, whether with money or in deed, providing them with the things they require, preparing their food, and carrying out their wishes so that they need not cease their Torah study. He should take care not to disparage their learning, lest they flag in their efforts to study. He should praise their good deeds so that they gain strength in their service, and he should provide them with the books they need, a house of study, and so forth. Anything that strengthens and supports those who toil in Torah derives form these two attributes. Each person should contribute whatever he can, however little or much. Ultimately, whatever a person can do to honor the

פֶּרֶק שְׁמִינִי

הֵיאַךְ יַרְגִּיל הָאָדָם עַצְמוֹ בְּמִדּוֹת נֶצַח, הוֹד, יְסוֹד. וְאוּלָם בְּתִקּוּנֵי הַנֶּצַח וְהַהוֹד קְצָתָם מְשֻׁתָּפִים לִשְׁנֵיהֶם וּקְצָתָם מְיֻחָדִים כָּל אֶחָד לְעַצְמוֹ.

וְהִנֵּה, רִאשׁוֹנָה, צָרִיךְ לְסַיֵּעַ לוֹמְדֵי הַתּוֹרָה וּלְהַחֲזִיקָם, אִם בְּמָמוֹנוֹ אוֹ בְּמַעֲשֵׂהוּ וּלְהַזְמִין לָהֶם צָרְכֵי שִׁמּוּשׁ הַזְמָנַת מָזוֹן וַהֲפָקַת כָּל רְצוֹנָם, שֶׁלֹּא יִתְבַּטְּלוּ מִדִּבְרֵי תוֹרָה, וּלְהִזָּהֵר שֶׁלֹּא לִגְנוֹת תַּלְמוּדָם, שֶׁלֹּא יִתְרַפּוּ מֵעֵסֶק הַתּוֹרָה, אֶלָּא לְכַבְּדָם וּלְהַלֵּל מַעֲשֵׂיהֶם הַטּוֹבִים, כְּדֵי שֶׁיִּתְחַזְּקוּ בַּעֲבוֹדָה, וּלְהַזְמִין לָהֶם סְפָרִים צוֹרֶךְ עֵסְקָם וּבֵית מִדְרָשׁ וְכָל כַּיּוֹצֵא שֶׁהוּא חִזּוּק וְסַעַד לְעוֹסְקֵי הַתּוֹרָה, הַכֹּל תָּלוּי בִּשְׁתֵּי מִדּוֹת הַלָּלוּ, כָּל אֶחָד כְּפִי כֹחוֹ, הַמְּעַט הוּא אִם רָב.

Torah and strengthen its observance — whether verbally, physically, or financially — arousing people's hearts to Torah and inspiring them to hold fast to it, is rooted in these two *sefirot*, which are called 'those who adhere to it and support it.'

Furthermore, he who toils in Torah study must learn from every person. As it is written, "From all my teachers, I have gained wisdom..." (*Tehillim* 119:99), for complete Torah knowledge is not gained from a single teacher. Thus, by learning from everyone, a person becomes worthy of being a vehicle for *netzach* and *hod*, which are the 'students of the L-rd' (*Yeshayahu* 54:13), and one who teaches Torah is on the level of *tiferet*. Therefore, when a man sits and learns, in this merit, *tiferet* flows into *netzach* and *hod*, and he actually attains their level.

Now, when a person learns Scripture, which comes from the Right, he has a specific association with *netzach*, and when he learns Mishnah, which comes form the Left, he has a specific association with *hod*. But Talmud includes everything, for it cites proofs for the laws of the Mishnah from Scripture, thereby completing them both.

How should a person train himself in the attribute of *yesod*? To avoid wasteful emission, he must be extremely careful of the kind of speech that leads to licentious thoughts. Needless to say, he should not use foul language; he should even be on his guard against pure speech that leads to licentious thoughts. This idea can be derived from an examination of the verse "Do not allow your mouth to bring sin to your flesh..." (*Kohelet* 5:5) — that is, "Do not let your mouth utter words that bring holy

סוֹף דָּבָר, כָּל מַה שֶּיַרְבֶּה בָּזֶה לְכַבֵּד הַתּוֹרָה וּלְהַחֲזִיקָהּ בְּדִבּוּר בְּגוּפוֹ וּבְמָמוֹנוֹ וּלְעוֹרֵר לֵב הַבְּרִיּוֹת אֶל הַתּוֹרָה שֶׁיִּתְחַזְּקוּ בָּהּ, הַכֹּל נִשְׁרָשׁ בִּשְׁתֵּי סְפִירוֹת אֵלּוּ, מִפְּנֵי שֶׁהֵם נִקְרָאִים "מַחֲזִיקִים בָּהּ וְתוֹמְכֶיהָ".

עוֹד צָרִיךְ הָעוֹסֵק בַּתּוֹרָה, שֶׁיִּלְמַד מִכָּל אָדָם, כְּדִכְתִיב (תהלים קי"ט, צ"ט): "מִכָּל מְלַמְּדַי הִשְׂכַּלְתִּי". כִּי אֵין הַתּוֹרָה מִשְׁתַּלֶּמֶת אֵצֶל רַב אֶחָד, וְכֵיוָן שֶׁהוּא נַעֲשָׂה תַלְמִיד לַכֹּל, זוֹכֶה לִהְיוֹת מֶרְכָּבָה אֶל נֶצַח וְהוֹד לְמוֹדֵי ד', וְהַמַּשְׁפִּיעַ אֵלָיו תּוֹרָה הוּא בְּמַדְרֵגַת תִּפְאֶרֶת, וַהֲרֵי בִּהְיוֹתוֹ יוֹשֵׁב וְלוֹמֵד זוֹכֶה אֶל הַתִּפְאֶרֶת שֶׁיַּשְׁפִּיעַ בְּנֶצַח וְהוֹד וְהוּא בְּמַדְרֵגָתָם מַמָּשׁ.

וְהִנֵּה, בִּהְיוֹתוֹ לוֹמֵד מִקְרָא, שֶׁהוּא מִן הַיָּמִין, יֵשׁ לוֹ יַחַס פְּרָטִי אֶל הַנֶּצַח, וּבִהְיוֹתוֹ לוֹמֵד מִשְׁנָה, שֶׁהוּא מִן הַשְּׂמֹאל, יֵשׁ לוֹ יַחַס פְּרָטִי אֶל הַהוֹד, וְהַגְּמָרָא הַכְּלוּלָה בַּכֹּל, שֶׁמְּבִיאָה רְאָיָה לְדִינֵי הַמִּשְׁנָה מִן הַכָּתוּב הֲרֵי זֶה תִּיקוּן לִשְׁנֵיהֶם יַחַד.

וְאוּלָם הֵיאַךְ יַרְגִּיל הָאָדָם עַצְמוֹ בְּמִדַּת הַיְסוֹד — צָרִיךְ הָאָדָם לְהִזָּהֵר מְאֹד מֵהַדִּבּוּר הַמֵּבִיא לִידֵי הִרְהוּר, כְּדֵי שֶׁלֹּא יָבוֹא לִידֵי קֶרִי. אֵין צָרִיךְ לוֹמַר שֶׁלֹּא יְדַבֵּר נְבָלָה, אֶלָּא אֲפִילוּ דִּבּוּר טָהוֹר הַמֵּבִיא לִידֵי הִרְהוּר רָאוּי לְהִשָּׁמֵר מִמֶּנּוּ. וְהָכִי דָּיֵּיק לִישְׁנָא דִּקְרָא (קהלת ה', ה'): "אַל תִּתֵּן אֶת פִּיךָ לַחֲטִיא אֶת בְּשָׂרֶךָ", הִזְהִיר שֶׁלֹּא

flesh [the Sign of the Holy Covenant] to wasteful emission." The verse continues: "why should G-d be angry because of your voice?" If this "voice" refers to obscenities, why is the expression "to bring sin" used in the first part of the verse? Uttering obscenities is itself a sin! Rather, even if the words themselves are not sinful but pure, if they give rise to licentious thoughts, he must be on his guard against them. For this reason, the verse uses the expression "to bring sin...why should G-d be angry": For since these words to bring sin, even though they themselves are permissible, G-d is angry with the voice that utters them, for the resulting evil act reverts to the voice and words that caused it. This is the extent to which one must be careful regarding the Sign of the Covenant, entertaining no licentious thoughts, lest he cause destruction.

Further care is necessary, since *yesod* also corresponds to 'the Covenant of the Rainbow,' which is arched above only to shoot arrows at the attribute of *malchut*, the target of the arrows. This refers to guarding the seminal drop, which shoots forth like an arrow "to produce branches and bear fruit" (*Yechezkel* 17:8). Just as the 'bow' in the higher worlds is never drawn except when aimed at the aforementioned target, a man should not draw his bow — that is, cause himself in any way to have an erection — unless it is directed towards the proper target: his wife, when she is in a state of purity, at the time of union. He should never go beyond this limit, lest the attribute of *yesod* become flawed, G-d forbid. This requires great care, mainly in guarding himself from licentious thoughts.

יִתֵּן פִּיו בְּדִבּוּר שֶׁמֵּבִיא לְהַחֲטִיא בְּשַׂר קֹדֶשׁ אוֹת בְּרִית בְּקֶרִי, וּכְתִיב (שם): "לָמָּה יִקְצוֹף הָאֱלֹהִים וגו'", וְאִם הוּא נִבְלוּת הַפֶּה, מַאי "לַחֲטִיא", הֲרֵי הוּא בְּעַצְמוֹ חָטָא. אֶלָּא אֲפִילוּ שֶׁהַדִּבּוּר לֹא יִהְיֶה חֵטְא, אֶלָּא דִבּוּר טָהוֹר, אִם מֵבִיא לִידֵי הִרְהוּר צָרִיךְ לְהִזָּהֵר מִמֶּנּוּ, וְלָזֶה אָמַר "לַחֲטִיא אֶת בְּשָׂרְךָ לָמָּה יִקְצוֹף", יִרְצֶה, אַחַר שֶׁמַּחֲטִיא יִקְצוֹף עַל אוֹתוֹ קוֹל אֲפִילוּ שֶׁיִּהְיֶה מֻתָּר, כִּי עַל יְדֵי פְּעוּלָה רָעָה הַנִּמְשֶׁכֶת מִמֶּנּוּ חָזַר הַקּוֹל וְהַדִּבּוּר רַע. כָּל כַּךְ צָרִיךְ זְהִירוּת לְאוֹת בְּרִית לְהַרְהֵר וְלֹא יַשְׁחִית.

וְעוֹד צָרִיךְ לִיזָּהֵר, שֶׁהַיְסוֹד הוּא אוֹת בְּרִית הַקֶּשֶׁת, וְהַקֶּשֶׁת אֵינָהּ דְּרוּכָה לְמַעְלָה אֶלָּא לְשַׁלֵּחַ חִצִּים לְמִדַּת הַמַּלְכוּת, שֶׁהִיא מַטָּרָה לַחֵץ, שׁוֹמֶרֶת הַטִּפָּה הַיּוֹרָה כַּחֵץ לַעֲשׂוֹת עָנָף וְלָשֵׂאת פְּרִי, וּכְשֵׁם שֶׁמֵּעוֹלָם לֹא יִדְרוֹךְ הַקֶּשֶׁת הָעֶלְיוֹן אֶלָּא לְנוֹכַח הַמַּטָּרָה הַנִּזְכֶּרֶת, כָּךְ הָאָדָם לֹא יִדְרוֹךְ הַקֶּשֶׁת, וְלֹא יַקְשֶׁה עַצְמוֹ בְּשׁוּם צַד, אֶלָּא לְנוֹכַח הַמַּטָּרָה הָרְאוּיָה, שֶׁהִיא אִשְׁתּוֹ, בְּטָהֳרָתָהּ, שֶׁהוּא עֵת הַזִּוּוּג, וְלֹא יוֹתֵר מִזֶּה שֶׁיִּפְגּוֹם הַמִּדָּה הַזֹּאת, חַס וְחָלִילָה. וּמְאֹד מְאֹד צָרִיךְ זְהִירוּת, וְעִיקַּר הַשְּׁמִירָה בִּהְיוֹתוֹ שׁוֹמֵר עַצְמוֹ מִן הַהִרְהוּר.

Chapter 9

How should a person train himself in the attribute of *malchut*? First of all, his wealth should not make him proud. Rather, he should always behave like a poor person, standing before his Maker like a pauper, begging and pleading. Even one who is wealthy should accustom himself to this attitude, considering that none of his possessions belong to him and that he is forsaken and requires the constant mercies of his Creator, having nothing but the bread the eats. He should humble his heart and afflict himself, especially at the time of prayer, for this is a very effective aid. In contrast, the verse states: "But your heart may then grow haughty, and you may forget..." (*Devarim* 8:14), for forgetfulness is common amid pride. This is the attitude to which King David made himself well-accustomed, saying: "...for I am alone and humbled" (*Tehillim* 25:16). Since each member of a man's household must fend for himself, what can each one do for him? Of

פֶּרֶק תְּשִׁיעִי

הֵיאַךְ יַרְגִּיל הָאָדָם עַצְמוֹ בְּמִדַּת הַמַּלְכוּת. רִאשׁוֹנָה לְכוּלָן, שֶׁלֹּא יִתְגָּאֶה לִבּוֹ בְּכָל אֲשֶׁר לוֹ וְיָשִׂים עַצְמוֹ תָּמִיד כְּעָנִי וְיַעֲמִיד עַצְמוֹ לִפְנֵי קוֹנוֹ כְּדַל שׁוֹאֵל וּמִתְחַנֵּן. וּלְהַרְגִּיל עַצְמוֹ בְּמִדָּה זוֹ, אֲפִילוּ שֶׁיִּהְיֶה עָשִׁיר, יַחֲשׁוֹב, שֶׁאֵין דָּבֵק עִמּוֹ מִכָּל אֲשֶׁר לוֹ מְאוּמָה, וְהוּא נֶעֱזָב, צָרִיךְ לְרַחֲמֵי הַבּוֹרֵא תָּמִיד, שֶׁאֵין לוֹ כָּל דָּבָר אֶלָּא הַלֶּחֶם אֲשֶׁר יֹאכֵל. וְיַכְנִיעַ לִבּוֹ וְיַעֲנֶה עַצְמוֹ, וּמַה גַּם בְּעֵת תְּפִילוֹתָיו, שֶׁזּוֹ סְגוּלָה נִפְלָאָה. וּלְהֵיפֶךְ מִזֶּה נֶאֱמַר (דברים, ח', י"ד): "וְרָם לְבָבְךָ וְשָׁכַחְתָּ", שֶׁשִּׁכְחָה הַחִיצוֹנִית מְצוּיָה שָׁם, וְדָוִד הִתְנַהֵג בְּמִדָּה זוֹ הַרְבֵּה, שֶׁאָמַר (תהלים כ"ה, ט"ז): "כִּי יָחִיד וְעָנִי אָנִי". שֶׁהֲרֵי כָּל אַנְשֵׁי בֵיתוֹ כָּל אֶחָד וְאֶחָד צָרִיךְ לַעֲזוֹר לְעַצְמוֹ, מַה כֻּלָּם אֵלָיו.

what help will even his wife and children be when he stands in judgment before the Creator? And when his soul departs, will they accompany him beyond the grave? What good are they to him on his day of judgment, from the entrance to his grave and beyond? Therefore, a person should humble and perfect himself according to the secret of this attribute.

A second, extremely important method is explained in the *Zohar*. A man should exile himself, wandering from place to place for the sake of Heaven, thereby becoming a vehicle for the exiled Shechinah. He should think to himself: "Behold, I am in exile, but I have all my implements with me. But what about the honor of the Supreme One, for the Shechinah is exiled without any implements, for they have gotten lost as a result of the exile?" For this reason, he should manage with as little as possible — as the verse states: "make yourself implements for exile (*Yechezkel* 12:3) — and let the exile humble his heart, while he binds himself to Torah. Then the Shechinah will be with him.

He should also impose an 'expulsion order' upon himself, always banishing himself from the comforts of home, just as Rabbi Shimon bar Yochai and his comrades banished themselves to toil in Torah. Better still, he should weary his legs by trudging from place to place without horse or wagon. Concerning such a person, it is stated: "...his hope שברו is with the L-rd, his G-d" (*Tehillim* 146:5), deriving from the word שבר, meaning 'breaking,' for he breaks his body for the honor of the Supreme One.

Another aspect of the attribute of *malchut* and one of

אֲפִלּוּ אִשְׁתּוֹ וּבָנָיו מַה יוֹעִילוּהוּ בִּהְיוֹתוֹ נִשְׁפָּט לִפְנֵי הַבּוֹרֵא אוֹ בְּעֵת סִלּוּק נִשְׁמָתוֹ. כְּלוּם יְלַוּוּהוּ אֶלָּא עַד קִבְרוֹ, מָה הֵם לוֹ בְּעֵת דִּינָיו מִפֶּתַח הַקֶּבֶר וְאֵילָךְ? לְפִיכָךְ יַשְׁפִּיל וִיתַקֵּן עַצְמוֹ בְּסוֹד הַמִּדָּה הַזֹּאת.

עוֹד שְׁנִיָּה פֵּרְשׁוּ בְּסֵפֶר הַזּוֹהַר (ויקהל קצ״ח, ב׳) וְהִיא חֲשׁוּבָה מְאֹד. יִגְלֶה מִמָּקוֹם לְמָקוֹם לְשֵׁם שָׁמַיִם, וּבָזֶה יַעֲשֶׂה מֶרְכָּבָה אֶל הַשְּׁכִינָה הַגּוֹלָה, וִידַמֶּה עַצְמוֹ, ״הֲרֵי אֲנִי גָּלִיתִי וַהֲרֵי כְּלֵי תַשְׁמִישִׁי עִמִּי, מַה יַּעֲשֶׂה כָּבוֹד גָּבֹהַ שֶׁגָּלְתָה שְׁכִינָה וְכֵלֶיהָ אֵינָם עִמָּהּ, שֶׁחָסְרוּ בְּסִבַּת הַגָּלוּת״. וְלָזֶה יְמַעֵט בְּכֵלָיו בְּכָל יְכָלְתּוֹ, כְּדִכְתִיב (יחזקאל י״ב, ג׳): ״כְּלֵי גוֹלָה עֲשֵׂה לָךְ״. וְיַכְנִיעַ לְבָבוֹ בַּגּוֹלָה וְיִתְקַשֵּׁר בַּתּוֹרָה, וְאָז שְׁכִינָה עִמּוֹ.

וְיַעֲשֶׂה לְעַצְמוֹ גֵרוּשִׁין וְיִתְגָּרֵשׁ מִבֵּית מְנוּחָתוֹ תָּמִיד, כְּדֶרֶךְ שֶׁהָיוּ מִתְגָּרְשִׁים רַבִּי שִׁמְעוֹן וַחֲבֵרָיו וְעוֹסְקִים בַּתּוֹרָה. וּמַה גַּם אִם יְכַתֵּת רַגְלָיו מִמָּקוֹם לְמָקוֹם בְּלִי סוּס וָרֶכֶב, עָלָיו נֶאֱמַר (תהלים קמ״ו, ה׳): ״שִׂבְרוֹ עַל ד׳ אֱלֹהָיו״. וּפֵירְשׁוּ בּוֹ (זוהר ויקהל קצ״ח, א׳) לָשׁוֹן ״שֶׁבֶר״, שֶׁהוּא מְשַׁבֵּר גּוּפוֹ לִכְבוֹד גָּבֹהַּ.

עוֹד מִמִּדַּת הַמַּלְכוּת מִדָּה חֲשׁוּבָה מְאֹד מִשְּׁאָר הָעֲבוֹדָה כֻּלָּהּ,

the most important (since it is the gateway to a person's Divine service) is fear of the L-rd, the glorious and awesome One. Now, fear itself is extremely dangerous, in that it can cause harm and allow entry to the 'external forces.' For if a person is afraid of suffering, death, or Gehinom, he fears the external forces themselves, since suffering, death, and Gehinom are results of their activity. However, proper fear is fear of the L-rd, which is achieved by pondering three things:

1) The greatness of Him Who fashioned all things extends over all existence. For man fears the lion, the bear, violence, fire, and a falling ruin, which are only minor emissaries. Why, then, should he not fear the great King, with the fear of His greatness resting upon his face? He should say, "How can lowly man sin against such a great Master? For if he angered a bear, it would gobble him up, whereas, because the Holy One, Blessed Be He, overlooks insult, is this reason not to fear His awesomeness and greatness?"

2) Divine providence is constantly at work, watching over and examining each person. Now, a slave always fears his master when in his presence, and man is always in the presence of the Creator, Who carefully inspects all his ways. Thus, he should be afraid and terrified to nullify His commandments.

3) Since He is the root of all souls, all of them rooted in the *sefirot* He emanates, and a transgressor damages His sanctuary, should he not fear that the King's Sanctuary is soiled by his evil deeds?

4) Flawed deeds repel the Shechinah Above. One

וְהִיא, לִירְאָה אֶת ד' הַנִּכְבָּד וְהַנּוֹרָא. וְהִנֵּה הַיִּרְאָה מְסוּכֶּנֶת מְאֹד לִיפָּגֵם וּלְהִכָּנֵס בָּהּ הַחִיצוֹנִים. שֶׁהֲרֵי אִם הוּא יָרֵא מִן הַיִּסּוּרִים אוֹ מִן הַמִּיתָה אוֹ מִגֵּיהִנָּם הֲרֵי זוֹ יִרְאַת הַחִיצוֹנִים, שֶׁכָּל פְּעוּלוֹת אֵלּוּ מִן הַחִיצוֹנִים. אָמְנָם הַיִּרְאָה הָעִיקָרִית, לִירְאָה אֶת ד'. וְהוּא שֶׁיַּחֲשׁוֹב בִּשְׁלֹשָׁה דְבָרִים:

הָא' — לִהְיוֹת גְּדוּלָתוֹ שֶׁל יוֹצֵר הַכֹּל עַל כָּל נִמְצָא. וַהֲרֵי הָאָדָם יָרֵא מִן הָאֲרִי, מִן הַדּוֹב, מִן הָאַנָּס, מִן הָאֵשׁ, מִן הַמַּפּוֹלֶת, וְאֵלּוּ הֵם שְׁלוּחִים קְטַנִּים, וְלָמָּה לֹא יִירָא מִן הַמֶּלֶךְ הַגָּדוֹל וְיִהְיֶה פַּחְדוֹ עַל פָּנָיו מִגְּדוּלָתוֹ וְיֹאמַר, "הֵיאַךְ יֶחֱטָא הָאָדָם הַנִּבְזֶה לַאֲדוֹן רַב כָּזֶה, וַהֲרֵי אִלּוּ הָיָה דוֹב יֹאכְלֵהוּ, וְאִילּוּ הַקָּבָּ"ה סוֹבֵל עֶלְבּוֹן, מִפְּנֵי זֶה לֹא יִירָא מִפַּחְדוֹ וּגְדוּלָתוֹ?"

הָב' — כַּאֲשֶׁר יְדַמֶּה הַשְׁגָּחָתוֹ תָּמִיד, שֶׁהוּא צוֹפֶה וּמַבִּיט בּוֹ וַהֲרֵי הָעֶבֶד יָרֵא מֵרַבּוֹ תָּמִיד בִּהְיוֹתוֹ לְפָנָיו, וְהָאָדָם תָּמִיד לִפְנֵי הַבּוֹרֵא וְעֵינוֹ פְּקוּחָה עַל כָּל דְּרָכָיו, יִירָא וְיִפְחַד הֵיאַךְ יְהֵא מְבַטֵּל מִצְווֹתָיו.

הָג' — הֱיוֹתוֹ שׁוֹרֶשׁ כָּל הַנְּשָׁמוֹת, וְכוּלָם מוּשְׁרָשׁוֹת בִּסְפִירוֹתָיו, וְהַחוֹטֵא פּוֹגֵם הֵיכָלוֹ, וְלָמָּה לֹא יִירָא. הֵיאַךְ יִהְיֶה הֵיכַל הַמֶּלֶךְ מְלוּכְלָךְ מִמַּעֲשָׂיו הָרָעִים.

should fear lest he cause this great evil of diverting the King's love from the Queen.

These kinds of fear set a person on the right path towards perfecting this attribute, enabling him to cleave to it.

Furthermore, a man should take great care to behave in such a way that the Shechinah will cleave to him and not depart from him. Now, as long as a man has not married, the Shechinah is not with him, since she relates to man mainly via the female aspect. For man stands between two female aspects — his wife below in the physical world, who receives "sustenance, clothing, and conjugal rights" from him; and the Shechinah above him, who blesses him with all these so that he will give again and again to the wife he has chose in the covenant of marriage. His position corresponds to *tiferet*, which stands between the two female aspects of the *sefirot* — *Imma Ila'ah* (*binah*), which provides for all of *tiferet*'s needs; and *Imma Tata'ah* (*malchut*), which receives "sustenance, clothing, and conjugal rights," i.e., *chesed*, *din*, and *rachamim*, as is known. But the Shechinah will not come to him unless he emulates the pattern of the higher reality.

Now, sometimes a man separates from his wife for one of three reasons: 1) she is a *niddah*; 2) he toils in Torah study and therefore separates himself from her on weekdays; 3) he is traveling and guards himself from sin. At these times, the Shechinah cleaves and binds herself to him and does not leave him, so that he is not abandoned and alienated. Rather, he is always complete, possessing both male and female elements.

הד' — יִרְאֶה שֶׁפְּגָם מַעֲשָׂיו הֵם דּוֹחִים שְׁכִינָה מִלְמַעְלָה וְיִירָא הֵיאַךְ יִגְרוֹם הָרָעָה הַגְּדוֹלָה הַזֹּאת לְהַפְרִיד חֵשֶׁק הַמֶּלֶךְ מִן הַמַּלְכָּה.

וְהַיִּרְאָה שֶׁהִיא כַּיּוֹצֵא בָזֶה, הִיא יִרְאָה הַמְיַשֶּׁרֶת הָאָדָם אֶל תִּקּוּן הַמִּדָּה הַזֹּאת וְהוּא דָבֵק בָּהּ.

עוֹד זְהִירוּת הַרְבֵּה צָרִיךְ לִיקַח הָאָדָם לְעַצְמוֹ, לַעֲשׂוֹת שֶׁתִּהְיֶה שְׁכִינָה דְּבֵקָה עִמּוֹ וְלֹא תִפָּרֵד מִמֶּנּוּ. וְהִנֵּה, הָאָדָם בְּעוֹד שֶׁלֹּא נָשָׂא אִשָּׁה — פְּשִׁיטָא שֶׁאֵין עִמּוֹ שְׁכִינָה כְּלָל, כִּי עִקַּר שְׁכִינָה לָאָדָם מִצַּד הַנְּקֵבָה, וְהָאָדָם עוֹמֵד בֵּין שְׁתֵּי הַנְּקֵבוֹת, נְקֵבָה תַּחְתּוֹנָה גַשְׁמִית, שֶׁהִיא נוֹטֶלֶת מִמֶּנּוּ שְׁאָר כְּסוּת וְעוֹנָה, וְהַשְּׁכִינָה הָעוֹמֶדֶת עָלָיו לְבָרְכוֹ בְּכֻלָּם שֶׁיִּתֵּן וְיַחֲזוֹר וְיִתֵּן לְאֵשֶׁת בְּרִיתוֹ כְּעִנְיַן הַתִּפְאֶרֶת שֶׁהוּא עוֹמֵד בֵּין שְׁתֵּי הַנְּקֵבוֹת, אִימָּא עִילָאָה, לְהַשְׁפִּיעַ לוֹ כָּל הַצּוֹרֶךְ, וְאִימָּא תַּתָּאָה, לְקַבֵּל מִמֶּנּוּ שְׁאָר כְּסוּת וְעוֹנָה, חֶסֶד, דִּין וְרַחֲמִים, וְלֹא תָבוֹא אֵלָיו שְׁכִינָה אִם לֹא יְדוּמֶּה אֶל מְצִיאוּת הָעֶלְיוֹן.

וְהִנֵּה, לִפְעָמִים הָאָדָם פּוֹרֵשׁ מֵאִשְׁתּוֹ לְאַחַת מִשָּׁלֹשׁ סִיבּוֹת. הָא' — לִהְיוֹתָהּ נִדָּה, הַב' — שֶׁהוּא עוֹסֵק בַּתּוֹרָה וּבוֹדֵל מִמֶּנָּה כָּל יְמֵי הַחוֹל, הַג' — שֶׁהוּא הוֹלֵךְ בְּדֶרֶךְ וְשׁוֹמֵר עַצְמוֹ מִן הַחֵטְא. וּבִזְמַנִּים אֵלּוּ הַשְּׁכִינָה דְּבֵקָה וּקְשׁוּרָה עִמּוֹ וְאֵינָהּ מַנַּחַת אוֹתוֹ, כְּדֵי שֶׁלֹּא יִהְיֶה עֲזוּב וְנִפְרָד, אֶלָּא לְעוֹלָם אָדָם שָׁלֵם זָכָר וּנְקֵבָה

Since the Shechinah unites with him, a man should take care not to cause her to separate from him when he is traveling. He should act with alacrity (and be rewarded) in reciting the Prayer for Travelers and in holding fast to the Torah. As a result, the Shechinah, which guards his way, stands by him always, since he is careful to avoid sin and study Torah. So, too, when his wife is a *niddah*, the Shechinah stands by him if he observes the laws of separation properly. Then, on the night of her purification, on Shabbat night, or on returning from his travels — each of these being the proper time for fulfilling the precept of cohabitation — the Shechinah Above is open and ready to receive holy souls. Thus, a man should cohabit with his wife at these times. This way, the Shechinah is always with him, as expounded in the *Zohar* on "Bereishit."

One should cohabit with his wife when the Shechinah is in place, that is, between the 'two arms' — *chesed* and *gevurah*. However, when the community is in distress, the Shechinah is not between the two arms, and cohabitation is forbidden, as the *Tikkunim* on "Bereishit" expounds.

To unite with 'the King's daughter,' so that she never separate from him, one must first don all sorts of adornments and fine garments. These are the perfection of all the attributes we have mentioned. After perfecting himself by these means, he should always concentrate on receiving the Shechinah while studying Torah and bearing the yoke of the precepts, according to the secret meditation on Unification. But this [Unification] depends

וַהֲרֵי שְׁכִינָה מִזְדַּוֶּגֶת לוֹ, צָרִיךְ אָדָם לִיזָּהֵר שֶׁלֹּא תִּפָּרֵד שְׁכִינָה מִמֶּנּוּ בִּהְיוֹתוֹ יוֹצֵא לַדֶּרֶךְ, וְיִהְיֶה זָרִיז וְנִשְׂכָּר לְהִתְפַּלֵּל תְּפִלַת הַדֶּרֶךְ וְלֶאֱחוֹז בַּתּוֹרָה, שֶׁבִּסִיבָּה זוֹ שְׁכִינָה, שֶׁהִיא שְׁמִירַת הַדֶּרֶךְ, עוֹמֶדֶת לוֹ תָּמִיד, בִּהְיוֹתוֹ זָהִיר מִן הַחֵטְא וְעוֹסֵק בַּתּוֹרָה. וְכֵן בִּהְיוֹת אִשְׁתּוֹ נִדָּה, שְׁכִינָה עוֹמֶדֶת לוֹ כְּשֶׁשּׁוֹמֵר הַנִּדָּה כָּרָאוּי. אַחַר כָּךְ, בְּלֵיל טָהֳרָתָהּ, אוֹ בְּלֵיל שַׁבָּת, אוֹ בְּבוֹאוֹ מִן הַדֶּרֶךְ, כָּל אֶחָד מֵהֶן זְמַן בְּעִילַת מִצְוָה הִיא, וּשְׁכִינָה נִפְתַּחַת לְמַעְלָה לְקַבֵּל נְשָׁמוֹת קְדוֹשׁוֹת, גַּם אִשְׁתּוֹ רָאוּי לְפְקוֹד אוֹתָהּ, וּבָזֶה שְׁכִינָה תָּמִיד עִמּוֹ. כֵּן פֵּירְשׁוּ בַּזּוֹהַר פָּרָשַׁת בְּרֵאשִׁית (מ״ט, א׳).

הַפְּקִידָה לְאִשְׁתּוֹ צָרִיךְ שֶׁתִּהְיֶה דַּוְקָא בִּזְמַן שֶׁהַשְׁכִינָה בִּמְקוֹמָהּ, דְּהַיְינוּ כְּשֶׁהִיא בֵּין שְׁתֵּי זְרוֹעוֹת. אָמְנָם בִּזְמַן צָרַת הַצִּבּוּר שֶׁאֵין הַשְׁכִינָה בֵּין שְׁתֵּי זְרוֹעוֹת, אָסוּר. וְכֵן פֵּירְשׁוּ בַּתִּקּוּנִים פָּרָשַׁת בְּרֵאשִׁית (תִּקּוּן ס״ט).

הָרוֹצֶה לְהִזְדַּוֵּוג עִם בַּת הַמֶּלֶךְ וְשֶׁלֹּא תִּפָּרֵד מִמֶּנּוּ לְעוֹלָם, צָרִיךְ תְּחִלָּה שֶׁיְּקַשֵּׁט עַצְמוֹ בְּכָל מִינֵי קִשּׁוּטִים וּמַלְבּוּשִׁים נָאִים, וְהֵם תִּקּוּנֵי הַמִּדּוֹת הַנִּזְכָּרוֹת כּוּלָּם. וְאַחַר שֶׁתִּיקֵן עַצְמוֹ בַּתִּקּוּנִים, יְכַוֵּין לְקַבְּלָהּ עָלָיו בִּהְיוֹתוֹ עוֹסֵק בַּתּוֹרָה וְנוֹשֵׂא עוֹל מִצְווֹת בְּסוֹד כַּוָּנַת

on personal purification and sanctification. And once one is pure and holy, he should meditate on providing the Shechinah with the "sustenance, clothing, and conjugal rights" a man is obliged to provide for his wife:

1) In all his deeds, he should bestow the spiritual bounty of the Right upon the Shechinah, thereby sustaining her.

2) By means of *gevurah*, he should cover the Shechinah so that the external forces cannot rule her. That is, there should be no trace of the *yetzer hara* in his fulfillment of the precepts, meaning that he should not fulfill them for the sake of physical pleasure or the prospect of imagined honor and so forth. For the *yetzer hara* is found in any precept performed for pleasure, honor, etc., and from this, the Shechinah flees, for performing a precept this way is improper.

Therefore, he must 'cover the nakedness' of the Shechinah and conceal it always, so that these forces will not dominate her. How should this be done? All his deeds should be for the sake of Heaven, with no trace of the *yetzer hara*. In addition, tefillin and tzitzit are powerful shields for the Shechinah, preventing the external forces from ruling her. He should wear them always.

3) He should unite with *tiferet* at the time of reciting the Shema and by setting times for Torah study. And when he sets a time for everything, he should intend that this time is set aside for the Shechinah, the King's daughter. This idea is hinted at in the *Tikkunim*.

הַיִּחוּד תָּמִיד, וּמִיָּד הִיא נִשֵּׂאת לוֹ וְאֵינָהּ פּוֹרֶשֶׁת מִמֶּנּוּ. וְזֶה בִּתְנַאי שֶׁיִּטַהֵר וִיקַדֵּשׁ עַצְמוֹ. וְאַחַר שֶׁהוּא טָהוֹר וְקָדוֹשׁ, יְכַוֵּן לְקַיֵּים לָהּ שְׁאָר כְּסוּת וְעוֹנָה, שֶׁהֵם שְׁלֹשָׁה דְּבָרִים שֶׁחַיָּיב הָאָדָם לְאִשְׁתּוֹ. הָא׳ — לְהַשְׁפִּיעַ לָהּ בְּכָל מַעֲשָׂיו שֶׁפַּע מִן הַיָּמִין לִמְזוֹנָהּ.

הַב׳ — לְכַסּוֹת עָלֶיהָ מִצַּד הַגְּבוּרָה, שֶׁלֹּא יִשְׁלְטוּ בָהּ הַחִיצוֹנִים, שֶׁלֹּא יִהְיֶה צַד יֵצֶר הָרָע בְּעֵסֶק מִצְוֹתָיו, כְּגוֹן לְהֲנָאַת הַגּוּף וּלְתִקְוַת הַכָּבוֹד הַמְדוּמֶּה וְכַיּוֹצֵא, שֶׁיֵּצֶר הָרָע מָצוּי בְּאוֹתָהּ מִצְוָה וְהִיא בּוֹרַחַת מִמֶּנּוּ, מִפְּנֵי שֶׁהִיא עֶרְוָ״ה.

אִם כֵּן צָרִיךְ לְכַסּוֹת הָעֶרְוָה וּלְהַסְתִּירָהּ תָּמִיד שֶׁלֹּא יִשְׁלוֹט בָּהּ. כֵּיצַד — כָּל מַעֲשָׂיו לְשֵׁם שָׁמַיִם בְּלִי חֵלֶק לַיֵּצֶר הָרָע. וְכֵן תְּפִילִין וְצִיצִית הֵם מְגִינִים גְּדוֹלִים בַּעֲדָהּ שֶׁלֹּא יִשְׁלְטוּ הַחִיצוֹנִים בָּהּ, וְיִהְיֶה רָגִיל בָּהֶם.

הַג׳ — לְיַחֲדָהּ עִם הַתִּפְאֶרֶת בְּעוֹנַת קְרִיאַת שְׁמַע בִּקְבִיעוּת עִתִּים לַתּוֹרָה, וּכְשֶׁיִּקְבַּע עוֹנָה לְכָל דָּבָר. יְכַוֵּן שֶׁזֶּהוּ עוֹנַת הַשְּׁכִינָה בַּת מֶלֶךְ. וְיֵשׁ רֶמֶז לָזֶה בְּתִקּוּנִים.

Chapter 10

In the *Zohar*'s commentary on "*Bereishit*," Rabbi Shimon bar Yochai explains the Torah's great and wonderful advice as to how a person can be bound to Supernal Holiness and conduct his life according to it, never becoming separated from the *sefirot* Above: He must act at the right time — that is, by knowing which *sefirah* dominates at a particular time, he can bind himself to it and carry out the adjustment associated with the ruling attribute.

The work begins at night, at the time of preparing for sleep. The ruling quality is then 'night,' the attribute of *malchut*; sleep is like death, and the 'Tree of Death' rules. What should one do? First, he should prepare to bind himself to the secret of Sanctity, that is, the secret of *malchut* in its aspect of holiness. For this purpose, when preparing for sleep, he should concentrate his heart on completely accepting the yoke of Heaven upon himself.

פרק עשירי

פֵּירֵשׁ רַבִּי שִׁמְעוֹן בְּפָרָשַׁת בְּרֵאשִׁית (זוהר בראשית יא, א) עֵצָה
רַבָּה וּגְדוֹלָה מִן הַתּוֹרָה, הֵיאַךְ יִתְקַשֵּׁר הָאָדָם בִּקְדוּשָׁה הָעֶלְיוֹנָה
וְיִתְנַהֵג בָּהּ וְאַל יִפָּרֵד מִן הַסְּפִירוֹת הָעֶלְיוֹנוֹת תָּדִיר. וְצָרִיךְ הָאָדָם
בָּזֶה לְהִתְנַהֵג כְּפִי הַזְּמַן. רוֹצֶה לוֹמַר לָדַעַת אֵיזוֹ סְפִירָה שׁוֹלֶטֶת
וּלְהִתְקַשֵּׁר בָּהּ וְלַעֲשׂוֹת הַתִּקּוּן הַמִּתְיַחֵס אֶל הַמִּדָּה הַשּׁוֹלֶטֶת.

וְהִתְחִיל מֵהַלַּיְלָה, עֵת שְׁכִיבַת הָאָדָם עַל מִטָּתוֹ, וַהֲרֵי הַשְּׁלִיטָה
הִיא לַיְלָה, מִדַּת הַמַּלְכוּת, וְהוּא הוֹלֵךְ לִישׁוֹן, הַשֵּׁינָה הִיא כְּעֵין
מִיתָה וְאִילָנָא דְמוֹתָא שַׁלְטָא, מַה יַּעֲשֶׂה? יְתַקֵּן וִיקַדֵּים לְהִתְקַשֵּׁר
בְּסוֹד הַקְּדוּשָׁה, דְּהַיְינוּ סוֹד מִדַּת הַמַּלְכוּת בִּבְחִינַת קְדוּשָׁתָהּ, וְלָזֶה
יֵלֵךְ עַל מִטָּתוֹ וִיקַבֵּל עוֹל מַלְכוּת שָׁמַיִם שְׁלֵימָה בְּכַוָּונַת

On rising at midnight, he should wash his hands of the *kelipah* that dominates them, remove the evil from his flesh, and recite the blessing. He should then restore the Shechinah through Torah study. About this, it is written (*Mishlei* 6:22), "When you lie down, it will guard you" from the forces of evil, and "when you awaken, it will speak with you" and be bound to you, and you to it. Then, his soul will rise to Gan Eden together with the Shechinah, which enters there with the righteous. *Tiferet* will also come there to delight with the righteous, and with him in their company, for they all listen to his voice. This way, a person journeys together with the Shechinah from a state of sleep and death to the secret of Supernal Life, where he becomes bound up in the mystery of Gan Eden, and *tiferet*, which shines upon the righteous in Gan Eden, begins to shine upon him. This is the explanation of the *Zohar* on "*Terumah*."

At dawn, he prepares to enter the *beit knesset*, binding himself to the three Partriarchs. At the entrance to the *beit knesset*, he should recite the verse "And I, through Your abundant kindness, come into Your house; I bow toward Your holy sanctuary in awe of You" (*Tehillim* 5:8), merging himself with the secret of *tiferet*, for man comprises *chesed*, *gevurah*, and *tiferet*, and he enters the *beit knesset* (which is *malchut*) and meditates on the qualities of the three Patriarchs when reciting this verse. "Your abundant kindness" corresponds to Avraham. "I bow toward Your holy sanctuary" corresponds to Yitzchak, for 'bowing' — that is, lowering one's stature towards the attribute of judgment and allowing himself to be pushed

הַלֵּב. קָם בַּחֲצוֹת לַיְלָה, יִטּוֹל יָדָיו מֵהַקְּלִיפָּה הַשּׁוֹלֶטֶת עֲלֵיהֶם
וְיַעֲבִיר רָעָה מִבְּשָׂרוֹ וִיבָרֵךְ וִיתַקֵּן הַשְּׁכִינָה בְּעֵסֶק הַתּוֹרָה וְעַל זֶה
נֶאֱמַר עָלֶיהָ (משלי ו', כ"ב): "בְּשָׁכְבְּךָ תִּשְׁמוֹר עָלֶיךָ" — מִן
הַחִצוֹנִים — "וַהֲקִיצוֹתָ הִיא תְשִׂיחֶךָ", וְיִתְקַשֵּׁר עִמּוֹ וְהוּא עִמָּהּ
וְיִתְעַלֶּה דְיוֹקַן נִשְׁמָתוֹ בְּגַן עֵדֶן עִם הַשְּׁכִינָה הַנִּכְנֶסֶת שָׁם עִם
הַצַּדִּיקִים, וְהַתִּפְאֶרֶת יָבוֹא שָׁם גַּם הוּא לְהִשְׁתַּעֲשֵׁעַ עִם הַצַּדִּיקִים
וְעִמּוֹ בְּחֶבְרָתָם, שֶׁכֻּלָּם מַקְשִׁיבִים לְקוֹלוֹ. הֲרֵי מַמָּשׁ נָסַע עִמָּהּ
מֵהֲמִיתָתוֹ וְהַשֵּׁנָה אֶל סוֹד הַחַיִּים הָעֶלְיוֹנִים וְנִקְשָׁר בְּסוֹד גַּן עֵדֶן
וְהִתְחִיל לְהִתְנוֹצֵץ עָלָיו אוֹר הַתִּפְאֶרֶת הַמִּתְנוֹצֵץ בְּגַן עֵדֶן עַל
הַצַּדִּיקִים. וְכֵן פֵּרֵשׁ בְּפָרָשַׁת תְּרוּמָה (ק"ל, ב).

הִשְׁכִּים וְעָלָה עַמּוּד הַשַּׁחַר, הִתְחִיל הוּא גַּם כֵּן לָבוֹא לִיכָּנֵס
לְבֵית הַכְּנֶסֶת וְקָשַׁר עַצְמוֹ בִּשְׁלֹשָׁה אָבוֹת. בְּפֶתַח בֵּית הַכְּנֶסֶת אָמַר
(תהלים ה', ח'): "וַאֲנִי בְּרוֹב חַסְדְּךָ אָבוֹא וגו'", וְכוֹלֵל עַצְמוֹ בְּסוֹד
הַתִּפְאֶרֶת אָדָם, כָּלַל חֶסֶד וּגְבוּרָה וְתִפְאֶרֶת, וְנִכְנַס לִכְנֶסֶת מַלְכוּת,
וּמְכַוֵּין בַּפָּסוּק בִּשְׁלֹשָׁה אָבוֹת. "בְּרוֹב חַסְדְּךָ" — דָּא אַבְרָהָם:
"אֶשְׁתַּחֲוֶה אֶל הֵיכַל קָדְשֶׁךָ" — דָּא יִצְחָק, דְּמִסִּטְרֵיהּ הִשְׁתַּחֲוָיָה
לִכְפּוֹף קוֹמָתוֹ נֶגֶד מִדַּת הַדִּין לִהְיוֹת נִדְחֶה מִפָּנֶיהָ, וְאָז הַשָּׁעָה נִדְחֵית

aside by it — comes from the aspect of Yitzchak. Then his prayer will be in a propitious time, for the outflow of compassion will be drawn downwards upon this attribute to sweeten it. "In awe of You" corresponds to Ya'akov, who said, "How awesome is this place..." (*Bereishit* 28:17).

This is how a person merges himself with these qualities in thought, speech and action. For thought is the meditation we mentioned, speech is reciting the verse, and action is coming to the *beit knesset* and bowing towards the sanctuary. Before the *Amidah*, he stands in the *beit knesset*, his mouth a wellspring flowing with prayer, unifying *yesod*, the source of the wellspring, and the well into which it opens, which is the *beit knesset*. And he rectifies the Shechinah with all the power of his concentration during prayer.

When he leaves the *beit knesset*, he ascends to the secret of Torah and binds himself to it, according to the mystical explanation of the quality of 'day.' He should continue this way the whole day until the time of the afternoon prayer, when he binds himself to *gevurah*. For in the morning, he binds himself to *chesed* in his prayers, during the day to *tiferet*, and towards evening to *gevurah*, coming to the *beit knesset* to perform the mystical Unification of *gevurah*, just as he does in the morning prayer with *chesed*. All this is according to the quality of 'day.'

Between these two prayers, he also binds the Shechinah to himself by means of his meal, with which he shows kindness to the 'poor woman.' As Hillel the Elder said: "A righteous man knows the soul of his animal..." (*Mishlei* 12:10). This should be one's intention in eating — to do

מִפָּנָיו, כִּי יִימָשֵׁךְ שֶׁפַע הָרַחֲמִים מִלְמַעְלָה עָלֶיהָ לְמַתְּקָהּ. "בְּיִרְאָתֶךָ"
— דָּא יַעֲקֹב, כְּתִיב בֵּיהּ (בראשית כ"ח, י"ז): "מַה נּוֹרָא הַמָּקוֹם
הַזֶּה".

הֲרֵי כָּלַל בָּהֶם בְּמַחֲשָׁבָה דִּבּוּר וּמַעֲשֶׂה, כִּי מַחֲשָׁבָה שֶׁזָּכַרְנוּ
הִיא הַכַּוָּנָה, הַדִּבּוּר הוּא הַפָּסוּק, וְהַמַּעֲשֶׂה — הַבִּיאָה לְבֵית הַכְּנֶסֶת
וְהִשְׁתַּחֲוָיָתוֹ נֶגֶד הֵיכָלוֹ. קֹדֶם תְּפִלָּה עוֹמֵד בְּבֵית הַכְּנֶסֶת, פִּיו מָקוֹר
נוֹבֵעַ תְּפִלָּה וְיִחוּד יְסוֹד, מְקוֹר הַבְּאֵר נִפְתָּח בַּבְּאֵר שֶׁהוּא בֵית
הַכְּנֶסֶת, וּמְמַתֵּק שְׁכִינָה בְּכָל יְכֹלֶת כַּוָּנַת בִּתְפִלָּתוֹ.

יוֹצֵא מִשָּׁם, עוֹלֶה בְּסוֹד הַתּוֹרָה וּמִתְקַשֵּׁר בָּהּ בְּסוֹד מִדַּת הַיּוֹם,
וּמִתְנַהֵג עִמָּהּ כָּל הַיּוֹם עַד שְׁעוֹת מִנְחָה, שֶׁמִּתְקַשֵּׁר בִּגְבוּרָה, שֶׁהֲרֵי
בַּבֹּקֶר נִקְשָׁר בְּחֶסֶד בִּתְפִלָּתוֹ, וּבַיּוֹם בְּתִפְאֶרֶת בְּעֵסֶק הַתּוֹרָה, וּבָעֶרֶב
בִּגְבוּרָה. וְכָל זֶה בְּמִדַּת יוֹם שֶׁהוּא בָא לְבֵית הַכְּנֶסֶת לְיַחֵד בְּסוֹד
הַגְּבוּרָה כְּדֶרֶךְ שֶׁעָשָׂה בְּצַד הַחֶסֶד.

וּבֵין זֶה לָזֶה קוֹשֵׁר הַשְּׁכִינָה עִמּוֹ בִּסְעוּדָתוֹ שֶׁגּוֹמֵל חֶסֶד עִם
הָעֲנִיָּה הַזֹּאת, כְּמוֹ שֶׁהָיָה הִלֵּל הַזָּקֵן אוֹמֵר (עיין ויקרא רבה פרק
ל"ד): "יוֹדֵעַ צַדִּיק נֶפֶשׁ בְּהֶמְתּוֹ" (משלי י"ב, י), וְזוֹ תִּהְיֶה כַּוָּנָתוֹ
בִּסְעוּדָתוֹ, לִגְמֹל חֶסֶד לַנֶּפֶשׁ בְּהֵמָה וּלְקַשְׁרָהּ בְּסוֹד הַמָּזוֹן.

kindness to his animal soul and bind it according to the secret of Eating.

After the time of the afternoon prayer has passed, and he has been bound to *gevurah*, he should wait for night, until *tiferet* descends to *malchut*. Thus, he is with *malchut* from the beginning of the night. He should bind himself to *malchut* and enter the *beit knesset* with this intention. As he binds himself below, *tiferet* comes to its place of lodging. When he exits the *beit knesset*, he should unite himself with *malchut* alone, according to the secret of Accepting the Yoke of the Kingdom of Heaven.

This is his daily schedule, corresponding to the cycle of the *sefirah*, so that he always cleaves to the light of the dominant *sefirah*. This advice is found chiefly in the *Zohar* on "*Bereishit*," and the rest of it has been gathered from many places in the *Zohar*. This is a comprehensive system by which man can always bind himself to holiness, with the Crown of the Shechinah never departing from his head.

וְאַחַר שֶׁעָלָה לִשְׁעַת הַמִּנְחָה וְנִקְשַׁר בִּגְבוּרָה, הַמֵּתִּן לָעֶרֶב וְיָרַד הַתִּפְאֶרֶת אֶל הַמַּלְכוּת, וַהֲרֵי הוּא עָמָּהּ בִּתְחִילַת הַלַּיְלָה, וְקוֹשֵׁר עַצְמוֹ בָּהּ, וְנִכְנַס לְבֵית הַכְּנֶסֶת עִם הַכַּוָּנָה הַנִּזְכֶּרֶת לְעֵיל, וְקוֹשֵׁר עַצְמוֹ לְמַטָּה, תִּפְאֶרֶת בָּא לִמְלוֹנוֹ. יָצָא מִבֵּית הַכְּנֶסֶת, יְיַחֵד עַצְמוֹ מַמָּשׁ בְּמַלְכוּת לְבַד, וּבְסוֹד קַבָּלַת עוֹל מַלְכוּת שָׁמַיִם. וְזֶהוּ תְּקוּפָתוֹ בַּיּוֹם עִם תְּקוּפַת הַסְּפִירָה וּלְעוֹלָם דָּבֵק בְּאוֹר הַשּׁוֹלֵט.

עֵצָה זוֹ עִיקָרָה בְּפָרָשַׁת בְּרֵאשִׁית וְהַשְּׁאָר מְקַבֵּץ מִמְּקוֹמוֹת רַבִּים מֵהַזּוֹהַר וְהִיא עֵצָה כּוֹלֶלֶת לְהִתְקַשֵּׁר הָאָדָם תָּמִיד בִּקְדוּשָׁה וְלֹא יֶחֱסַר עֲטוּר הַשְּׁכִינָה מֵעַל רֹאשׁוֹ.

תהלה אביע לרוכב בשמי שמי קדם שזכני להתחיל ולהשלים הספר הנורא הזה, הלא אם קטן הוא לעינים — ראש שבטי ישראל הוא, בו יבין וישכיל האדם כי כל פעולותיו, הן טובות הן להפך חס ושלום, עושים רושם למעלה, כאשר עיני המעיין תחזינה. ושמעתי מאשר שאהבה נפשי, הלא הוא החכם כבוד מורנו ורבנו הרב רבנו גדליה ישמרהו צורו וגואלו, בן הרב המחבר, שהוא אחד מהשבעים תמרים אשר שתל אביו הרב, זכרונו לחיי העולם הבא.

יהי רצון מלפני אבינו שבשמים שיאמר עלי "משה זכה וזיכה את הרבים" ולעשות ספרים הרבה. אמן כן יהי רצון.

כה אמר הצעיר משה בסולה.

Notes on Chapter 1

Tomer Devorah: Regarding this title, see the introduction to this edition. The first edition, printed in Venice in 1579, is subtitled: "Regarding the right path a man should choose for himself: his self-isolation, his prayers, and the contemplation of his ways."

for man to emulate: The word *"adam,"* man is related to the word *"adameh,"* "I will be compared to," as in "...I will be compared to the One above" (*Yeshayahu* 14:14), hinting that man must emulate his Creator (Rabbi Menachem Azariah De-Fano, *Asarah Ma'amarot, ma'amar "Eim Kol Chai,"* pt. II, ch. 33; Rabbi Yeshayahu Hurwitz, *Shelah,* pp. 3a, 20b).

to emulate his Creator: This is one of the positive commandments listed by Rambam (*Sefer HaMitzvot, aseh* 8; *Mishneh Torah, Hilchot De'ot* 1:5) and by *Sefer HaChinuch* (mitzvah 611), based on the verses "...you shall go in His ways" (*Devarim* 28:9) and "to go in all His ways" (ibid. 11:22). *Sifri* (*"Eikev"*) explains, "Just as the Holy One, Blessed Be He, is called 'Compassionate,' you should be compassionate; just as the Holy One, Blessed Be He, is called 'Gracious,' you should be gracious; just as the Holy One, Blessed Be He, is called 'Righteous,' you should be righteous; just as the Holy One, Blessed Be He, is called 'Pious,' you should be pious." Expounding the verse "Follow the L-rd, your G-d..." (*Devarim* 13:5), the Gemara derives the practical implications of this concept: "Emulate the attributes of the Holy One, Blessed Be He: Just as the Holy One, Blessed Be He, clothes the naked...so should you; just as the Holy One, Blessed Be He, visits the sick...so should you; just as the Holy One, Blessed Be He, consoles the bereaved, so should you..." (*Sotah* 14a).

the Supernal Form: Ramak is referring to the configuration of the *sefirot* in the world of *Atzilut*, which is called *Adam HaElyon* in Kabbalah (intro., pt. 3; *Pardes Rimonim, sha'ar* 4, chs. 5-6; *Shnei Luchot HaBrit* (*Shelah*), "Beit Yisrael," p. 5c).

in both image (*tzelem*) and likeness (*demut*): Cf. *Bereishit* 1:26-27.

image (*tzelem*) and likeness (*demut*): The image, or *tzelem*, of man is the human mold of his physical form, which links his body and soul. This mold derives from the configuration of the *sefirot*. The likeness, or *demut*, of man refers to the soul enclothed in the body, which reflects the *Atzmut*, or "Infinite Light," which illuminates the *sefirot* (intro., pt. 3; *Pardes Rimonim, sha'ar* 31, ch. 4; *Shelah*, "Beit Yisrael," p. 6c; *Nefesh HaChaim, sha'ar* 1, ch 1; Rashi, *Bereishit* 1:26).

physical form reflects the Supernal Form: Regarding how man's physical form parallels the *sefirot*, see *Pardes, sha'ar* 21, ch. 2, and *sha'ar* 31, chs. 8-9.

his actions: Cf. *Avot* 1:17 — The essential thing...is the deed."

the Thirteen Supernal Attributes of Mercy: The *Zohar* explains that the thirteen attributes mentioned by Moshe are for the sake of life in this world, whereas the thirteen mentioned by Michah are for the sake of the life of the soul ("*Idra*," vol. 3, p. 13).

of *keter*: The Supernal Attributes of Mercy, which derive from *keter*, are pure compassion and contain no severe judgment, in contrast to the thirteen attributes mentioned by Moshe (*Pardes, sha'ar* 8, ch. 3; *Eilimah Rabbati, ma'ayan* 3, *tamar* 4, ch. 14).

these Thirteen Attributes: The Thirteen Attributes of Mercy mentioned in *Michah* are of a higher order (deriving from *keter*) than those mentioned by Moshe (*Shemot* 34:6-7), which derived from *Ze'ir Anpin*. Thus, they are recited by the prophet not in the form of prayer but as praise and adulation of the Holy One, Blessed Be He. In contrast, the thirteen attributes recited by Moshe are a plea for mercy, and they have been established in the liturgy as such (*Eilimah Rabbati, ma'ayan* 3; *tamar* 4, ch. 14; *Rosh HaShanah* 17b).

1. *Who is G-d like You*:

a tolerant King: the word נעלב implies one who bears embarrassment and abuse in silence; cf. *II Divrei HaYamim* 36:16.

His view: "No one faithful to the Holy One, Blessed Be He, should think that any event, great or insignificant, occurs by chance, G-d forbid. Rather, everything is by Divine providence. That is, everything is watched over not by means of various powers — be they angels, the Throne of Glory, or the *sefirot* — but by the Infinite One Himself" (*Eilimah Rabbati, ma'ayan* 1, *tamar* 5, ch. 1).

man is...nourished and sustained: Not only is man sustained, but so are the life force of the *sefirot*, the *merkavot* ("vehicles" of Divine revelation), the angels, and the entire work of Creation from beginning to end. This is the meaning of the phrase "You give life to them all" (*Nechemiah* 9:6), upon which our sages comment, "Read not מחיה, give life, but מהווה, bring into existence (*Pardes, sha'ar* 6, ch. 8)." Thus, everything draws its existence and life force from the Holy One, Blessed Be He.

at that very moment, bestowing abundant vitality upon him: It is as if G-d himself performs the act, because He gave man free choice, and it is as if He limits His Omnipotence for the sake of this free choice. Thus, man forces the Holy One, Blessed Be He, to fulfill his will, so to speak. This is a terrible insult (*Michtav MeEliyahu,* vol. 3, p. 69).

G-d does not withhold: "...even for the worst of sins, for the very day that Israel made the golden calf, manna descended from heaven. And although the worshippers of the golden calf offered some of this manna as a sacrifice to the idol, the following day manna descended as usual" (*Tanchuma,* "*Ki Tissa*" 14).

as He did with Yaravam: See *I Melachim* 13:4.

the ministering angels refer: See *Pirkei Heichalot,* ch. 25.

man should emulate: "Said Rabbi Alexandri: Whoever hears himself being cursed but remains silent...becomes a partner of the Holy One, Blessed Be He. For [He] hears the nations of the world mocking Him in His presence. Although He could annihilate them instantly, He remains silent. Thus, when King David heard himself being cursed, he, too, remained silent" (*Midrash Tehillim* 86).

2. *Who pardons iniquity:*

Who pardons iniquity: This attribute is especially evident on Yom Kippur. As it is written: "For on this day He will grant you forgiveness to purify you from your sins..." (*VaYikra* 16:30)

(*Reishit Chochmah, sha'ar'' "HaAhavah,"* ch. 11, p. 93b).

a destructive creature is created: See *Pardes, sha'ar* 25, ch. 3.

in the *Mishnah*: See *Avot* 4:11.

against himself: "Your evil will torment you..." (*Yirmeyahu* 2:19). The evil a person does is itself his punishment, for it separates him from G-d (*Ikkarim*, ch. 43, par. 3).

a single accuser: Kabbalah takes this phrase literally — a person's sins create a destructive demon (*Pardes, sha'ar* 25, ch. 3; *Zohar*, "*Kedoshim*," p. 83b).

would cease to be: Created by the sins of the transgressor, the destructive accuser ceases to exist once these sins have been expiated. (See Rambam, *Mishneh Torah, Hilchot Teshuvah*, for a full exposition of the requirements for atonement.)

our sages: See *Sanhedrin* 111a; *Bereishit Rabbah* 22:11; and *Yalkut Shimoni*, "*Bereishit*" 38.

nourish: שאר also means "nourish." (See *Pesachim* 36b).

3. *And forgives...transgression*:

through an emissary: Cf. *Targum Onkelos* and Rashi's commentary on *Shemot* 33:14, "I will no longer send an angel. I myself will accompany you." Cf. ibid. 33:3-4.

rectifies the perversion: This is a tremendous kindness on the part of the Holy One, Blessed Be He, for He Himself plunges down, so to speak, into the person's impurity to receive his repentance (*Michtav MeEliyahu*, vol.2, p. 80).

the filth of...sins: Sin and evil are called "vomit and filth" in Tanach (cf. *Yeshayahu* 28:8; also see *Moreh Nevuchim*, pt. III, ch. 8).

too shamed: There is a lofty level of awe of G-d stemming from a sense of shame, called in Kabbalah ירא בושת (*Tikkunei Zohar*, p. 5b; *Reishit Chochmah, sha'ar "HaYirah,"* ch. 3,. 13d, and ch. 11, p. 96d; cf. "The brazen is headed for Gehinom, but the shame-faced for Gan Eden [*Avot* 5:20]).

the filth of his garments: Cf. "And Yehoshua was dressed in soiled garments and standing before the angel. [The angel] said...'Remove the soiled garments from upon him'; [the angel] said to him, 'Behold, I have caused your iniquity to pass from upon you, and I dress you in fine new robes' " (*Zechariah* 3:3-4). Rashi explains: "Since the sins were compared to soiled garments, the verse compares merits to clean, new robes."

Ramak, however, explains that these garments are not simply allegorical. Depending on a person's actions, the life force enclothing his soul is drawn from holy sources or their opposite. Garments drawn from holy sources are called clean and new; those drawn from impure sources are called stained and worn (*Pardes, sha'ar "HaNeshamah,"* ch. 11).

4. [*And forgives the transgression of*] the remnant of His heritage:

she'er bassar: Cf. *VaYikra* 18:6, 12; *Michah* 3:3.

the spouse: The Holy One, Blessed Be He, betrothed the entire Jewish people when He gave us the Torah on Mount Sinai (*Ta'anit* 26b; *BeMidbar Rabbah* 12:8).

our sages explain: See *Shir HaShirim Rabbah* 9:4; *Zohar, "Sifrei Torah," "VaYeitzei,"* p. 156b.

"My daughter," "My sister," and "My mother": See *Shir HaShirim Rabbah* 3:25; *Pesikta DeRav Kahane* 1:5.

a people close to Him: Cf. *Devarim* 4:7.

the pain of Israel extends to...'dual visage': See *Zohar*, vol. 1, p. 120b.

peleh: פלא and אלף have identical letters but in reverse order. *Peleh* derives from the phrase היפלא מה׳ דבר — "Is anything too wondrous for G-d?" (*Bereishit* 18:14) (*Pardes, sha'ar "Archei HaKinuyim,"* פלא). This level is so sublime that anger and pain have no place there; hence the literal meaning of the way *Yeshayahu* 63:9 is *written*, with an *aleph*, לא צר — "He is not afflicted." Nevertheless, the way it is *read*, with a *vav*, לו, implies that Israel's suffering penetrates even the level of *keter* (ibid.; *Zohar*, vol. 1, p. 120b).

'dual visage': This refers to the *sefirot* of *tiferet* and *malchut* (*Pardes, sha'ar "Miut HaYare'ach," sha'ar "Archei HaKinuyim,"* ערך דו).

the world is mainly conducted: Thus, Israel's suffering arouses the compassion of the Holy One, Blessed Be He, and He conducts the world with kindness and mercy (*Pardes, sha'ar* 31, ch. 11).

each person has a part of all others: See *Tanya*, ch. 32; *Derech Mitzvotecha, mitzvat "Ahavat Yisrael."*

a multitude of people: As it is written, "In a multitude of people is the king's glory..." (*Mishlei* 14:28). And as we pray, "Bless us, O our Father, *all of us as one*, with the light of Your countenance..." (*Amidah*) (*Tanya*, ch. 32).

our sages explain: See *Berachot* 47b.

all [the people of] Israel are guarantors for one another: See *Shevuot* 39a.

blemishes...his own soul: See *Pardes, sha'ar "HaNeshamah,"* chs. 10-11; *Reishit Chochmah, sha'ar "HaYirah,"* chs. 7-10.

cherish his friend's honor as his own: See *Tanchuma, "BeShal-*

lach" 26; cf. *Avot* 4:12; Rambam, *Hilchot De'ot* 6:3.

love your fellow Jew as yourself: Hillel said, "This is the whole Torah; all the rest is commentary" (*Shabbat* 31a).

5. *He does not maintain His anger forever.*

His anger forever: Cf. "For His wrath endures but for a moment..." (*Tehillim* 30:6).

as Israel's benefit requires: "All that I did, I did only for Israel's benefit" (*Yalkut Shimoni, Yeshayahu* 60, *remez* 4).

to chastise: "One should chastise [the sinner] in private, speaking to him in a pleasant manner, using gentle words....One who rebukes his fellow should initially not use harsh words, thereby shaming his fellow. As the verse states, '...do not bear sin because of him' [*YaYikra* 19:17]. ... From here [we deduce] that it is forbidden to shame another Jew...and even though it is not punishable by lashes, it is a grave sin" (Rambam, *Mishneh Torah, Hilchot De'ot* 6:7-8; *Sefer HaMitzvot*, *aseh* 205; *lo ta'aseh* 305).

they would accept the rebuke: For it is forbidden to rebuke one who will not listen (*Yevamot* 65b).

permitted to hate...as regards his sin: See *Pesachim* 113b. But this permission applies only as regards the sin itself. As regards the sinner's soul, which is part of G-d above (see *Iyyov* 31:2), one must love him (*Tanya* ch. 32). Thus, one must help him unload and load his donkey (*Tal Torah* on *Pesachim* 113b).

abandon: עזוב means both "help" and "abandon." See *Targum Onkelos*, which understands Ramak's interpretations as the plain meaning of the verse.

a religious obligation...with love: The precept of loving one's fellow Jew extends only to a Jew who is "your fellow in Torah and mitzvot" (*Sefer HaChinuch, aseh* 243; *Semag, aseh* 9; *Hagahot Maimoniot* on *Mishneh Torah, Hilchot De'ot* 6:3), whereas one is commanded to hate a sinner (*Sefer HaChinuch, aseh* 238 et al.) However, this commandment applies only to a colleague in Torah and mitzvot who has sinned and been rebuked but has not repented (see *Shevuot* 30a). Moreover, from the verse the *Chinuch* quotes, it is clear that in its author's view the obligation to hate a sinner absolutely applies only to heretics (see *Shabbat* 116a; Ramban, *Devarim* 7:9; *Tal Torah* on *Pesachim* 113b).

This is Rambam's opinion as well: "One who believes in all [Thirteen] Principles of Faith is part of the Jewish people, and it is a mitzvah to love him and show him compassion...even if he transgressed because of passion or because he was overcome by his evil nature.... But if one denies one of these principles, he is not part of the Jewish people and is called a heretic...and it is a mitzvah to hate him" (*Peirush HaMishnayot, Sanhedrin* 10, Principle 13).

Thus regarding one who is neither a colleague in Torah and mitzvot nor a heretic. Hillel exhorts us, "Be of the disciples of Aaron...loving the creatures and drawing them to Torah" (*Avot* 1:12). That is, if some are so far from Torah and the service of G-d that they are called simply "creatures," they must be lovingly attracted to Torah and Divine service (see *Tanya*, ch. 32).

to draw the person closer with love: "Today, pushing sinners away does not close the gap in the Jewish people — it widens the gap! Therefore, we must bring sinners back by binding them with "ropes of love" [*Hoshea* 11:4] and placing them in beams of light as best we can" (*Chazon Ish, Yoreh De'ah* 2:16).

6. *For He delights in kindness*:

elsewhere: See *Pardes, sha'ar* "HaHeichalot," end ch. 5; *Zohar*, "Pikudei," p. 253a.

Go in between the *galgal*, beneath: See *VaYikra Rabbah* 26 (end).

a man's hand: This image represents acts of charity and kindness (*VaYikra Rabbah* 26 [end]).

under the wings: *Sha'arei Gan Eden* explains that the hand was concealed by the wings of the *keruvim*, thereby representing one of the most desirable forms of charity: that which is given in secret (*Yoreh De'ah* 249:7).

our sages have said: See *Yevamot* 63a-b.

7. *He will again show us compassion*:

The perfectly righteous cannot stand: See *Berachot* 34b; *Zohar*, "*Chayei Sarah*," p. 129c. For a reconciliation of the conflicting opinions regarding the status of the righteous and the repentant, see *Shelah*, "*Bayit Gadol*," (pp. 26b-c).

where repentant sinners stand: "A penitent should subdue himself to the same extent that he clung to evil, until he smashes the evil to which his sin drove him. This way, he will return his soul to holiness — but with the advantage of rectifying not only himself but the forces of evil he has overthrown" (*Pardes, sha'ar* "*HaNeshamah*," ch. 10).

Why is the letter ה: See *Menachot* 29b. There it also states that this world was created with the letter *hei* and the World to Come with the letter *yud*. Thus, repentance, represented by the letter *hei*, is possible in this world only. Cf. "One hour of repentance and good deeds in this world is better than all life in the World to Come..." (*Avot* 4:17).

ascend to the narrow gap: To fulfill the will of the Creator, one should seek to enter through the narrow gap used by the pious (*Chovot HaLevavot, sha'ar* "*HaTeshuvah*," ch. 10).

much more than the righteous: "For what reason does the letter *hei* have a roof? Said the Holy One, Blessed Be He, 'if [the sinner] returns to Me, I will attach to him a crown like Mine' " (*Menachot* 29b).

the fifth palace of Gan Eden: "In the fifth palace stand all those who have returned in perfect repentance...and even the perfectly righteous cannot ascend to that palace and stand there" (*Zohar*, "Bereishit," p. 39a).

תשוב ה, when he returns the ה: See *Zohar*, "Naso," "Ra'aya Mehemna," p. 122a. The gist of the *Zohar* is as follows: The letter *hei*, the final letter of the four-letter Name of G-d (The Tetragrammaton), represents the Divine power through which the world was created (*Menachot* 29b). Through sin, a person places a barrier between himself and G-d (cf. "Only your sins have separated between you and the L-rd, your G-d" [*Yeshayahu* 59:2]). Thus, he "dislocates" the letter *hei* from the other three letters of the Divine Name. Therefore, one who "returns the *hei*" by repudiating evil and repenting smashes the barrier he created and reunifies the Divine Name.

8. *He will vanquish our iniquities*:

the secret of vanquishing iniquity: "The Holy One, Blessed Be He, vanquishes and hides sins beneath the Throne of Glory in order that merits can prevail" (Rashi on *Arachin* 8b).

the precepts are compared to a grapevine: See *Kiddushin* 40a; *Sotah* 46a; *Zohar*, "Ra'aya Mehemna" III, p. 253a; and *Midrash Tehillim* 114.

budding, it's blossoms bursting forth: Cf. *Zohar*, vol. I, p. 192a.

which ou sages interpret: See *Midrash Shochar Tov* 5 and *Sabbat* 149b. The full rabbinic statement reads, "You do not dwell with evil, and evil does not dwell with You." Also see *Zohar*, vol. I, p. 52b.

no reward in this world: "There is no reward for mitzvot in this world" (*Kiddushin* 39b).

bliss of His presence: Cf. "One hour of repentance and good deeds in this world is better than all of life in the World to Come; and one hour of bliss in the World to Come is better than all of life in this world" (*Avot* 4:17).

as bribes: Cf. *Devarim* 10:17 and Ramban ad loc.

as if he burnt the Torah: See *Kiddushin* 39b.

the radiance of the Shechinah: This term refers to the indwelling Divine Presence (cf. *Shemot* 25:8).

collects the debt...bestows the reward: "Credit is never exchanged for debt or vice versa. Rather, reward is bestowed for observing the precepts and punishment is administered for transgressions" (*Sifri*, "*Berachah*").

to build an edifice: Cf. "Who are called builders? These are Torah scholars, who occupy themselves with building the world" (*Shabbat* 114a).

and form a precious garment: The precepts one performs in this world enwrap his soul before it enters Gan Eden. By virtue of this garment, the soul enters the Divine Presence (*Zohar*, vol. II, pp. 210a-b and 229a-b, and vol. III. p. 169a; *Pardes, sha'ar* 31, ch. 7; cf. *Bereishit Rabbah* 19:6).

he should...be appeased...just as the Holy One, Blessed Be He, does: "A person should learn from his Creator, as Rabbi Yochanan said: 'Even when the Holy One, Blessed Be He, is angry, He remembers the deeds of the righteous...and vanquishes the sins [of the transgressor]...and recalls the good deeds he did,' as is written in *Berachot* 54b" (*Reishit Chochmah, sha'ar "HaAnavah,"* ch. 1).

9. *And You will cast all their sins into the depths of the sea*:

the iniquity of Haman reverts: See *Esther* 9:25.

Erase my sin: This prayer is part of the Yom Kippur liturgy.

but not by way of severe suffering: This prayer is part of the daily morning blessings.

You are just: Cf. *Nechemiah* 9:33. The Midrash comments: "Said the Holy One, Blessed Be He, to the ministering angels: Come, I will show you the righteousness of [the Jews]. For I have heaped difficulties and trials upon them in this world...and they have not rebelled. Instead, they call Me the Righteous One and themselves wicked, saying 'We have sinned, we have acted perversely, we have willfully transgressed.... And You are just' " (*Pesikta*, sec. 36, on the verse "Rejoice and be glad").

purged: See *Yoma* 86a.

Zohar: See vol. II, p. 262b.

any animal that is party to a transgression: See *VaYikra* 20:15-16 and *Sanhedrin* 54a-b.

the stones...the sword...must be buried: See *Sanhedrin* 45b. Alternatively, Rambam explains that they must be buried lest they be remembered to the transgressor's detriment (*Mishneh Torah, Hilchot Sanhedrin* 15:9).

head...arms...legs: The final exile is symbolized by the legs, the longest limbs of the body, for this exile is the lengthiest of all (see *Tikkunim, tikkun* 21).

the arrows: These arrows symbolize the emissaries that deliver punishments.

will be spent but not on Israel: See *Sotah* 9a and Rashi on *Devarim* 32:23.

who are called "the depths of the sea": See *Zohar*, vol, III, p. 101b.

he is like your brother: See *Makkot* 3:15.

10. *Show faithfulness to Ya'akov*:

faithfulness: אמת here means "*showing* faithfulness." That is, the prophet prays that G-d will keep His promise never to abandon Ya'akov (*Bereishit* 28:15). See Rashi, Radak, and *Metzudat David* on *Michah* 7:28.

Israel refers to a higher level than...Ya'akov: The name "Ya'akov" suggests guile and deceit, whereas the name "Israel" means royalty and nobility (see Rashi on *Bereishit* 32:29 and 35:10). Ramak explains that according to Kabbalah, "Ya'akov" refers to the *sefirah* of *malchut*, which descends into this world of falseness and deceit, much as Ya'akov had to deal with Eisav and Lavan, while "Israel" refers to the *sefirah* of *tiferet*, which is called "*emet*" — truth and faithfulness — represented by Ya'akov's victory over his enemies (*Pardes, sha'ar "Archei Ha-Kinuyim*," ערך יעקב, ערך אמת).

to the strict requirements of the Law: But one who goes beyond the minimum requirements of the Law is pious. (See *Bava Kamma* 99 b ff.; *Bava Metzia* 24b; Rambam, *Mishneh Torah, Hilchot De'ot* 1:5; Bartenura on *Avot* 5:10; and *Reishit Chochmah, sha'ar "HaAhavah*," ch. 11, p. 96c.)

also has this aspect: "The same measure a man uses is in turn used for him" (*Megillah* 12b, *Sotah* 8b). That is, both collectively and individually man's actions determine how the world is run. This is a cardinal principle of Ramak's philosophy. See

Shiur Komah, ch. 7, par. 17; *Pardes, sha'ar* 7, ch. 4.

11. *Kindness to Avraham*:

to Avraham: Why is Ya'akov mentioned before Avraham? Since Ya'akov represents "those individuals of average spiritual stature, who do not know how to go beyond what the Law requires," their merits perhaps cannot justify the bestowal of goodness and benevolence on the world. Therefore, the prophet asks that G-d's grace be bestowed on the Jewish people as the heirs of the Avraham, whose conduct surpassed the requirements of the Law and who represents unlimited kindness, which draws down the corresponding quality from Above (*Sha'arei Orah*, end *sha'ar* 7).

the strict execution of justice: Thus, we are promised correspondingly, "All who ignore their natural feelings have their transgressions ignored" (*Yoma* 23a).

among his friends: This is a positive commandment (Rambam, *Mishneh Torah, Hilchot De'ot* 6:2).

12. *Which You have sworn to our fathers*:

the merit of their fathers: Although this idea seems to contradict the premise that "the merit of the *Avot* no longer protects the wicked" (*Shabbat* 55a and *Tosafot* ad loc., דיה אמר ושמואל), the Midrash states: "Rabba Acha said: The merit of the *Avot* stands forever; we always recall their merit and say: '...G-d, your L-rd, is merciful; He will not abandon you or destroy you, and He will not forget your Patriarchs' covenant, which he swore to them' [*Devarim* 4:31]" (*VaYikra Rabbah* 36 [end]).

to whom I swore: Alternatively, Rabbeinu Tam points out that although the *merit* of the Patriarchs might be exhausted, G-d's *covenant* with them is eternal, and this is what we recall (*Tosafot* on *Shabbat* 55a, ד״יה ושמואל). (Also see Rashi on *Bereishit* 22:14; *Sha'arei Orah, sha'ar* 7.)

as he can: "One who sees someone sinning is obliged to return him to the good path. This is a positive commandment.... And if he does not accept the rebuke, he should be rebuked a second time and a third and so on...until the sinner hits him, saying, 'I will not listen' " (Rambam, *Mishneh Torah, Hilchot De'ot* 6:7). The Gemara states: "Rebuke him even a hundred times" (*Bava Metzia* 31a).

13. *From days of old*:

days of old: By quoting *Yirmeyahu* 2:2, Ramak implies that "days of old" refers to the exodus from Egypt and the receiving of the Torah on Mount Sinai. However, other commentaries associate "days of old" with the oath G-d made to Avraham during the binding of Yitzchak (*Bereishit* 22:16-18). Thus, all three Patriarchs are mentioned here (*Metzudat David*, Rashi).

in your youth...on the day of your marriage: This verse refers to the exodus from Egypt and the receiving of the Torah on Mount Sinai (*Zohar*, vol. III, p. 103b; Rashi; *Metzudat David*).

a special treasure: סגולה is the Hebrew word used here. Cf. *Targum*, Rashi, and Ibn Ezra on *Shemot* 19:5. Also see *Kohelet* 2:8, *I Divrei HaYamim* 29:3; and Radak, *Shorashim*.

includes all the others: It is the completion and perfection of them all (*Zohar*, vol. III, p. 103b).

in the "Idra": See *Zohar*, vol. III, p. 134b. The "*Idra*" is one section of *Zohar*, "*Nasso*," vol. III, pp. 127b-145a.

not find...unworthy: Even the wicked and the idolaters of Israel are called "sons of the Almighty" (*Kiddushin* 36a). "Even when [the Jews] are spiritually impure, the Shechinah is with them" (*Yoma* 56b). "Even the worthless among you is as full of mitzvot as a pomegranate [is full of seeds]" (*Berachot* 57a).

according to his behavior will the outflow: "The entire world and the way it is conducted depend on man. If he does good, the world will be conducted in a proper and orderly fashion. If he does bad, the Almighty will conduct the world with harsh judgments and severities" (*Shiur Komah*, ch. 7, par. 17; *Pardes*, sha'ar 7, ch. 4). As mentioned, this is a cardinal principle of Ramak's philosophy. Cf. two oft-quoted statements of our sages: "Measure for measure" (*Shabbat* 105b, *Nedarim* 32a, *Sanhedrin* 90a) and "The same measure a man uses is in turn used for him" (*Megillah* 12b; *Sotah* 8b).

Notes on Chapter 2

Keter: (crown) is the highest and most encompassing *sefirah*. So sublime that it is called "the most hidden of all hidden things" (*Zohar*, vol. I, p. 147a; *Pardes, sha'ar* 5, ch. 4), *keter* is thus referred to as *"ayin"* — nothingness (*Zohar*, vol. III, p. 256b).

humility: The Hebrew ענוה (humility) derives from the word עני, poor, for a poor person is subdued, and from the word עִנּוּי, self-affliction, for fasting and the like are humbling (*Reishit Chochmah, Sha'ar "HaAnavah,"* p. 213a).

all-encompassing: "The quality of humility must imbue a man's thought, speech, and deed...the way he walks...dresses...his relations with others...his learning...his emotions...his prayers" (*Shelah, sha'ar "HaOtiot,"* אות ע).

the most sublime of all attributes: This is because humility derives form *keter*, the most sublime *sefirah*, as explained above (*Avodah Zara* 20b; *Reishit Chochmah, sha'ar "HaAnavah,"* p. 213d ff.).

one reason: Ramak does not explain the other reason.

should lower his gaze: One should always gaze downwards as if standing in prayer (Rambam, *Mishneh Torah, Hilchot De'ot* 5:8).

to minimize his own worth: "Said the Holy One, Blessed Be He, to Israel, 'I love you, for even when I bestow greatness upon you, you minimize your worth before Me'." (*Chullin* 89b). "The Holy One, Blessed Be He, rests His Shechinah only on those who are...humble" (*Nedarim* 38a).

lowers his heard: The Holy One, Blessed Be He, will straighten and raise up over all men those who lower their heads" (*Zohar*, vol. II, p. 232).

none so patient and humble...in His attribute of *keter*: "Everywhere you find His might, you find His humility" (*Megillah* 31a; *Reishit Chochmah, sha'ar "HaAnavah,"* p. 213b).

from the highest to the lowest: The idiom used in the Talmud is "from the horns of the ibex to the eggs of lice" (*Avodah Zarah* 3b).

they could not exist for even a moment: On the phrase "and You give life to them all" (*Nechemiah* 9:6), Ramak comments: "Read not only, 'give life,' but 'bring into being.' ...G-d creates beings *ex-nihilo* every moment. Thus, giving them life and creating them are one and the same, for if the [G-d given] life force were removed, everything would instantly cease to exist" (*Pardes, sha'ar,* 6, ch. 8; *Eilimah Rabbati,* sec. 2, ch. 1; *Reishit Chochmah, sha'ar "HaKedushah,"* end ch. 7; *Shelah, sha'ar "HaOtiot,"* pp. 48b, 70a). Also see Rambam, *Mishneh Torah, Hilchot Yesodei HaTorah* 1:3, 5, and *Moreh Nevuchim* pt. I, ch. 69, and pt. II, ch. 13).

very important: "The Holy One, Blessed Be He, did not create even a single thing for nothing" (*BeMidbar Rabbah*, 18:18; *Zohar*, vol. I, p. 23a).

it is absolute compassion: See *Zohar*, "*Idra Rabba*," vol. III, p. 129a; *Pardes*, *sha'ar* 8, ch. 3.

the Primal Torah: "There are many aspects of Torah. There is the aspect of Torah in *chochmah*, whence Torah emanates.... Regarding this [aspect], our sages said: 'The overflow of wisdom (*chochmah*) above is Torah' [*Bereishit Rabbah* 17:7]. This is also explained in the *Zohar*: 'There is no Torah without wisdom (*chochmah*), and there is no wisdom without Torah, for they are one and the same level and one and the same thing...' [*Zohar*, vol. III, p. 81a]. This is called *HaTorah HaKedumah*, the Primal Torah. And even though Torah's place here below is in *tiferet*, its roots are above in the depths of *chochmah*" (*Pardes*, *sha'ar* "*Archei HaKinuyim*," ערך תורה).

in *Zohar*, "*VaYakhel*": See vol. II, p. 217b.

forehead: The forehead is a metaphor for atonement and expiation. Thus, the *kohen gadol* wore the *tzitz* (forehead plate) on his forehead at all times in order to make the Temple sacrifices acceptable before G-d and to expiate errors therein (particularly ritual impurity). (See *Shemot* 28:36-38 and Rashi ad loc.; *Mena. hot* 25a; and *Zohar*, "*Idra Rabba*," vol. III, p. 129a). The *tzitz* also atoned for brazenness and arrogance (*VaYikra Rabbah* 10; *Zohar*, "*Idra Rabba*," vol. III, p. 129a; "*Ra'aya Mehemna*," vol. III, p. 174b; *Pardes*, *sha'ar* "*Archei HaKinuyim*," ערך ציץ).

chochmah **in the *metzach* of *Atik*:** This is an extremely elevated level of *keter*. See *Zohar*, "*Idra Rabba*," vol. III, p. 129a; *Pardes*, *sha'ar* 8, ch. 3.

whence all severities are appeased: "There is no 'Left Side' [i.e., harsh judgment] in *Atik*" (*Zohar*, "*Idra Rabba*," vol. III, p. 129a).

towards all creatures: One should never arouse strife or controversy concerning any person, great or small. One should be pleasant to all people, including gentiles (*Reishit Chochmah*, *sha'ar* "*HaAnavah*," p. 214b).

the Mishnah: See *Avot* 3:10.

ears...eyes...nose: The sanctification of these organs is discussed at length in *Reishit Chochmah*, *sha'ar* "*HaKedushah*," chs. 8-9.

ears: Interestingly, although both the *Zohar* and *Reishit Chochmah* place the rectification of the eyes before that of the ears ("*Idra Rabba*," vol. III, pp. 136b-138b; *sha'ar* "*HaAnavah*," p. 214b), Ramak reverses the order. Perhaps he follows the sequence of Eve's sin — first she *listened* to the serpent, then "the woman *saw* that the tree was good to eat and desirable to the eyes" (*Bereishit* 3:1-6) — as implied by his subsequent reference to "the words and speech of the Serpent."

the secret of Supernal 'Listening': "This is a metaphor for the powers of *gevurah* [the attribute of might or power in the sense of severity], which receives the prayers and cries of man" (*Pardes*, *sha'ar* "*Archei HaKinuyim*," ערך אזן).

the words and speech of the Serpent have no entry: Cf. "no black magic נחש affects Ya'akov" (*BeMidbar* 23:23). On this phrase Ramban comments: "The Jewish people [is] not subject to the angels and the stars...such that [the Jews] can be harmed by anyone using occult powers or black magic."

you shall not accept a false report: See *Pesachim* 118a and *Sanhedrin* 7a.

the Supernal 'Eye': This image symbolizes Divine providence (See *Reishit Chochmah, sha'ar* "HaAnavah," p. 214b). Cf. "Behold, the eye of the L-rd is directed towards those who fear Him toward those who hope for His kindness" (*Tehillim* 33:18).

he should not close his eyes to...suffering: "The Holy One, Blessed Be He, counts the tears of those who weep over [the misfortunes] of the upright, and He stores them in His treasury" (*Shabbat* 105b).

the Supernal 'Eye' is ever open: Cf. "Behold, the Guardian of Israel neither slumbers nor sleeps" (*Tehillim* 121:4). The *Zohar* states: "If the Supernal Eye closed for a single moment, nothing could exist. For this reason, Divine providence is called 'an open eye' " (*Zohar*, "Idra Rabba," vol. III, p. 129b). See *Eilimah Rabbati*, pt. 1, *tamar* 5 (p. 80ff.).

always looking at the good: The Holy One, Blessed Be He, always watches over and shows compassion to the Jews, even if they transgress. So, too, man should be generous and forgiving (*Reishit Chochmah, sha'ar* "HaAnavah," ch. 1, p. 214b, and *sha'ar* "HaAhavah," ch. 11, p. 93c).

the nose: The nose symbolizes the acceptance of man's prayers and pleas, which the Torah describes as "a pleasing scent for the L-rd" (*Tikkunei Zohar, tikkun* 70, p. 165b; *Pardes, sha'ar* "Archei HaKinuyim," ערך חוטם). Commenting on the verse "For the sake of My name I will delay My anger (אפי), and for the sake of My praise I will be patient (אחטם) (*Yeshayahu* 48:9), Rashi, *Metzudat David*, and Radak connects the words חוטם (nostrils) and אף (nose or anger).

face should always shine: Such a face fulfills the verse "May the L-rd make His countenance shine upon you" (*BeMidbar* 6:25), which is recited daily as part of the Priestly Blessing

(*Reishit Chochmah, sha'ar* "*HaAnavah*," p. 214c). *Targum Onkelos* renders this verse "May the L-rd cause His Shechinah to enlighten you...."

with a cheerful countenance: Cf. *Avot* 1:15.

mouth: The mouth symbolizes Torah: "*Malchut* is the mouth, which we call the Oral Torah" (*Tikkunei Zohar*, intro. ,ד״יה פתח אליהו).

no ugly words: "Rabbi Yehoshua ben Levi said: 'A person should never utter unseemly words' " (*Pesachim* 3a).

frivolous talk: "One who engages in frivolous chatter transgresses a positive and a negative commandment" (*Yoma* 19b).

to open His sources: "Since man is part of G-d Above, if his deeds are pure and forthright, and he is bound with 'ropes of love' [*Hoshea* 11:4] to the roots of holiness...his soul will become a channel whereby the *sefirot*, from the very highest to the lowest, pour forth benevolence" (*Pardes, sha'ar* 32, ch. 1).

these severities are inactive...*keter* reigns: The severities are nullified by the radiance of *keter*, which is all compassion (see *Zohar*, "*Idra Rabbah*," vol. III, p. 129a; *Pardes, sha'ar* 8, ch. 3).

sweetened...the delight of Shabbat: See *Zohar*, vol. II, pp. 88a-b; *Eilimah Rabbati*, pt. 1, *tamar* 5, ch. 6 (p. 82).

the courts do not sit in judgment on Shabbat: See *Beitzah* 5:2.

which he repels: See *Pardes, sha'ar* 32, ch. 1.

the *sefirah* Above pertaining to...severity: Here Ramak refers to the *sefirah* of *gevurah*.

the main quality...the key...is humility: Regarding all other characteristics, the mean, is the proper measure. However, a person should be humble to the utmost degree (*Shelah, sha'ar* "*HaOtiot*," אות ע; Rambam, *Mishneh Torah, Hilchot De'ot* 2:7, 1:5).

does not see his value...considers himself nothing: From the continuation of this paragraph, it is evident that Ramak urges humility not only in relation to the Holy One, Blessed Be He, but in relation to man, as in "Be of humble spirit before all men" (*Avot* 4:10). Cf. "in my eyes I was lowly" (*II Shmuel* 6:22); "And I am a worm, not a man — the shame of mankind and the despised of the people" (*Tehillim* 22:7). See *Shelah, sha'ar* "*HaOtiot*," אות ע, p. 51b.

despicable and loathsome thing: See *Zohar*, vol. II, p. 1a.

all other qualities are drawn after it: "Words of Torah are preserved only in one who treats himself as if he didn't exist. As the verse states: 'And *chochmah* derives from *ayin* (nothingness)...' [*Iyyov* 28:12]" (*Sotah* 21b). See following note:

to view itself as nothing: Thus, *keter* is called *ayin* — nothingness (*Zohar* vol. III, pp. 256b, 290a; vol. II, pp. 42b, 121a; *Pardes, sha'ar* "*Archei HaKinuyim*," ערך אין).

flee...from honor: Cf. "Envy, lust, and honor drive a man from the world" (*Avot* 4:21); "To acquire Torah, one must have forty-eight qualities:...distancing oneself from honor, not being arrogant about his learning..." (ibid. 6:6); and "Do not chase after glory" (*Derech Eretz Zuta*, ch. 2). Also see *Reishit Chochmah, sha'ar* "*HaAnavah*," ch. 2, p. 116d; *Sefer Chassidim*, ch. 84.

a person should constantly recall his sins: "The rabbis taught: Sins a person confessed on Yom Kippur he should not reconfess the following Yom Kippur.... Rabbi Eliezer ben Yaakov said: How much more praiseworthy it is to confess again, for the verse states, '...my sin is always before me' [*Tehillim* 51:5]" (*Yoma* 86b). Many authorities follow the latter opinion (Rambam, *Mishneh Torah, Hilchot Teshuvah* 2:8; *Semag, aseh* 16; *Tur Shulchan Aruch* 607:4). Also see *Zohar*, vol. 1, p. 73b.

his strength and vitality: "A healthy and whole body is among the ways of G-d, for it is impossible for one to gain any understanding and knowledge of the Creator when he is "ill" (Rambam, *Mishneh Torah, Hilchot De'ot* 4:1).

afflicted with contempt and shame: "These are minor sufferings, which, if accepted with love, atone for all his sins" (*Reishit Chochmah, sha'ar "HaAnavah,"* ch. 3, p. 120c).

respect all creatures: "Love all creatures, and honor them" (*Derech Eretz Zuta,* ch. 1).

Whose wisdom is contained in all creatures: The verse "You have made them all with wisdom" (*Tehillim* 104:24) may be understood literally — everything G-d creates contains His wisdom. See Ibn Ezra ad loc.

it affects the honor of their Creator: "Everything the Holy One, Blessed Be He, created, He created for His glory" (*Yoma* 38a). Thus, one who despises or disparages His creation despises or disparages the Creator.

to seek the wisdom in them: "Rabbi Akiva said: 'The Holy One, Blessed Be He, made everything in such a way that great wisdom can be learned from all things. As the verse states: "G-d has made everything for His sake..." [*Mishlei* 16:4] [i.e., for the sake of understanding His wisdom — see *Targum Yonatan*].' Rabbi Elazar said: 'We learn it from this verse: "G-d saw all that He had made, and indeed it was very good..." [*Bereishit* 1:31]. What is the meaning of *"very* good"? [Good enough] to learn supernal wisdom therefrom' " (*Zohar,* vol. II, p. 15b).

even the wicked: Regarding this somewhat controversial topic, see ch. 1's notes on the phrases "permitted to hate...as regards his sin" and "a religious obligation...with love." Also see *Shevet*

Mussar, ch. 37.

by covering up their flaws...their defects: As it is written, "...love covers all sins" (*Mishlei* 10:12).

...if this poor...fellow were very rich...why should he lack honor: Cf. "Rabbi Meir said: 'Look not at the vessel but at what it contains' " (*Avot* 4:20).

he is superior to me...since he is plagued and crushed: "For him whom G-d loves, He chastises..." (*Mishlei* 3:12). The Gemara calls these "sufferings of love" (*Berachot* 5b), with which the Holy One, Blessed Be He, afflicts the sinless in order to increase their reward in the World to Come (Rashi ad loc.). "Rava said...: 'Everyone the Holy One, Blessed Be He, desires, He crushes with suffering...' " (*Berachot* 5a).

which cleanse one of sin: "Suffering scours away sin" (*Berachot* 5a, *Yoma* 3:4 [32b], and Bartenura and Rashi ad loc.).

Notes on Chapter 3

chochmah: *Chochmah* represents G-d's first creative activity (*Pardes, sha'ar* 5, ch. 4; *Targum Yerushalmi,* Bereishit 1:1). It is thus called "the beginning," from which everything else derives (*Zohar,* vol. I, p. 3b). *Chochmah* is not apprehensible until it becomes enformed in *binah* (cf. *Zohar,* vol. I, p. 15b).

hidden and exceedingly exalted: "Even though *chochmah* is called 'being' in relation to the 'nothingness' of *keter,* [*chochmah's*] being is incomprehensible and exceedingly refined" (*Pardes, sha'ar* 5, chs. 4-5).

spread out over all creation..."You have made them all in *chochmah*": "You have made them all *bechochmah*" can be understood in two interrelated ways — in *chochmah* or by *chochmah.* The former interpretation implies that creation is founded in *chochmah* (*Eitz Chaim, sha'ar* 25, ch. 1). This is apparently Ramak's intention. The latter sense implies that *chochmah* is the tool of creation, as will be explained in the text and notes.

pervade all his actions: "Just as a sage is recognized by his wisdom and knowledge...he should be recognized by his activities; his eating, his drinking...his speech, his walk, his dress..." (Rambam, *Mishneh Torah, Hilchot De'ot* 5:1).

to benefit and influence others with *chochmah*: Cf. " 'Let the wise man not take pride in his wisdom.... But in this [he] should take pride — in gaining wisdom and knowledge of Me, for I am the L-rd, Who does kindness, justice, and charity on earth, for these are what I desired,' says the L-rd" (*Yirmeyahu* 9:22-23). The commentaries explain that "knowledge of Me" means doing kindness, justice, and charity, for this is what G-d does (Radak, Mahari Kra ad loc.). As the Gemara states: "The purpose of *chochmah* is repentance and good deeds" (*Berachot* 17a.) Also see *VaYikra Rabbah* 35.

***chochmah* Above has two aspects:** See *Eilimah Rabbati*, pt. 2, *tamar* 6, ch. 31, pp. 91c-92a. Also see *Pardes, sha'ar "Archei HaKinuyim,"* ערך חכמה.

overseeing the other *sefirot*: See *Eilimah Rabbati* pt. 2, *tamar* 6, ch. 31, pp. 91c-92a.

a person should have two aspects: Though our sages debate whether man's *chochmah* resides in the head or the heart (*Yalkut Shimoni, Mishlei,* beg. ch. 1), according to Ramak, *both* opinions are correct, since the attribute has two aspects.

communion in solitude: "One way of cleaving to the Holy One, Blessed Be He, is to be in solitude part of the day and contemplate the greatness of the Creator" (*Reishit Chochmah, sha'ar "HaAhavah,"* ch. 10).

what is proper for him and his needs: On the verse "Her husband is well-known at the gates..." (*Mishlei* 31:23, the *Zohar* comments: "This refers to the Holy One, Blessed Be He, Who makes Himself known and attaches Himself to each person according to his heart's capacity to cleave to *chochmah*" (vol. 1, p. 103b).

not to give more...not go beyond the limits: See Rambam, *Moreh Nevuchim*, pt. 1, ch. 33.

the Supernal Thought: In this context, this term refers to the highest level of *chochmah*. See *Tikkunei Zohar, tikkun* 19, p. 40, and *tikkun* 69, p. 115a; *Pardes, sha'ar "Archei HaKinuyim,"* ערך מחשבה.

contemplates everything that exists: Cf. "All of them are looked over in one glance" (*Rosh HaShanah* 18a).

bringing near those who have strayed...to proper conduct: Moshe and King David were chosen to lead the Jewish people because, as shepherds they'd shown concern for their flocks, feeding and guiding them according to their needs (*Shemot Rabbah* 2:2-3).

The Supernal Thought guides the highest worlds: *Chochmah* oversees all the other *sefirot* (*Pardes, sha'ar* 4, ch. 5).

chochmah **gives life:** See *Tikkunim*, end *tikkun* 22. In addition, the numerical value of חכמה equals that of החיים (Z. W. Ashkenazi).

chochmah **is the source of all existence:** See *Zohar*, vol. III, p. 10b. In this sense, the term "*bechochmah*" in the verses "You have made them all *bechochmah*..." (*Tehillim* 104:24) and "G-d has founded the earth *bechochmah*" (*Mishlei* 3:19) means with or by *chochmah* rather than in *chochmah*, an interpretation explained in an earlier note on this chapter. In this context, *chochmah* is the instrument of Creation, and everything derives from it (see *Eitz Chaim, sha'ar* 42, ch. 1). The commentaries on the *Zohar* ad loc. explain that *chochmah* here refers to the Torah, as in "The Holy One, Blessed Be He, looked into the Torah and created the world" (*Zohar*, vol. II, 161a-b). Also see *Sanhedrin* 38a; Ramban, *Bereishit* 1:1; *Moreh Nevuchim*, pt. II, ch. 30.

holy souls emanate from that source: See *Zohar*, vol. II, p. 174a; *Bereishit Rabbah* 1:4; *Eitz Chaim, sha'ar* 41, ch. 1.

Did I conceive this nation: Although the straightforward sense of the verse seems to undercut Ramak's intention, *Or HaChaim* explains: "Our sages teach, 'Anyone who teaches his friend's child Torah is as if he gave birth to him' [*Sanhedrin* 19b]. Therefore, all the souls of the Jewish people in the desert were branches of Moshe's soul, and he was their father. Thus, the verse does not state: 'Am I the *father* of this people?' or 'Are they my *children*?' For in truth, he was their father, and they are called his children in terms of the Torah he taught them, although he didn't conceive or give birth to them" (Or HaChaim on *BeMidbar* 11:12).

take care...seek out...heal...nourish...and return: See *Zechariah* 11:16.

against treating food disrespectfully: See *Berachot* 50b; *Shulchan Aruch, Oruch Chaim* 171; *Zohar*, vol. I, p. 14b.

Rabbi Yehudah the Prince was punished: See *Bava Metzia* 85a.

compassion shields against severity: "Compassion prevents severities from destroying the world. The world is conducted through compassion and endures because of it" (*Zohar*, vol. I, p. 180b).

the light of *chochmah*...**his suffering disappeared:** Rabbi Yehudah stopped suffering because *chochmah* is absolute compassion (*Pardes, sha'ar* 8, ch. 5).

one should not disparage any creature: "There is nothing in the world that a person must push away from himself and treat disdainfully, for all...are acts of truth, and all...are necessary in the world" (*Zohar*, vol. II, p. 68b). Similarly, "The Holy One, Blessed Be He, did not create a single thing in this world without a purpose" (*BeMidbar Rabbah* 18:18; *Zohar*, vol. I, p. 23a).

uproot plants: Cf. "When you besiege a city...you must not destroy its trees..." (*Devarim* 20:19).

choose a noble death: "Rabbi Nachman said..., 'The Torah states: "love your fellowman as yourself" [*VaYikra* 19:18], that is, choose a noble death for him' " (*Sanhedrin* 45a). Although the Gemara is talking about the death penalty, Ramak extends this idea to all creatures.

carefully inspected: See *Chullin* 17b; *Shulchan Aruch, Yoreh De'ah* 18.

to raise them higher and higher: This is the mystical doctrine of *birur hanitzotzot*, the extrication and purification of the sparks of holiness imbedded within creation, elevating them from inanimate to plant life, animal life, and ultimately human life. For a full exposition of this idea, see *Eitz Chaim, sha'ar* 26, ch. 2; *sha'ar* 39, ch. 3; and *sha'ar* 50, ch. 3. Also see *Reishit Chochmah, sha'ar "HaKedushah,"* end ch. 15.

taking away...in order to benefit: Ramak refers to uprooting or slaughtering them in order to raise them to a higher level of being.

Notes on Chapter 4

binah: *Binah* means deriving one matter from another (*Chagigah* 14a, *Zohar Chadash*, p. 4a). *Chochmah* becomes known only through *binah* (*Tikkunei Zohar*, *tikkun* 22, p. 63b), which expands and elucidates it.

binah...**repentance**: Regarding the *Amidah* prayer, the Gemara asks: "Why did the sages place [the benediction regarding] repentance immediately after [the benediction regarding] *binah*? Because the verse states: '...and his heart will understand, and [then] he will repent and be healed' [*Yeshayahu* 6:10]" (*Megillah* 17b).

Kabbalah connects *binah* and repentance as follows: "*Binah* is called *teshuvah* [which means both repentance and returning]. For when *binah* is removed, harsh judgements are brought into the world...and the world is judged. And when *binah* returns to her children [i.e., the other *sefirot*] and pours forth compassion, this is called ordinary *teshuvah*. But when *binah* returns and reintegrates all the other levels within itself, enabling them to receive [Divine benevolence] from their highest level, this is complete *teshuvah*, since *binah* has returned, and so have all the other levels" (*Pardes, sha'ar* "*Archei HaKinuyim*," ערך תשובה. Also see *Zohar*, vol. III, p. 15b, and "*Ra'aya Mehemna*," p. 122a.

rectifies every flaw: "Nothing can withstand *teshuvah*, even idolatry and immorality..." (*Talmud Yerushalmi, Pe'ah* 1:1; *Zohar,* vol. II, p. 106a; *Zohar Chadash, "Bereishit,"* p. 19d).

binah **sweetens all severities:** "Stern judgments can be sweetened only at their source," which is *binah* (*Eitz Chaim, sha'ar* 13, ch. 1; *Mikdash Melech* on *Zohar*, vol. 1, p. 151a).

all his days...in repentance: Cf. "Rabbi Eliezer said: 'Repent one day before your death' [*Avot* 2:10]. His students asked him: 'Does a person know when he will die?' And he answered them, 'Therefore, *a fortiori*, he should repent today lest he die tomorrow. This way, all one's days will be spent in repentance' " (*Shabbat* 153a).

the higher level of repentance: Kabbalah posits two levels of *teshuvah*: "*Teshuvah* is תשוב ה, returning the *hei*. The latter *hei* is *teshuvah tata'ah*, 'inferior' *teshuvah*; the former *hei* is *teshuvah ila'ah*, 'superior' *teshuvah*" (*Zohar, "Ra'aya Mehemna,"* vol. III, p. 122a ff.). The gist of the *Zohar* is as follows:

The letter *hei* is both the second and fourth letter of the four-letter Name of G-d (the Tetragrammaton). The former *hei* represents *binah*, and the latter *hei* represents *malchut* (see *Pardes, sha'ar "Archei HaKinuyim,"* ערך תשובה). Through sin, a person "dislocates" the final *hei* from the Divine Name. Therefore, one who "returns the *hei*" by repudiating evil and repenting properly smashes the barrier he created and reunifies the Divine Name. However, since this *teshuvah* is only in regard to sin, it is "inferior." "Superior" *teshuvah* (returning the former *hei*, which represents *binah*) is not repentance for sin, it is Torah study based on love and awe of the Holy One, Blessed Be He, whereby the soul *returns* to its highest level and cleaves to Him Whom emanated it. See *Likutei Amarim, sha'ar "HaTeshuvah,"* chs. 5-10; Rambam, *Mishneh Torah, Hilchot Teshuvah* 10:2-3; and ch. 1's notes on the seventh attribute ("He will show us compassion").

the secret of the Jubilee: "The Jubilee is *binah*, for the fifty years of the Jubilee cycle [see *VaYikra* 25:8 ff.] correspond to the fifty gates of *binah* [explained at length in *Pardes, sha'ar* 13]. And *binah* is called 'jubilee' when the fiftieth gate shines into all the gates of *binah*, pouring out abundant blessing and goodness. Now, this occurs when the fiftieth gate cleaves to *chochmah* — then it is called 'jubilee,' and the world is full of compassion and abundant goodness, freedom and redemption" (*Pardes, sha'ar "Archei HaKinuyim,"* ערך יובל).

the root of the external forces: The severities are first aroused in *binah* (*Zohar*, vol. II, p. 175b, and vol. III, p. 118b).

secret of the River Dinur: Mentioned in *Daniel* 7:10, the River Dinur is a river of fire that issues forth from G-d's burning anger (Rabbeinu Sa'adiah Gaon, *Metzudat David*). The Gemara (*Chagigah* 13b) and *Zohar* (vol. II, p. 211b) state that this river pours forth from the sweat of the *chayot* mentioned in Yechezkel's vision of the *merkavah* (*Yechezkel* 1:5ff.).

the River Dinur itself is included in Holiness: See *Zohar*, vol. II, p. 211b.

the pleasing scent of the sacrifices: Regarding the sweetening of the severities through this scent, see *Zohar*, vol. 1, p. 70a; and *Pardes, sha'ar* 8, ch. 12.

also achieves this effect: See our note on the phrase "*binah* sweetens all severities" earlier in this chapter.

only the aspects of holiness: Besides restoring one's holiness, repentance transforms evil into good. Cf. "His deliberate transgressions become like merits" (*Yoma* 86b), i.e., the transgressions themselves are transformed into good through repentance (Rashi and Maharsha ad loc.). Similarly, Chazal explain that one should serve the Creator "with all your heart" (*Devarim* 6:5), that is, with both the evil inclination and the good inclination (*Berachot* 54a).

Kayin himself was evil, and he derived from evil: See *Zohar*, vol. I, p. 54a, and vol. II, p. 167b.

be uplifted: The Hebrew word שאת connotes both lifting up and forgiving. See Ramban, *Bereishit* 4:7.

via the root of your soul: The soul is rooted in *chochmah*, which is pure goodness and compassion (*Pardes, sha'ar* 8, ch. 5), as explained in the previous chapter.

a sweet Supernal root: All things derive from *chochmah*, which is total goodness, as explained in the previous chapter.

transgressions may be turned into merits: See *Yoma* 86b.

transforming themselves into good rather than becoming nullified: See Rashi and Maharsha on *Yoma* 86b.

kina demisavuta: This derivation is a play on the words קין (Kayin) and קינא (nest).

the state of Adam's sin...would have been to his credit: That is, by rectifying Adam's sin, Kayin would have transformed it into merit, which would have been to his credit.

the Son Brings Merit to His Father: See *Sanhedrin* 104a; *Zohar*, vol. II, 273b, and vol. III, 57a.

Kayin did not desire to repent: See *Zohar Chadash, "Bereishit,"* p. 19d.

all its branches will eventually become sweetened: This sweetening will occur when the verse "...and I will remove the spirit of impurity from the earth" (*Zechariah* 13:2) is fulfilled. See Rambam, *Mishneh Torah, Hilchot Melachim* 12.

purifies his evil inclination and transforms it into good: See *Berachot* 54a; *Zohar*, "*Ra'aya Mehemna,*" vol. I, p. 43a, and vol. III, p. 277a.

he should also repent in some way: "Every night a person should examine all his actions of that day in order to repent before his Master..." (*Zohar*, vol. I, pp. 191a, 220a).

Notes on Chapter 5

the secret of *chesed* **is to love G-d:** The attribute of *chesed* is the manifestation and actualization of G-d's absolute, gratuitous, and unlimited benevolence and kindness (*Zohar*, vol. II, p. 168b; *Pardes, sha'ar* 8, ch. 1). When a person lovingly cleaves to his Creator from the depths of his heart and soul, the Holy One, Blessed Be He, showers him with love, kindness, and benevolence. This is the secret of the verse "As in water, the face reflects the face, so does the heart of man to man" (*Mishlei* 27:19) (*Reishit Chochmah, sha'ar* "*HaAhavah*," ch. 1, p. 53c; also see *Likutei Amarim*, ch. 46).

whether he receives good...or suffering: "A person is obliged to bless G-d for bad things, just as he does for good things. As the verse states, 'You shall love the L-rd, your G-d, with all your heart, with all your soul, and with all your might' (*Devarim* 6:5) — with whatever measure He metes out to you" (*Berachot* 54a). Similarly, on the verse, "I will surely delight the L-rd; let my soul rejoice in my G-d..." (*Yeshayahu* 61:10), the *Zohar* comments: "Since the verse states 'in the L-rd,' why does it state, 'in my G-d'? But this is what Israel said: If compassion is showered upon us, 'I will surely delight in *the L-rd*' [י - ה - ו - ה], signifying compassion]; and if harsh judgments come upon us, 'let my soul rejoice in my *G-d* [אלהי, signifying judgment]" (vol. II, p. 90b). Also see *Berachot* 60b.

Faithful are the wounds inflicted by a loving friend: Such wounds cause one to improve his ways (*Metzudat David*).

thereby including all attributes in the attribute of *chesed*: Cf. "All that the Merciful One does is for the best" (*Berachot* 60b). Also see *Zohar*, vol. I, p. 181a; *Mechilta*, "*Yitro*" 10; *Reishit Chochmah, sha'ar "HaAhavah,"* ch. 2, p. 54b.

Divine conduct...from the attribute of *malchut*: This idea is explained in ch. 9.

connected to *chesed*: See *Pardes, sha'ar "Archei HaKinuyim,"* ערך חסד.

Nachum Ish Gamzu, who would always say: See *Ta'anit* 21a.

"This, too, is for the good!": That is to say, "This, too," even though it appears to stem from the attribute of severity, "is for the good," i.e., for the sake of kindness, in order to purify the soul (*Reishit Chochmah, sha'ar "HaAhavah,"* ch. 5, p. 230a).

***chesed*, which is called 'good':** See *Zohar*, vol. II, p. 168b. Nevertheless, there is a difference between *chesed* (kindness) and goodness. On the verse "Only goodness and kindness shall follow me all the days of my life..." (*Tehillim* 23:6), the *Zohar* asks: "Since goodness is mentioned in the verse, why is kindness also mentioned? And since kindness is mentioned, why is goodness also mentioned? Either of them would have sufficed! However, 'goodness' is entirely inward and does not flow downward, whereas 'kindness' spreads out below to sustain all, righteous and wicked" (vol. 2, p. 168b).

The *Tikkunim* states: See intro., p. 1b. Cf. *Zohar*, vol. III, pp. 222b, 281a.

a pious, kindhearted person: This is a translation of the Hebrew word *chasid*, i.e., one who does *chesed*.

who does kindness (*chesed*) to his Creator: The *chasid* desires only to reveal G-dliness in the world and "perfect the world under the sovereignty of the Almighty" ("*Aleinu*"). Ramak explains that we can restore the Shechinah to this world through acts of kindness and benevolence towards our fellowmen. The *Tikkunim* calls this process "uniting the Holy One, Blessed Be He, with His Shechinah."

provide him with all the necessities of his sustenance: This idea can possibly be explained in the following way: A person's birthday is comparable to Rosh HaShanah, when Adam himself was created. (*Yalkut Shimoni*, "*Pinchas*" 782). And just as a person's sustenance is set aside for him on Rosh HaShanah (*Beitzah* 16a), so, too, is it on his birthday.

the birth of *tiferet* from *binah*: See *Pardes*, *sha'ar* 8, ch. 17; *Or Ne'erav*, pt. 6, ch. 1.

***tiferet* will tend toward the aspect of *gevurah*:** Since *tiferet* is a synthesis of *chesed*, symbolized by the right arm, and *gevurah*, symbolized by the left arm (see *Tikkunim*, intro., ד״ה פתח אליהו), the predominance of severity at its "birth" will cause it to tend toward *gevurah*. Ideally, *tiferet* should emerge on the right, the side of *chesed*, as Ramak proceeds to convey. See *Zohar*, vol. II, p. 219b.

its birth will be difficult: The synthesis of *chesed* and *gevurah*, such that *tiferet* tends towards the right, will be difficult to achieve.

as we pray: Ramak is referring to the Rosh HaShanah liturgy.

on the side of light: This is the side of *chesed*, which is often referred to as "day" and "light" in Kabbalah. See *Pardes, sha'ar* "*Archei HaKinuyim*," ערך אור, ערך יום.

eager to fulfill the commandments: "For love, which derives from *chesed*, is the key to the fulfillment of the entire Torah" (*Reishit Chochmah, sha'ar* "*HaAhavah*," ch. 3, p. 57d; *Zohar*, vol. III, p. 263b). Also see Rambam, *Peirush HaMishnayot, Avot* 1:3, and *Mishneh Torah, Hilchot Teshuvah* 10:2; Rambam, *Shemot* 20:8.

circumcising every aspect of 'husk' or 'foreskin': The husk and foreskin represent the physical manifestations of evil, which separates between man and G-d (cf. *Yeshayahu* 59:2) and prevents the revelation of holiness in the world, particularly in man. Both the physical foreskin and the 'foreskin' of the heart must be circumcised (See R. Yitzchak Luria, *Ta'amei HaMitzvot* "*mitzvot milah*").

yesod: This *sefirah* corresponds to the "sign of the Holy Covenant [of circumcision]," where circumcision takes place (See *Tikkunim*, intro., ד"ה פתח אליהו).

One should pursue: One who pursues sinners in order to return them to their Creator is worthy of very great reward (*Zohar*, vol. II, p. 128b).

who cause the foreskin to grow on yesod: This description refers to sinners. See *Zohar*, vol. II, p. 128b.

circumcising the foreskins of their hearts: Cf. *Devarim* 10:16. This circumcision means removing the *yetzer hara* (the evil urge) (*Sukkah* 52a).

renders the Supernal Tzaddik 'without a foreskin': That is to say, the supernal *sefirah* of *yesod*, which is called "*tzaddik*," can pour forth goodness and plenty to the world unhindered (*Pardes, sha'ar "Archei HaKinuyim," ערך צדיק*; Rabbi Y. Gekitilia, *Sha'arei Orah*, ch. 2). Cf. "...the tzaddik is the foundation (*yesod*) of the world" (*Mishlei* 10:25).

worthy of the priesthood: See *BeMidbar* 25:10-13.

the Shechinah is lovesick: In exile, the Shechinah is banished from its place and separated from the other *sefirot* (*Zohar*, "*Ra'aya Mehemna*," vol. III, pp. 219a, 74a; *Tikkunei Zohar*, and *tikkun* 25, p. 70b, *tikkun* 69, p. 106a).

unification: When the *sefirot* are unified, the revelation of the Divine Presence is restored to the world. Here, the subject is the unification of *tiferet* and *malchut*. See *Pardes, sha'ar* 8, ch. 18ff.

in the hands of man: The unification of these two *sefirot* depends on "arousal from below" (אתערותא דלתתא), a Kabbalistic term signifying man's Divine service (*Pardes, sha'ar* 8, ch. 19). Elsewhere Ramak writes: "The entire world and the way it is conducted depend on man. If he does good, the world will be conducted in a proper, orderly fashion" (*Shiur Komah*, ch. 7, par. 17).

"Sustain me...spread apples before me: Regarding this translation, see Radak, *Shorashim*, רפד.

The *Tikkunim* expounds this: See *Tikkunei Zohar, tikkun* 19, p. 39b; also see *tikkun* 64, p. 95a.

the 'two arms': *Chesed* is the right arm, and *gevurah* the left (*Tikkunim*, intro., ד"ה פתח אליהו). Of course, this imagery should not be understood literally. See *Pardes, sha'ar*, "*Archei Ha-Kinuyim*, ערך ימין.

illness: As will be explained shortly, *tiferet* is also "ill" as a result of *malchut*'s exile.

to bind *malchut* between *netzach* and *hod*...for this is the proper place: See *Pardes, sha'ar* 9, ch. 4.

red and white...the side of *chesed*: Red represents *gevurah*, the powers of severity, and white represents *chesed*, the powers of kindness. *Malchut* blends both these aspects, as explained above, but ideally it should tilt towards *chesed* (*Pardes, sha'ar* 10, chs. 3-4; *Or Ne'erav*, pt. 6, ch. 4).

sick with the sins: Cf. *Shofetim* 10:16.

isolated from her in this world: The *Shechinah* is in exile, imprisoned and encumbered among the evil husks (*kelipot*) (*Eitz chaim, sha'ar* 47, ch. 6; *Zohar*, vol. III, pp. 74a ff., 79a, and vol. II, p. 189a).

"Like a bird who wanders...": The Shechinah is often compared to a bird. See *Tikkunei Zohar*, intro., p. 1b; *Zohar*, "Ra'aya Mehemna," vol. III, p. 278a.

so is a man: The "man" here is *tiferet*.

return to his place: There, he will receive the outpouring of benevolence from *binah*.

until he returns her to her place: See *Zohar*, vol. III, p. 278a. The *Zohar* continues: "Therefore, when one returns in repentance, it is as if he has restored the Holy One, Blessed Be He,and His Shechinah to their proper place. This is the secret of Redemption."

he is ill because of our transgressions: The *Zohar* interprets this verse as referring to Moshiach (vol. II, p. 212a).

visit them and attend to their needs by studying Torah: These actions unify the *sefirot* in question by drawing down light and benevolence from the higher *sefirot* (*Pardes, sha'ar* 8, ch. 19).

yesod and *malchut*: These two *sefirot* are called "poor" because they have nothing of their own, depending instead on the outpouring of goodness and beneficence from Above (*Pardes, sha'ar "Archei HaKinuyim," ערך צדיק, וערך עני*; *Tikkunei Zohar, tikkun* 21, p. 58a).

The *Tikkunim* explains: See *Tikkunei Zohar, tikkun* 18, pp. 33a, 37a, and *tikkun* 70, p. 131b.

four times daily: *Kedushah* is recited once in the morning repetition of the *Shemoneh Esreh*, once in the afternoon repetition, once in the "*Yotzer Or*" prayer, and once in the "*U'Va LeTzion*" prayer.

utter one hundred blessings daily: See *Menachot* 43b.

leket...*shichechah*...*pe'ah*: See *VaYikra* 19:9-10; *Devarim* 24:19.

the Supernal 'sheaf,' which is *binah*: *Binah* gathers in and binds the first three *sefirot* — *Keter, chochmah*, and *binah* — within itself (*Pardes, sha'ar "Archei HaKinuyim," ערך עומר*).

tiferet **is a stranger to *malchut***: This is because *malchut* is in exile, as explained (*Zohar, "Ra'aya Mehemna,"* vol. III, p. 278).

ma'aser ani: See *Devarim* 14:28-29.

'*ma'aser*' the tithe: מעשר, tithe, derives from the root עשר, ten. Thus, *malchut* is called *ma'aser* because it is the tenth *sefirah*.

refers to *tiferet* and *yesod*: See *Tikkunei Zohar, tikkun* 6, p. 21a.

the mystical explanation of exile: Ramak refers to exile of the Shechinah.

searching for what they have lost: That is, they are searching for the Shechinah, which is lost among the *kelipot*. Other versions read not אבדתם, they have lost, but עבודתם, their service, meaning that *tiferet* and *yesod* are "searching for their mode of service."

be brought into that place: That is, *tiferet* and *yesod* must be guided to and united with *malchut* in order to rectify it and release the Shechinah from captivity.

the explanation in the *Zohar*: "Rabbi Yehudah said to Rabbi Yose: 'Open your lips and review words of Torah, for the Shechinah rests upon you.' Whenever one reviews words of Torah, the Shechinah descends and unites [with him], and how much more so when one is on a journey, for then the Shechinah precedes those who are pure in their faith in the Holy One, Blessed Be He" (*Zohar*, vol. I, p. 115b). Also see *Chesed LeAvraham, ma'ayan* 2, *nahar* 62).

some other way: That is, they bring about unification not through Torah study exclusively but, for example, through acts of charity and kindness, as has just been explained.

in the *Tikkunim*: See *Tikkunei Zohar*, intro., pp. 1b-2b.

provide them with food: Through the unification of *tiferet* and *yesod* with *malchut*, light and benevolence are drawn down from the higher *sefirot*. This drawing down is analogous to providing guests with food.

the guarded wine: This wine has been "stored in the grapes since the six days of Creation" — that is, the secrets of Torah that will be revealed only to the righteous in the World to Come (*Zohar*, vol. I, pp. 135b, 192a; also see *Berachot* 34b).

the sweetened milk: This milk represents *chesed* that is further sweetened by the outflow from *binah* (*Pardes, sha'ar* "Archei HaKinuyim," ערך חלב, and *sha'ar* 8, ch. 6).

Ya'akov to Rachel: Ya'akov corresponds to the *sefirah* of *tiferet*, and Rachel to the *sefirah* of *malchut* (*Pardes, sha'ar* "Archei Ha-Kinuyim," ערך רחל, ערך יעקב).

Ra'aya Mehemna: See *Zohar*, vol. III, pp. 3b, 244a.

in their Supernal form: This refers to their pure form in the higher worlds (specifically, the World of Emanation [*Atzilut*]) rather than as these *sefirot* descend and enclothe themselves to give rise to the attributes of man's soul.

to be with them: This refers to the unification of all the *sefirot*.

concentrating...to achieve its parallel Above: "Since man is part of G-d Above, if his deeds are pure and forthright and his soul — which rises through all the worlds and levels — is bound with 'ropes of love' [*Hoshea* 11:4] to the roots of holiness, then through righteous deeds and proper intentions...he unifies the *sefirot* with a firm bond and becomes the channel whereby all the *sefirot*, from the highest to the lowest, pour forth their influence" (*Pardes*, *sha'ar* 32, ch. 1).

verbalize: Such was the custom of Rabbi Abba (*Zohar*, vol. II, p. 88a).

"...in your mouth and in your heart to do it": This verse alludes to thought, speech, and deed.

conceal themselves and disappear into their sheaths: See *Eitz Chaim*, *sha'ar* 7.

correct and cleanse: These acts parallel the purification of the body (the *taharah*) before burial.

enclothe them in white: This parallels the white shrouds in which a dead body is wrapped.

carrying them on one's shoulders: This is how the dead are carried.

beyond the level of the 'shoulder': This is the level of *binah* (see *Pardes*, *sha'ar* "Archei HaKinuyim," ערך כתף.) Thus, as Ramak continues, "Above this level is the hidden secret, which is incomprehensible."

[Hashem] buried [Moshe] in the valley: See *Sotah* 9b, 14a; Rashi, and Ralbag on *Devarim* 34:6.

valley...Thirteen: The word used here for valley, גי, has a numerical value of 13.

in the *Tikkunim*: See *Tikkunim* on *Zohar Chadash*, p. 154a.

aspects that face downwards: See notes on ch. 1.

the upper level of Eden: According to Kabbalah, there are two levels of Gan Eden (Paradise). The higher level is in *binah*, and the lower in *malchut*. However, Eden itself (as distinct from Gan Eden) is the *chochmah* of *keter* and the source of the higher Gan Eden. See *Pardes*, *sha'ar* "*Archei HaKinuyim*," ערך עדן.

a bride to the *chuppah*: The bride here symbolizes *malchut* (see *Pardes*, *sha'ar* "Archei HaKinuyim," ערך כלה), and the wedding canopy (*chuppah*) represents the World of Emanation (*Atzilut*). Thus, *malchut* is unified with all the other *sefirot* (see ibid., ערך חופה). Regarding this unification, see ibid., *sha'ar* 8, ch. 18.

the secret of Prayer: See *Zohar*, vol. II, pp. 133b, 200b, and vol. III, p. 230b.

until *yesod* is adjusted: See *Pardes*, *sha'ar* 7, ch. 2, and *sha'ar* 8, ch. 24.

sin...no unity or bond between the *sefirot*: Cf. "Only your sins have separated between you and your G-d, and your transgressions have hidden His countenance from you, so that He does not hear [your prayers]" (*Yeshayahu* 59:2).

man and his wife — that is, between *tiferet* and *malchut*: See *Pardes*, *sha'ar* 8, ch. 18.

acts of benevolence in the higher worlds: This refers to the unification of the *sefirot*, as explained.

Notes on Chapter 6

gevurah: *Gevurah* is the power of restraint. It is often called *din*, law and judgment, for it demands that *chesed* be distributed justly, in proportion to the recipient's merit (*Zohar*, vol. II, p. 175b; *Tikkunei Zohar*, intro. p. 17b). In a negative sense, *gevurah* represents harsh judgment or severity. *Gevurah* seeks to limit the outflow of *chesed* (*Pardes*, *sha'ar* 8, ch. 2). *Chesed* and *gevurah* thus oppose each other but are balanced and synthesized through *tiferet*.

Man was created with two inclinations: See *Berachot* 61a.

yetzer hatov...yetzer hara...chesed...gevurah: See Rabbi Yitzchak Luria, *Sha'ar HaKavanot*, *drush* "Shevi'i Shel Pesach." Also cf. " 'A wise man's heart is on his right side...' [*Kohelet* 10:2] — this is the *yetzer hatov* which is placed on the right;'...and a fool's heart is on his left' [ibid.] — this is the *yetzer hara*" (*BeMidbar Rabbah* 22; *Zohar*, vol. III, p. 263a). As explained in ch. 5, the right is synonymous with *chesed*, and the left with *gevurah*.

Zohar on *Bereishit*: See vol. I, p. 49a.

the *yetzer hatov* was created for the needs of the person: It urges him to serve his Creator and gain entry into Gan Eden (*Pardes, sha'ar* 25, ch. 3).

the *yetzer hara* was created for the sake of his wife: "If not for the *yetzer hara*, a man would not build a home or marry a wife..." (*Bereishit Rabbah* 9). The *yetzer hara* in itself is not disgusting and despicable, for its origin is holy (Rabbi Shlomo Wolbe, *Alei Shur*, pt. 1, ch. 7). Regarding the purpose of the *yetzer hara*, see *Pardes, sha'ar* 25, ch. 3.

***tiferet*...contains the quality of *chesed*...to the Right:** *Tiferet* synthesizes *chesed*, symbolized by the right arm, and *gevurah*, symbolized by the left (See *Tikkunim*, intro., ד״יה פתח אליהו). Ideally, *tiferet* should tend to the right, the side of *chesed*. See *Zohar*, vol. II, p. 219b; *Tikkunei Zohar, tikkun* 13, p. 29b.

***malchut* tends to the Left...*gevurah*:** See *Pardes, sha'ar* 10, ch. 4; *Or Ne'erav*, pt. 6, ch. 4.

beneficial: Cf. "Those who arouse the *yetzer hara* will fall into Gehinom" (*Eruvin* 19a).

in the higher worlds: The text literally reads "in the Supernal man." This term refers to the highest world, *Atzilut* (*Or Ne'erav*, pt. 7, ערך אדם), and to the *sefirah* of *chochmah* (ibid.; *Pardes, sha'ar*, "*Archei HaKinuyim*," ערך אדם).

a flaw in the higher worlds: However, Ramak points out that the *kelipot* (the evil husks that conceal G-dliness) do not enter the higher levels. Rather, sin causes the lower levels, particularly *malchut*, to derive sustenance from sources of impurity, thus defiling themselves until the sinner repents (*Pardes, sha'ar* 31, ch. 11, and *sha'ar* 25, ch. 6).

anger: "Whoever is enraged is as if he worships idols" (*Zohar*, vol. I, p. 27b, and vol. III, pp. 179a, 234b; Rambam, *Mishneh Torah, Hilchot De'ot* 2:3; cf. *Shabbat* 105b; *Nedarim* 22b).

bound and tied...cannot be activated: "A person should always wage war with his *yetzer hatov* against the *yetzer hara*. If he prevails, good. If not, he should occupy himself with Torah study. If this does not suffice, he should read the Shema. If this, too, is insufficient, he should call to mind the day he will die" (*Berachot* 5a, according to Rashi and Maharsha). Hence, the *yetzer hara* is bound through Torah study and proper observance of the commandments. See *Tikkunei Zohar, tikkun* 21, p. 60a.

sweetened *gevurot*: See *Pardes, sha'ar* 31, ch. 10, and *sha'ar* 25, ch. 3.

providing my wife with clothes: A woman is the counterpart of the Shechinah in this world. The clothing a man must provide for his wife (See Shemot 21:10) thus corresponds to the adornment of the Shechinah.

restoring the Shechinah: As mentioned in the introduction, *tikkun* has several meanings in Kabbalah. Regarding the ten *sefirot*, which are called the ten *tikkunim* in *Petach Eliyahu* (Tikkunei Zohar, intro.), Ramak explains: "These...are called *tikkunim*, because they 'reinstate' Him Who emanated them. For through them the power and might of the Holy One, Blessed Be He, is revealed..." (*Pardes, sha'ar* 4, ch. 5). In this sense, *tikkun* means restoring the Shechinah to its rightful place (see *Shir HaShirim Rabba* 5:1) by providing it with a proper "dwelling" and appropriate "clothing" (i.e., Torah and mitzvot) (*Pardes, sha'ar* 31, ch. 11; *Tanchuma,* "*Nasso*" 16).

He continues: "Alternatively, the intention [in calling them tikkunim] is that they rectify the world, for through them the Emanator runs the world" (*Pardes, sha'ar* 4, ch. 5). In this sense, *tikkun* means rectifying or perfecting.

the Shechinah is adorned by *binah*: See *Pardes, sha'ar* 8, chs. 21-22.

an aspect of *gevurah*...**includes all severities:** See *Pardes, sha'ar* "*Archei HaKinuyim*," ערך בינה.

binah's **abundant compassion sweetens:** "Stern judgments can be sweetened only at their source," which is *binah* (*Eitz Chaim, sha'ar* 13, ch. 1; *Mikdash Melech* on *Zohar* vol. I, p. 151a). Also see *Pardes, sha'ar* 31, ch. 10, and *sha'ar* 25, ch. 3.

the *yetzer hara* **fulfill[s] the Will of its Creator:** "All that the Holy One, Blessed Be he, made, Above and below, exists for the sake of revealing His glory and [performing] His service. Now, whoever saw a servant who turned against his master, doing the opposite of whatever was his master's will? It is the Will of the Holy One, Blessed Be He, that people constantly serve Him and go in the way of truth in order [that He may] reward them in many good ways. Now, since this is the Will of the Holy One, Blessed Be He, how can an evil servant [the *yetzer hara*] come and counteract [it] and tempt man to walk in an evil way, pushing him off the good path and urging him to disobey...the Holy One, Blessed Be He? Rather, surely the servant acts according to his master's wishes" (*Zohar*, vol. II, p. 163a; *Pardes, sha'ar* 25, ch. 3).

The *Zohar* offers a parable: A king cautioned his only son to resist the temptations of evil women. Then, in secret, the king hired a beautiful harlot to attempt to seduce his son, thereby testing his obedience and devotion to his father. The prince obeyed his father's wishes and ignored the woman's allurements. The king rejoiced greatly in his son's righteousness and bestowed upon him the greatest gifts and highest honors.

"Now, who brought all that glory to the prince? Surely, it was that woman...and she is to be praised on all counts: First, she fulfilled the king's wishes, and second, she enabled the prince to receive all that good and the king to love his son exceedingly (ibid.).

beneficial powers of the Left: See *Pardes, sha'ar* 8, ch. 21.

wealth and honor: Referring to the Torah, the verse states: "Long life is at its right, riches and honor at its left" (*Mishlei* 3:16).

the *yetzer hara* to love the Shechinah: On the verse "You shall love the L-rd, your G-d, with all your heart..." (*Devarim* 6:5), the Gemara states: " 'With all your heart' — with both inclinations: with the good inclination (*yetzer hatov*) and with the evil inclination (*yetzer hara*)" (*Berachot* 54a).

mystical explanation: See *Zohar,* vol. I, p. 133a.

"His left arm is under my head...and his right arm embraces me": Thus, our sages state: "Always, the left hand should repulse and, at the same time, the right hand should draw near. Never should both hands repulse" (*Sanhedrin* 107b; *Sotah* 47a; *Zohar,* vol. II, pp. 27a, 106b, and vol. III, p. 177b). In this context, the Left should be aroused to reunify the *sefirot* Above by "sweetening the severities," so that the Shechinah, or *malchut,* tends towards the Right, where the Union takes place.

by way of the Left Side: See *Zohar,* vol. I, p. 133a.

redirect all of them to his service of G-d, binding them to the Right: Cf. "When the Jews do the Will of the Omnipresent One, they transform Left [i.e., demerit] into Right [i.e., merit]..." (*Tanchuma, "BeShallach"* 15). In Kabbalah, this transformation is known as 'including or merging the Left into the Right' (*Zohar,* vol. II, p. 162b, and vol. III, p. 280; *Mikdash Melech* on *Zohar,* vol. I, p. 151a).

Notes on Chapter 7

tiferet: *Tiferet* harmonizes and synthesizes the boundless outpouring of *chesed* with the severe limitations of *gevurah*. Others can then endure the resultant blend, which hinges on their ability and worthiness to receive its outflow. Thus, *tiferet* is referred to as "truth," for it depends on the recipient's merit (*Zohar Chadash*, "Toldot," p. 26c, and "Yitro," p. 31b). Nevertheless, ideally *tiferet* tends towards *chesed* (*Pardes, sha'ar* 8, ch. 2, and *sha'ar* 9, ch. 3) and is therefore called *rachamim* — mercy or compassion (*Zohar Chadash*, "Yitro," p. 31b). In addition, *tiferet* is referred to as "beauty," for its harmonious blending of the *sefirot* is beautiful (*Tikkunei Zohar, tikkun* 70, p. 133b; and *Pardes, sha'ar* 8, ch. 17).

in Torah study: See *Tikkunei Zohar*, intro., p. 2b, and *tikkun* 3, p. 18b; *Pardes, sha'ar* 8, ch. 17. Cf. " 'L-rd, Yours is the greatness...the glory (*tiferet*)' [*I Divrei HaYamim* 29:11] — It was taught in the name of Rabbi Akiva: 'The glory' refers to the giving of the Torah" (*Berachot* 58a).

aloof through one's learning: Many of Chazal's statements bear out this thesis, such as: "Do not make [the Torah] a crown for self-aggrandizement" (*Avot* 4:5); " '[Torah] is not in the heavens' (*Devarim* 30:12) — That is, it will not be found in those who aggrandize themselves like the heavens by means of the Torah" (*Eruvin* 55a). See *Zohar*, vol. II, p. 101b.

humbles himself through words of Torah: The Mishnah lists humility as one of the forty-eight qualities necessary to acquire Torah (*Avot* 6:6).

to descend and lower itself: Cf. "Just as water leaves a high place and goes to a low place, words of Torah are preserved only in one of lowly bearing" (*Ta'anit* 7a).

to flow forth to *malchut*: See *Pardes, sha'ar* 8, ch. 18ff.

four *sefirot*: They are *netzach, hod, yesod,* and *malchut*.

three corresponding qualities: According to the *Zohar, netzach* and *hod* are "two halves of one body, like twins" (vol. III, p. 236a). Consequently, only three qualities correspond to these four *sefirot*.

"students of [the Torah of] the L-rd": See *Zohar*, vol. III, p. 61a. Also see *Metzudat Tzion*.

pleasant to his students: Cf. "The short-tempered cannot teach" (*Avot* 2:5).

the degree appropriate: That is, *chesed* and *gevurah* will blend in such a way that the recipient will benefit from the outflow of benevolence.

Eliyahu the Prophet appeared...[as a] loathsome pauper: See *Ta'anit 20a-b and Tosafot*, ד"ה נזדמן.

aloof from *yesod*: As mentioned, both *yesod* and *malchut* are "poor" (*Pardes, sha'ar "Archei HaKinuyim,"* ערך עני; *Tikkunei Zohar, tikkun* 21, p. 58a).

sages should highly esteem the poor: Cf. "One who gives a small sum to a poor person is blessed with six blessings. One who soothes a poor person with kind words is blessed with eleven blessings" (*Bava Batra* 9a). Also see *Avot DeRabbi Natan* 16.

the ignorant...the people of the L-rd...the secret of 'the Land': Although the term עם הארץ is generally derogatory, here Ramak applies it to the Jewish people, which embodies "the secret of 'the Land,' " that is, the Shechinah.

he casts them down to the external forces: On the verse "Israel is holy to the L-rd..." (*Yirmeyahu* 2:3), the *Zohar* comments: "We learn that the people of Israel are called holy. And because they are holy, it is forbidden for a man to call his friend a derogatory name..." (vol. II, p. 122a).

in the Gemara: "Why are the sons of Torah sages rarely sages themselves? Rav Ashi said: 'For they call people donkeys!' " (*Nedarim* 81a).

"women are of unstable temperament": See *Shabbat* 33b, *Kiddushin* 80b. That is, *malchut* is immature until the higher *sefirot* supply it with intellect. See *Eitz Chaim, sha'ar* 15, ch. 4, and *sha'ar* 13, ch. 5.

the category of 'the dust of the earth': Dust enclothes the power of growth. Thus, our sages state: "Beware of the sons of the ignorant, for from them Torah will come forth" (*Sanhedrin* 96a).

in the *Zohar*: See intro., p. 7a.

Rav Chaggai: See *Zohar,* vol. III, p. 158a.

Tikkunim: See the end of *tikkun* 26, p. 71a.

deciding the halachah according to the truth: The letters of the word הלכה — the law — are identical to those of הכלה — the bride. This "bride" refers to *malchut* (Z. W. Ashkenazi; also see *Pardes, sha'ar "Archei HaKinuyim,"* ערך הכלה). Truth (אמת) is synonymous with Torah and *tiferet* (ibid., ערך אמת). Cf. "There is no truth besides Torah" (*Yerushalmi, Rosh HaShanah* 3:8).

'controversy for the sake of Heaven': See *Avot* 5:17.

between the two opposing powers, *chesed* and *gevurah*: The "controversy" between *chesed* and *gevurah* benefits those who are due to receive the Divine efflux, as explained in the first notes on chs. 5-6. In addition, Hillel and Shammai, who represent the lenient view of the law (*chesed*) and the strict view (*gevurah*), respectively, epitomize controversy for the sake of Heaven (as mentioned in *Avot* 5:17). The law is almost always decided according to the school of Hillel (*Eruvin* 13b) in keeping with the aforementioned principle that *tiferet* should tend towards *chesed*.

Heaven (*tiferet*): *Tiferet* is called Heaven (שמים), for this word comprises two words: אש — fire, symbolizing *gevurah*, and מים — water, symbolizing *chesed* (*Pardes, sha'ar "Archei HaKinuyim,"* ערך שמים).

"it's end is love": A play on the words והב בסופה (*BeMidbar* 21:14). Even though interpretations of Torah may differ, if the dispute is for the sake of Heaven, "it's end is love" (*Kiddushin* 30b).

derives benefit from words of Torah: "Do not make [the Torah] a crown for self-aggrandizement or an axe with which to cut. So, too, Hillel used to say: 'He who exploits the crown [of Torah for his own ends] shall perish.... Whoever derives personal gain from words of Torah removes his life from this world' " (*Avot* 4:5). See Rambam, *Peirush HaMishnayot* ad loc.

impure thought: This phrase encompasses any position or premise that is not adopted for the sake of truth.

Notes on Chapter 8

netzach, hod: *Netzach* (victory, endurance, or eternity) and *hod* (majesty, splendor) are usually paired. The *Zohar* considers them "two halves of one body, like twins" (vol. III, p. 236a). They are an extension of the *sefirot* from which they derive — *chesed* and *gevurah*, respectively. Thus, *netzach* conquers the barriers that prevent the outflow of Divine benevolence, while *hod* restrains this outflow lest it be dissipated among unworthy recipients. This way, Divine majesty and splendor are preserved.

yesod: *Yesod* (foundation) unites Emanator and recipient, or, in the language of Kabbalah, *malchut* and the other *sefirot*. Just as *tiferet* mediates between *chesed* and *gevurah*, *yesod* mediates between *netzach* and *hod* (*Pardes*, *sha'ar* 8, ch. 24). Moreover, *yesod* blends, channels, and receives light from all the *sefirot* above it (*Tikkunei Zohar*, *tikkun* 21, p. 55b). This way, their emanations can issue forth to creatures.

some aspects in common: See the first note on this chapter.

carrying out their wishes: "Anyone who hosts a Torah sage, Scripture regards him as though he has sacrificed a *korban tamid*" (*Berachot* 10b). Similarly, providing for a sage is like providing for Shabbat and brings salvation to the provider (see *Zohar*, vol. III, p. 29b).

however little or much: See *BeMidbar* 13:18.

to honor the Torah: " '...those who support [the Torah] are fortunate' (*Mishlei* 3:18) — This refers to those who support Torah scholars" (*Zohar*, vol. III, p. 53b).

complete Torah knowledge is not gained from a single teacher: Cf. "Ben Zoma said: 'Who is wise? He who learns from every person' " (*Avot* 4:1); "One who learns from only one teacher will never see any sign of blessing" (*Avodah Zarah* 19a). As one of Ramak's teachers, Rabbi Shlomo HaLevi Alkabetz, explains, "Each individual has his portion in Torah, and no two people's portions are identical. Therefore, 'One who learns from only one teacher will never see any sign of blessing,' for teacher can transmit only his own portion to his students" (*Ayelet Ahavim* 19:10).

'students of the L-rd': "Rabbi Elazar said in the name of Rabbi Chanina: Torah scholars increase peace in the world, for it is said: 'All your children shall be students of [the Torah of] the L-rd; great will be the peace of your children' [*Yeshayahu* 54:13]" (*Berachot* 64a, *Yevamot* 122b).

Scripture...the Right...Mishnah...the Left: See *Zohar*, vol. I, p. 27b.

Talmud includes everything: See *Yerushalmi, Pe'ah* 2:4. The secrets of Torah, generally known as Kabbalah, are included in Talmud (Rambam, *Mishneh Torah, Hilchot Talmud Torah* 1:12).

wasteful emission: Both the Gemara (*Niddah* 13a) and the *Zohar* (vol. I, pp. 56, 188) consider this an extremely serious offense, for it causes great spiritual impurity.

speech: "The main cause of wasteful emission is sinning in the covenant of speech" (*Reishit Chochmah, sha'ar "HaKedushah,"* ch. 17, p. 209c).

to your flesh: Some commentators explain that this phrase refers to one's children, upon whom his sins ultimately devolve (Rashi, *Metzudot*). Others take the verse literally (Ibn Ezra, Malbim). Ramak's explanation satisfies both approaches: A person's words may cause him to sin through wasteful emission. This offense, in turn, may damage the children conceived afterwards.

Uttering Obscenities...a sin: See *Zohar*, vol. I, p. 76a, and vol. II, p. 249b; *Sefer HaChareidim*, ch. 24, par. 49; *VaYikra Rabbah* 24. Also see *Targum Onkelos* and Ibn Ezra on *Devarim* 23:15.

even if the words themselves are not sinful but pure: See *Tikkunei Zohar*, end of *tikkun* 13.

Sign of the Covenant: See *Bereishit* 17:10. "*Yesod*, the end of the torso, is the sign of the Holy Covenant" (*Tikkunei Zohar*, intro., דייה פתח אליהו).

'the Covenant of the Rainbow': See *Bereishit* 9:12-13.

the target of the arrows: Cf. *Eichah* 3:12. "The target" refers to *malchut* (*Tikkunei Zohar, tikkun* 13; *Pardes, sha'ar "Archei Ha-Kinuyim,"* ערך מטרה).

guarding himself from licentious thoughts: "One should not think licentious thoughts during the day and come to wasteful emission at night" (*Avodah Zarah* 20b). See Rashi ad loc.

Notes on Chapter 9

malchut: *Malchut* (kingship, royalty, sovereignty), the last of the ten *sefirot*, is uniquely "passive," having nothing but that which other *sefirot* pour into it (*Eitz Chaim, sha'ar* 6, ch. 5, and *sha'ar* 8, ch. 5). Thus, the *Zohar* compares *malchut* to the moon, which has no light of its own (vol. I, pp. 249b, 251b, and vol. II, p. 245b; *Tikkunei Zohar, tikkun* 44, p. 82b). Nevertheless, *malchut* brings creation into being, for nothing occurs among the lower beings without this *sefirah* (ibid., *tikkun* 19, p. 40b; *Zohar Chadash*, p. 11a). Thus, *malchut* is the architect of creation (*Pardes, sha'ar* 11, ch. 2). *Malchut* corresponds to the mouth (*Tikkunei Zohar*, intro., p. 17a) and thus represents the word of G-d (cf. *Avot* 5:1) and the revealed world (*Zohar*, vol. I, p. 1b, and vol. II, p. 127a).

his wealth should not make him proud: "The Holy One, Blessed Be He, gives a man wealth in order to support the poor and fulfill His commandments. If he does not do so and becomes proud in his wealth, [it] will become a curse" (*Zohar*, vol. I, p. 121). Also see *Avot* 4:9, 6:9.

having nothing but the bread he eats: Although our bread also comes from G-d, perhaps Ramak is alluding to the Talmudic comment that the verse "...[G-d] gave the Earth to man" (*Tehillim* 115:16) applies whenever we thank Him before benefiting from this world. See *Berachot* 35b; *Zohar*, vol. 33, pp. 44b, 270b.

especially at the time of prayer: The prayers of the poor supersede even those of Moshe and King David, for the prayers of the poor come from a broken heart (*Zohar*, Vol. III, p. 195a).

"for I am alone and humbled": We have translated the word עני as "humbled" rather than "poor." See *Metzudat Tzion*.

must fend for himself: This statement refers to spiritual matters.

in the *Zohar*: See vol. II, p. 198b.

exile himself: "[Self-imposed] exile atones for sin, for it causes a person to be submissive and humble..." (Rambam, *Mishneh Torah, Hilchot Teshuvah* 2:4).

implements: These are: a lamp, a dish, a mat on which to sit or sleep, and either a lamp (*Nedarim* 40b) or a bag (*Eichah Rabbati* 1:22).

an expulsion order upon himself: Ramak, his brother-in-law, Rabbi Shlomo HaLevi Alkabetz (author of the "*Lecha Dodi*" prayer), and some of their comrades spent some time in self-imposed exile. Ramak kept a diary during one such exile — in the winter of 1538 — which later became *Sefer Geirushin*. There, he relates that they sometimes travel barefoot.

Rabbi Shimon bar Yochai and his comrades: See *Zohar*, vol. II, p. 198a.

as the gateway to: According to the Venice 1579 edition of *Tomer Devorah*, published by Rabbi Moshe Bassola, this is the correct reading. Other versions read not שער (gate) but שאר (remainder), which would be rendered: "and one that is more important than all the rest of a person's Divine service." The awe of G-d being the gateway to a person's Divine service is discussed at length in *Reishit Chochmah, sha'ar "HaYirah,"* preface to ch. 1. Moreover, the *Zohar* (intro., p. 11b) lists fear of G-d as the first commandment.

he fears the external forces: See *Zohar*, vol. I, p. 11b, and "*Ra'aya Mehemna*," vol. III, p. 263b; *Tikkunei Zohar, tikkun* 33.

proper fear is fear of the L-rd: "There are three types of fear: Two are of improper deviation.... The man who fears the Holy One in order that his children may live, and he who fears punishment in this world...or in the next. The third type of fear is the proper type: Man should be in awe of his Master, for He is the mighty Ruler and Source and Root of all worlds" (*Zohar*, intro., p. 11b). Cf. *Kohelet* 12:13.

three things: Ramak proceeds to list four things, suggesting that our text here is incorrect.

the greatness of Him Who fashioned all things: See *Reishit Chochmah, sha'ar "HaYirah,"* pp. 7a-d.

the fear of His greatness resting upon his face: See *Midrash Mishlei* 19.

man is always in the presence of the Creator: As the verse states: "...the earth is filled with His glory" (*Yeshayahu* 6:3).

Who carefully inspects all his ways: Cf. "...G-d searches the hearts [of man]" (*Mishlei* 17:3); "Your eyes are open upon all the ways of man" (*Yirmeyahu* 32:19). Also see *Chovot HaLevavot, sha'ar "Avodat Elokim,"* ch. 5.

rooted in the *sefirot*: "You have made garments for the *sefirot*, from which souls issue forth to man" (*Tikkunei Zohar*, intro.). Ramak explains how all souls emanate from the *sefirot* and descend from this elevated level to become enclothed in physical bodies (*Pardes, sha'ar* 4, ch. 6). See also *Zohar*, "*Ra'aya Mehemna*," vol. III, p. 29b; *Tikkunei Zohar, tikkun* 22, p. 65.

repel the Shechinah Above: See *Shir HaShirim Rabbah* 5:1; *Pirkei DeRabbi Eliezer* 18; *Zohar*, vol. II, pp. 20a, 37a, 85b.

alienating the King's love from the Queen: See *Zohar*, vol. III, pp. 16b, 74a.

via the female aspect: "The Shechinah dwells with one who has a wife" (*Zohar*, vol. I, p. 228b).

"sustenance, clothing, and conjugal rights": See *Shemot* 21:10.

give again and again: See Rashi on the blessing ויתן לך (*Bereishit* 27:28).

the wife he has chosen in the covenant of marriage: Cf. *Malachi* 2:14.

i.e., *chesed, din,* and *rachamim*: These terms correspond to kindness, judgment, or severity, and compassion, respectively.

niddah*: During her menstrual period, a woman is called a *niddah*, and her husband must separate from her. See *VaYikra* 15:19, where Rashi explains that the word *niddah* means "separated." Also see *Shulchan Aruch, Yoreh De'ah* 183, 188.

separates himself from her on weekdays: Scholars fulfill their marital duties on Shabbat (*Ketubot* 62b; *Shulchan Aruch, Orach Chaim* 241).

complete, possessing both male and female elements: See *Zohar*, vol. I, pp. 49b-50a.

the Prayer for Travelers: See *Berachot* 29b-30a.

the *Zohar* on *Bereishit*: See vol. I, pp. 49b-50a.

when the community is in distress: See *Eruvin* 63b; *Zohar*, vol. III, p. 71.

the *Tikkunim* on *Bereishit*: See *Tikkunei Zohar, tikkun* 69, p. 102b.

'the king's daughter': This title refers to the Shechinah.

meditation on Unification: This meditation refers to the Unification of the Shechinah with the Holy One, Blessed Be He (*Pardes, sha'ar* 32).

the Right...thereby sustaining her corresponds to sustenance: See *Tikkunei Zohar, tikkun* 69.

By means of *gevurah*, he should cover the Shechinah: See *Tikkunei Zohar, tikkun* 69.

for the sake of Heaven: "Let all your deeds be for the sake of Heaven" (*Avot* 2:12; *Zohar*, vol. III, p. 51b).

shields for the Shechinah: See *Zohar*, vol. I, p. 23b; *Tikkunei Zohar, tikkun* 69.

He should wear them always: Cf. "It is forbidden to divert one's attention from his tefillin while he is wearing them" (*Shulchan Aruch HaRav, Orach Chaim* 28:1). Consequently, it is customary not to wear tefillin constantly.

in the *Tikkunim*: See *Tikkunei Zohar, tikkun* 6, p. 18a.

Notes on Chapter 10

Zohar's commentary on *Bereishit*: See *Zohar*, intro. vol. I, p. 11a.

never becoming separated: See *Pardes, sha'ar* 31, ch. 5.

act at the right time: As the verses state: "He has done everything well in its proper time..." (*Kohelet* 3:11), and "Everything has its time, and there is a season for all desires..." (ibid. 3:1). Regarding the ramifications of this idea, see *Shulchan Aruch, Orach Chaim* 1.

adjustment: As mentioned in the introduction to this work, *tikkun* has several meanings in Kabbalah. Here, the word signifies rectification or perfection (*Pardes, sha'ar* 4, ch. 5).

'night,' the attribute of *malchut*: See *Zohar*, vol. I, p. 20b.

going to sleep is like death: "Sleep is one-sixtieth of death" (*Berachot* 57b; *Zohar*, vol. I, p. 169b, and vol. III, pp. 120b, 207a, 234b).

'Tree of Death': See *Pardes, sha'ar "Archei HaKinuyim," ערך עץ*.

accepting the yoke of Heaven: See *Zohar*, intro., p. 11a. Complete acceptance of the yoke of Heaven involves the recital of the Shema (see *Berachot* 13a-14b, 61b).

wash his hands of the *kelipah*: See *Zohar*, vol. I, p. 53b.

recite the blessing: Ramak refers to the blessing recited over the washing of the hands (*Shulchan Aruch, Orach Chaim* 4).

restore the Shechinah through Torah study: See *Pardes, sha'ar* 4, ch. 5.

"When you lie down...when you awaken": See *Metzudat David*.

his soul will rise to Gan Eden: See *Zohar*, vol. III, p. 213a; *Pardes, sha'ar* 11, chs. 1, 3.

listen to his voice: Cf. *Shir HaShirim* 8:13.

***Zohar* on "*Terumah*":** See vol. II, p. 173b.

at the entrance: I.e., *before* entering the synagogue. See *Zohar*, intro., vol. I, p. 11a; Rabbi Chaim Vital, *Sha'ar HaKavanot*, p. 3c.

man comprises *chesed, gevurah*, and *tiferet*: See *Pardes, sha'ar "Archei HaKinuyim," ערך אדם*; *Pardes, sha'ar* 31.

***beit knesset*, which is *malchut*:** See *Pardes, sha'ar "Archei HaKinuyim," ערך בית הכנסת*.

"...kindness" corresponds to Avraham: See *Pardes, sha'ar "Archei HaKinuyim," ערך אברהם*.

"I bow..." corresponds to Yitzchak: Yitzchak corresponds to the attribute of awe and judgment. See *Pardes, sha'ar "Archei HaKinuyim," ערך יצחק*.

in a propitious time: These words follow the verse cited above and conclude the prayer, which is recited upon entering the synagogue.

"In awe of You" corresponds to Yaakov: See *Pardes, sha'ar* "*Archei HaKinuyim*," ערך יצחק.

in thought, speech, and action: All the attributes mentioned in the preceding chapters must be acquired on all three levels: thought, speech, and action. See *Shelah, sha'ar* "*HaOtiot*," p. 51b.

yesod, **the source of the wellspring:** See *Zohar,* vol. I, p. 60.

quality of 'day': This corresponds to the *sefirah* of *tiferet,* the quality of Torah, as explained in ch. 7. Also see *Pardes, sha'ar* "*Archei HaKinuyim*," ערך יצחק.

by means of his meal: The concept of eating as part of one's Divine service is explained at length in *Reishit Chochmah, sha'ar* "*HaKedushah*," ch. 15.

as Hillel the Elder said: See *VaYikra Rabbah* 34:3.

"A righteous man knows the soul of his animal": In our edition of the Midrash, Hillel quotes a different verse: "A kind man does good to his soul..." (*Mishlei* 11:17).

his animal soul: "In every Jew, righteous or wicked, there are two souls. As it is written, '...I have made souls' [*Yeshayahu* 57:16], alluding to two souls. One soul originates in the *kelipah* and the *sitra achra* and is enclothed in the blood of a human being, giving life to the body, 'For the life of the flesh is in the blood...' [*Vayikra* 17:11] — this refers to the animal soul" (Rabbi Chaim Vital, *Sha'ar HaKedushah,* pt. 1, ch. 1; *Eitz Chaim, sha'ar* 50, ch. 2; *Likutei Amarim,* ch. 1).